To Dan

A Lakeland Mountain Diary

This is a book I return to
so often possibly as some
relief when I see a world
losing its moral compass.

The mountains never really
change they are ever dependable
even if the weather is not.

All my love

Grandad Tony

xx

A Lakeland Mountain Diary

From 40 Years in *The Guardian*

A. HARRY GRIFFIN

The Crowood Press

First published in 1990 by
The Crowood Press Ltd
Gipsy Lane
Swindon
Wiltshire SN2 6DQ

British Library Cataloguing in Publication Data
Griffin, A. Harry
A lakeland mountain diary : from 40 years publication in
the guardian.
1. Cumbria. Lake District. Description & travel
I. Title   II. The guardian
914.427804858

ISBN 1 85223 565 9

Picture credits
All photographs from the archives of the late Geoffrey Berry

Typeset by Butler & Tanner Ltd, Frome and London.
Printed in Great Britain by Billing & Sons Ltd, Worcester

Contents

Acknowledgements

Successive editors of *The Guardian* – W.P. Wadsworth, Alastair Hetherington and Peter Preston – have always encouraged my 'Country Diary' writings and I am most grateful to them for this. The illustrations in the text are all from the Geoffrey Berry Archive, housed in the Cumbria county library at Kendal and I greatly appreciate the courtesy and generosity of the library authority in allowing me to reproduce them. The late Geoffrey Berry, formerly secretary to the Friends of the Lake District, also illustrated most of my earlier books and was a close personal friend. On about half of the outings described in this book I was alone in the hills but on the others I enjoyed the stimulating company of friends. They include, especially, Ted Stacey, Ivan Waller, Keith Dixon and Sir John Johnson and there have been several others. All helped in my enjoyment of these fell days in all weathers. The manuscript was beautifully prepared from dog-eared cuttings, scribbled alterations and pages of my happy-go-lucky typing by Brenda Shepherd of Kendal who, besides neatness and dexterity, also has a fine feeling for words.

AHG
Kendal, Cumbria

In memory of Mollie

Royalties from the sale of this book will be devoted to St John's Hospice, Lancaster.

A Labour of Love

Unlike some cabinet ministers, actresses and distinguished writers whose private scribblings have occasionally, when revealed in print, shaken or titillated nations, I have never kept a diary – not a day-to-day one of ordinary, mostly boring happenings, anyway. For very many years I have, however, kept a *mountain* diary and, during the past 40 years, two of them. The first, the long-standing one, jotted down at night on my return from the hills, is no more than a brief note of the date, the weather, companions, if any, the names of the climbs or mountain round and any special feature of the day – say, a sighting of the Brocken Spectre or the depth of the snow. None of this hotchpotch of dates, names and meteorological statistics, if skipped through years later, is dull to me, for it can bring to life memories of almost-forgotten mountain days that have been such an important part of my life, but it is inconceivable that these bare bones could possibly be of general interest.

The second diary – my contributions to *The Guardian*'s 'Country Diary' every other Monday – is, however, rather more descriptive writing about some of my wanderings or scrambles in the Lakeland fells and a selection of these form the basis of this book. They have been assembled in monthly form, January to December, to give a picture of one man's Lakeland mountain year. It is not, of course, any one particular year but, rather, an amalgam of articles from the last 15 years, from 1976 to 1990. Incidentally, it may be of interest and perhaps encouraging to middle-aged or elderly people who feel they have become too old for the hills at, say, 50 or 60 to hear that all these outings, either lazy or strenuous, were done when I was between 65 and 80 years of age.

Towards the end of 1950 the late Mr W.P. Wadsworth, the editor of what was then *The Manchester Guardian*, wrote to me asking whether I would like to contribute to the paper's 'Country Diary' once a fortnight. George Muller of Cockermouth, who had been writing about the Lake District in *The Guardian* for many years, had died at the age of 75, and they wanted somebody to continue the pieces. It so happened that George had been an original member (from 1907) of the climbing club to which I belonged, and I knew him well – an active link with

Golden eagle country in Lakeland, with High Street in the background.

the early days of rock climbing, an authority on all outdoor matters in Cumbria, and a fine, sensitive writer. I can only assume he had mentioned me to Mr Wadsworth for I had never contributed to the paper before and doubt whether my scribblings elsewhere had been noticed within *The Guardian*'s august portals in Manchester. Delighted with the invitation I agreed to do my best and Mr Wadsworth's instructions were simple and to the point. 'Write about anything you like,' he ordered, 'but, for heaven's sake, keep off birds. We get all we want about these from the others.' He meant the other contributors to 'Country Diary'.

I started my fortnightly pieces on the first Monday in January 1951 and have continued them without a break, illness or holidays notwithstanding, ever since – 40 years of pages from a Lakeland mountain diary. It works out at 1,040 pieces and more than 260,000 words and, although I might have repeated myself here and there, writing about a corner that I had described years earlier, the diaries were topical, always referring to an outing of the previous week. I have enjoyed every minute of writing them, although I have sometimes been furious when *The Guardian*'s well-known gremlins have made a mess of my words or, very occasionally, when a piece – having been lost in the post or through some other mischance – has failed to appear.

By and large, during successive editorships, I have tried to follow Mr Wadsworth's instructions to 'keep off birds' – I am not very knowledgeable about them, anyway. I have though, written occasionally about mountain birds, especially since we now have golden eagles nesting and rearing their young on Lakeland crags again, after a break of 200 years. Otherwise, I have just tried to picture Lakeland, and especially the fells, as I have seen it during the changing seasons, passing on little things that interested me at the time. Sometimes I have kept off the fells and written about the dales and the villages, sports and pastimes and other matters while, occasionally, I have enthused about other areas such as the Yorkshire Dales, Scotland, the Alps, and (once) the Canadian Rockies. In this selection, however, I have tried to confine myself to Lakeland or its fringes and, wherever possible, kept on the high ground.

This is my second anthology of *Guardian* pieces. In 1976 Robert Hale published *A Year in the Fells*, based on my writings between 1951 and 1975. It is now out of print, and I have been persuaded to risk another peep into mountain memories by many readers who either do not know of its existence, or simply want more. The simple arithmetic of 40 years of diaries coinciding with my 80th birthday seemed a sufficiently reasonable excuse for doing it in this year.

Nearly all the pieces have been written in a room that has views, on a clear day, of the hills in four of the old counties – Cumberland, Westmorland, Lancashire and Yorkshire – when the memory of a recent walk, climb or mountain ski run, or perhaps just a peep at a waterfall or pool, was fresh in my mind. The remainder, a score or so from 1989, were compiled in my present study in a Kendal town flat. From there the main view is of rooftops, but Benson Knott, about 1,000 feet high, is out there beyond the Town Hall clock and, from bedroom windows, Whiteside Pike and White Howe in the Bannisdale fells and the Whinfell ridge can be seen, high above the town. The hills are now only about two miles further away than they were in my fellside eyrie and can still be easily reached, either by car and on foot, or in memory.

On about half of the outings described I was alone – a completely satisfying situation for the competent walker. You travel faster when you are alone and probably see more. Hardly any of the trips were planned; usually, they emerged from a last-minute decision while driving north or north-west into the fells. Having been up every hill, in all possible directions, on many occasions – perhaps a hundred times on some – having climbed on almost every crag and explored most of the gills, it is always a problem deciding where to go. Every time, though, there has been something new to see – perhaps a hidden pool or even just the sunlight lighting a crag from a 'new' angle.

There are several *Guardian* country diarists scribbling away in remote corners of the kingdom about quiet places, wild life of all kinds and the little things of the countryside. None of it is very world-shattering but, for people marooned in cities, it is perhaps a breath of country air or, in my case, mountain air. No doubt the fact that *The Guardian* has always kept the feature on the leader page, cheek by jowl with comments on important events of the day, national or international, is significant. People may sometimes tire of reading about the turmoils of government or violence in the cities and be happy, now and again, to read about simple things that hurt nobody. For many years we country diarists worked in decent obscurity, our identities limited to initials, but in May 1966 we were suddenly thrust into the limelight, the decision having been made, presumably at the highest level, that we should be named. No longer could we skulk in oblivion; from now on readers would know who we were. We would, henceforward, have to be most careful in our revelations and might even be stopped in the streets. Nothing much, in fact, has changed – except, perhaps, that we get more letters. And I have had hundreds over the years; most have been kindly, some ask for information, and occasionally some demand to know why I have 'revealed' the existence of some favourite place that will now be overrun by the hordes. (True, I have given away some secrets, but I have always tried to keep my more delectable and unspoiled corners to myself and never take readers by the hand in guidebook fashion.) Mostly, we country diarists don't know one another very well but in the 1970s *The Guardian* invited us all to lunch in London so that they could have a look at us, and so that we could meet one another. I seem to remember that we were a pretty ordinary bunch, but the talk over the wine was certainly wide-ranging, reflecting many diverse interests and enthusiasms.

There are 240 'Country Diary' pieces in this selection, 20 for each month, hopefully to convey something of the flavour of a year in the fells with all the widely-differing weather thrown in. The pieces have been used unaltered (except where the gremlins had been at them); they represent what I thought at the time, and I don't think my views

Tilberthwaite Gill near Coniston.

have changed much over the years. Where necessary, I have added explanatory notes at the end of some of the pieces and, here and there, as required, indicated when the diary was written. An attempt has been made to embrace most of the Lake District but readers may notice that the winter months, with much shorter days, have usually been spent on mountains nearer to home, leaving more distant places for the long hours of daylight in summer. All the trips have been done from home, there and back in the day – or often, in summer, in just a morning or evening – but at my age I don't get up especially early on cold mornings.

Reading through the manuscript I am a little ashamed of my earlier descriptive powers and limited vocabulary, noticing several repetitions of scenic wonders, and some rather naive portrayals of quite splendid sights that deserved more profound appraisal. This is how I felt at the time; perhaps, today, I would try to do better.

I realise my great good fortune in having been brought up on the verge of Lakeland, having been able to live and work inside its boundaries, within daily sight of the hills, and in enjoying the inestimable blessing of reasonably good health and fitness. The Lake District has changed – for the worse, in my opinion – during my lifetime, and especially during the 40 years of my *Guardian* writing, and the huge increase in mass tourism is bringing difficult problems. We are kicking the hills to death, spoiling some of the once-quiet places and, often, by our enthusiasms, destroying the very peace and quietude that the more discerning have always sought in the Lake District. At all costs we must fight to prevent the worst excesses of commercial development and refuse to allow the district to be cheapened or trivialised or standards lowered. The necessary balance between the preservation and, indeed, the enhancement of the natural amenities – the unspoiled fells, dales, lakes and woodlands and the native way of life – on the one hand, and the provision of appropriate facilities for public enjoyment on the other, must always be tilted firmly in favour of the former. No part of the Lake District should ever be 'the pot of gold at the end of the rainbow' for anybody, for this noblest corner of England – its first National Park – is more important than money, or the whim of governments. It is not disposable, nor for sale – not any part of it. For me, despite its gross over-use at holiday times and weekends (which turns away many who preferred the area in less crowded times), its eroded tracks, and the seaside-resort atmosphere of the more popular places, the Lake District is still the most beautiful place in England and I know where I can find quiet corners even on Bank Holidays. I have always returned from places abroad, some of

The Troutbeck Fells.

them outstandingly beautiful, with the feeling that I was glad to be
back home again among my own friendly little hills. I hope that this
will always be so but daily vigilance is required from all of us – including
those in high places – to ensure that the Lake District we love is not
ruined by greed, selfishness or apathy.

Winter Adventuring

JANUARY

The First Snow

New snow on the fells brings out the sculpturing as magically as a brass-rubbing or a print in a developing tank. Yesterday and for weeks past the fells, as seen from my windows, have been no more than dim, grey shapes, except when they have been invisible in the murk. But this morning, following overnight snow, they are suddenly revealed in startling clarity, with every crag and outcrop boldly etched in black against the gleaming white of gullies and fellsides. Not even summer sunshine on the clearest day can paint the actual shapes of the mountains so accurately. The effect, indeed, is almost stereoscopic. You feel you can see right into the corries, and cliffs and ridges are transformed from mere parts of a flat panorama into differently-distanced features standing proud against the background. The south-east corrie of Red Screes, for example, usually looks a dark, amorphous mass of rock and scree: today it is dramatised into an alpine scene of black crags and sharply-defined snow gullies. Similarly, the head of Kentmere has changed overnight from a rounded combe into a wild corner of rock and snow. I can even pinpoint, with exact precision, the source of the River Kent, just ten miles away. It was the snow that once first showed me that I could see a tiny segment of St Sunday Crag from my house. For years I had assumed the diminutive bump, peeping over the shoulder of Sallows, to be part of Caudale Moor but the snows made it all clear. Whether the new snow heralds the start of our outdoor winter it is difficult to say, but ski edges, crampon points and ice-axe blades are all sharpened in readiness.

Silence of the Snows

Absolute silence is a state rarely achieved – even in lonely hills. Almost always there is the noise of falling waters, however distant, the sighing of wind, the whisper of the grass, tiny sounds of moving sheep, a tinkle of sliding scree, or the faint drone of unseen aircraft. Only on a totally windless day, when the becks are frozen and the fells blanketed in snow, can you sometimes stand and savour the complete absence of sound – an utter quietude that is almost uncanny. I experienced this the other day on the east face of Wetherlam – nobody about, nothing moving, bright sunlight on frozen snows, and not enough wind, even on the summit, to flicker a burning match. The steep snow gully, to the right of Hen Tor, in perfect condition for crampons and axes, provided an exhilarating ladder to the heights, and a nearby gully proved a quick way down. For some time, after my climbs, I sat in retreating sunshine

Helvellyn, showing the tourist route in winter.

in the corrie enjoying the exceptional stillness of the late afternoon. Far to the east the sunset glowed pink on the snows of Helvellyn and Fairfield but the gloom of dusk already filled the valleys. Frequently I strained my ears for the slightest sound but it never came. Motor cars on the roads, quarrymen at work and all the bustling life of the dales only a mile or two away but no sound or sight of it on my slow slope. Not even a moving sheep or the trickle of a spring. At the summit I had slowly scanned the ring of snowbound fells for sight of the moving speck of some other pilgrim without success. So far as I could see I was quite alone in a white world, frozen into awesome immobility. Thus the often-overcrowded fell country on a rare day of winter perfection.

Kirkstone Ski Circus

A place in the fells to be avoided at all costs on snowy weekends is the summit of Kirkstone Pass. If you are a skier you will have to fight for space with youngsters careering about on toboggans, tea-trays, or plastic sheets, and if you leave your car there to go for a walk or climb you may run the risk of being prosecuted for illegal parking. Even if you merely wish to drive over the pass to Penrith or Windermere you may find the crossing more congested and frustrating than a city centre journey in the rush-hour. Compared with Kirkstone top on a winter weekend, Blackpool beach in summer could well be quieter and more relaxing. For the competent the skiing on Kirkstone is rather limited but, increasingly during recent winters, people in all parts of northern England have discovered that they and their children can play about in the snow at 1,500 feet without having to do any walking – with liquid refreshment available on the spot. The car parking on the pass is perfectly adequate throughout the year – except on these snow circus weekends when four times the space might be insufficient. To tackle the problem the planners are to spend many thousands of pounds this year to create more parking spaces, which might ease the problem next winter. One can only hope this unfortunately necessary development in a place of rare beauty so high in the fells – where telegraph poles were removed to preserve the scenery – will be done with the very greatest care and devotion. Meanwhile those who prefer peace and quietude in their winter hills will spend their weekends elsewhere. There are many better places – although perhaps not so handy for a drink.

[This was written in January, 1980. The extra car parking was provided but Kirkstone Pass is still a place to be avoided by the discerning at weekends when the snow circuses take over. Midweek, however – for the retired or unemployed –

it can often provide useful exercise or practice, especially when portable ski tows are in operation.]

A Winter Mountain

Of all our summits over 2,500 feet, Red Screes is the nearest to a motor road – and to alcoholic refreshment. Even more significant, in winter, is the fact that this road, Kirkstone Pass, is only a thousand feet or so below the summit, making the snows readily accessible and creating, on suitable weekends, the well-known ski circus. Since the pass is within 20 minutes' drive of my home I am often up there, especially in winter, the car laden with skis, ice-axes, crampons and the rest of the paraphernalia. If the Kirkstone snows are not deep enough, too icy or too crowded with noisy youngsters on sledges or tea-trays I leave my skis in the car and go climbing on the craggy, east face of Red Screes – handy enough for kicking up and down a couple of snow gullies and back home for lunch. These gullies – the huge, sabre-slash of Kilnshaw Chimney and the three couloirs up the headwall of the south-east corrie – are only of moderate difficulty but provide quite interesting winter routes to the summit, over steepish cornices for the experienced solo climber or good practice for beginners under instruction. Much more demanding ice routes can sometimes be found between the gullies or on and around Raven Crag in the corrie and there are other possibilities in the north-east corrie when snow conditions are good. Red Screes – the colour of the scree is particularly striking in summer sunshine after rain – is, therefore, a wonderfully convenient winter mountain with snow and ice climbing within five or ten minutes of the road and, for the skaters, a frozen tarn right on the summit. Sometimes, too, there's skiing in the south-east corrie.

An Alpine Afternoon

On one of the last splendid days of the old year I had left the winter sports circus on Kirkstone Pass for a late afternoon ascent of an enticing snow gully on Red Screes. The merry cries and laughter of the skiers and careering children on toboggans or, even faster, on plastic macs, pursued me up the lower slopes. Looking down, the pass seemed blocked with toy motor cars; the police would be having a busy time. But, once in the great white bowl of the corrie, I was in a new world of frozen silence where nothing moved. A shoulder of fell hid me from the holiday jollity and the only sound was the crunch of boots on the crusted snow. Due south, Windermere, a gleam of silver, snaked into the haze, and eastwards, the sunshine burnished the snows on St Raven's Edge. Ladders of footsteps led up some of the gullies but the one I had chosen – shadowed from the westering sun – was unmarked. A straightforward ascent, with a satisfying pull over the beginnings of a cornice, and I was back in the sunshine on the summit snow fields. Two people, up from London for a holiday look at mountain Lakeland, had a tremendous view over 1,000 square miles of sunlit snow peaks. You may pay £100 or more to enjoy a view like this in the Alps; on the right day in our own fells you can capture much the same serenity and solitude in an easy hour from the car. As the sun sank behind the Langdale Pikes I came down another much-laddered gully towards the last of the holiday crowds. The nursery slopes, already gripped by the night frost, were shadowed and almost deserted, but the evening sun still glowed on the white switchback line of the Troutbeck Fells.

Flies on a White Wall

Sunshine on high snows reaching the horizon, silvered slopes with blue shadows, and not a breath of wind; difficult to visualise a more perfect winter day in the hills. The climb started above and beyond Grisedale Tarn, frozen over and thickly covered in snow so that its considerable area merged with the fellside and, to a stranger, might not have been there. About a dozen other climbers were also at work in the shadowed Tarn Crag gullies – from the pass we must have looked like black flies on a white wall. Progress was unhurried, conversation quiet, the only sounds the pecking of holds, the swish down the slope of falling ice chips, and the occasional hammering in of 'dead-man' belays. For the steepening cornice the snow had turned to reliable ice and we stepped out, in turn, into the dazzling sunlight – so often the perfect reward for a winter climb. Equipment stored away, most parties strolled easily to the summit of Dollywaggon Pike – this day a superb viewpoint. The nearby, east-facing cliffs of High Crag and Nethermost Pike were curtained in white ice and Cock Cove below might have been the amphitheatre of winter giants. A mile away across the valley, walkers, black specks against the snow, could be seen crossing the white whaleback of Fairfield and the rock ridges of St Sunday Crag were transformed into alpine grandeur.

The Dollywaggon path above Grisedale Tarn, with Fairfield in the background.

Winter Perils

The sad discovery at New Year of the frozen bodies of two youths, huddled together by the summit cairn of Scafell Pike, was a grim reminder of the winter perils of the fells. As I write on a murky January afternoon of warm drizzle, wet mists and the grass still green and growing, winter still seems far away, although the snows have been and gone, twice. But we know that hard weather must lie ahead and statistics underline the likelihood of forthcoming accidents, and even tragedies, on our winter mountains. The greatest risk at this time is of hypothermia – the loss of heat to the central core of the body that insidiously reduces mental faculties and can quickly lead to serious exposure and, if not dealt with in time, to death. And the most serious contributory factor is not so much the cold and the wet but the wind. For this reason, completely windproofed garments are essential wear in the Lake District mountains in winter – besides extra food, torches, ice-axes and, under certain conditions, crampons or nailed boots. And a wise precaution, adopted by all members of mountain rescue teams, national park rangers and responsible mountaineers, is to carry a plastic bag for covering the body in an emergency – a tiny bundle, weighing a few ounces only, stuffed in the rucksack.

[I wrote this fifteen years ago, in January 1976, but the winter dangers of the hills to the inexperienced or foolhardy are still the same and, sadly, tragedies happen each year. Visitors should realise that weather conditions in the valleys give little or no indication of the likely conditions on the winter hills. Ice-axes should always be carried, although they may not be needed, when there is seen to be snow on the fells and crampons may be necessary, even for ordinary walkers, if there is much ice about or the snow is frozen hard.]

Ice for Climbing

Years ago we searched for good ice on the frozen lakes and tarns, hoping to be the first to cut threes and loops with our skates. Kindly old Lovell Mason of Ambleside, then well into his eighties, always beat us on to Rydal Water but I have memories of moonlight skating on Tarn Hows and even of a skating carnival on Windermere in 1928 or 1929 with the lake frozen all over, cars parked on the ice, braziers to warm yourself and excursion trains bringing hundreds of skaters from London and the south. We don't seem to get these winters so often nowadays but the search for ice goes on – today, more often, ice for climbing. During the last ten years or so new Scottish ice-climbing techniques have spread to the Lake District and increasing numbers of climbers, both local and from further afield, are now trying out their sharply-angled metal axes and front-pointing skills on every bit of steep ice they can find. Any small crag or outcrop sheeted with water-ice – there are several convenient ones in the Red Screes corries above Kirkstone Pass – may be good enough for practice and, recently, frozen waterfalls in some of the gills have given good sport. The splendid fall of Whorneyside Force in Hell Gill, Oxendale, for example, has been frozen into startling immobility – a rare challenge for experts. Years ago winter climbing in Lakeland meant slow step-cutting up the Great End gullies – just like the Edwardian climbers in their Norfolk jackets and nailed boots; today, the best of the new ice-men are tackling in winter quite hard summer rock climbs. Moss Gill on Scafell, Great Gully on The Screes, North West on Pillar Rock and Intermediate Gully on Dow Crag have all had their winter ascents in recent years.

[Even harder ice routes than these – this was written nine years ago – are now being done in hard winters in Lakeland but the climbing and skiing seasons have come much later in recent years and ideal conditions do not now occur so frequently as they did in the past.]

The Spectre of the Brocken

A snow gully winding up through the crags on the east face of Wetherlam took us through thick hill fog towards the summit. All we could see were ourselves – dim shapes against the snow. A compass gave direction. Fifty feet below the summit the grey gloom lightened overhead and then, suddenly, we stepped into dazzling sunlight. All that could be seen was a square hundred yards of summit rocks, steaming in the sunshine. The rest of Lakeland lay buried beneath mile after mile of writhing cotton wool, lit from above by sun streaming down from a cloudless sky. Minutes later we had our first revelation. The white blanket sank slightly and there, seven miles to the north-west, just peeping above the cloud, were the rocky summits of the Scafells – the highest land in England. So clear were these distant summits, across the sea of fog, they seemed within throwing distance. We basked in the sunshine and the fantastic scene, only ourselves and the Scafells, so far as we could see, above the white boiling mists – and then turned down into the cloud. And, immediately, we had our second revelation – a perfect Brocken Spectre, with two concentric rainbows, apparently straddling a rock ridge 200 yards away. Seeing the Spectre, a giant apparition striding the mountains, the first visitors to the Alps were often alarmed but, for many years now, the sighting has been accepted as a simple reflection phenomenon, caused by the shadow of the observer being thrown on to the mist by sunlight. All the same, the appearance of the eerie colossus can make a mountain day – this was only my fifth Spectre in 50 years of mountain wandering.

[Since then, January 1978, I've seen one more Brocken Spectre, from near the start of the Climbers' Traverse on Bowfell. The apparition seemed to be straddling the top of Stake Pass. The Wetherlam Spectre was unusual in that it carried a double 'glory' – the only time I have seen this.]

Ski Mountaineering

The return of the snows provided a day, sandwiched between others of mist and rain, when an otherwise disappointing winter outdoors suddenly became worthwhile. From the lane above Ings the Coniston and Langdale fells looked carved out of icing sugar – a line of white fairy castles sparkling in the morning sunlight. Gritting lorries eased the passage over the ice-bound Kirkstone Pass and the snow reached down a few hundred feet above the glass-calm surface of Ullswater. From the former Greenside mines Raise was climbed on skis fitted with skins – the first time this had been possible this winter – and the ridge traversed to White Side. Clichés are difficult to avoid. The sky, right across the firmament, really was a ceiling of cloudless blue, the sunshine blazed on the glinting snow slopes, and there was not a breath of wind. Nearly 3,000 feet below, the Vale of Keswick was a patchwork of brown, green and gold, dotted with sunlit grey or white blobs of houses and farms. Behind rose the gleaming white backcloth of Skiddaw and Blencathra, with Bassenthwaite Lake curving to the north-west. The only people about were a dozen youngsters on an Outward Bound course, edging across the snow with their ice-axes and peering over the ice-bound cliffs. Powder snow – snow that has never melted – is not often encountered on our fells but it was powder that day with snow that swirls about you at every turn. The descent was made in slow swings in untracked snow all the way down to Keppel Cove and almost back to the mines. On the way down I was joined by another skier – on a brief holiday from South Wales. 'What a day!' he cried exultantly, but the next day we were back to rain and fog, and the snows disappeared.

Winter Perfection

It was the sort of day you sometimes see pictured in old Chinese paintings – sun-kissed snow mountains soaring above mist-laden valleys into skies of willow-plate blue. Most remarkable were the trees and hedges – every branch, twig and leaf hanging in crusted hoar frost so that we drove through a magical landscape out of Lakeland into the Northern Pennines. Smoke rose straight from cottage chimneys, ice crackled under our wheels in the narrow, winding lanes and the 100 feet high, snow-plastered lattice masts on the fell-top radio station, miles away, pointed like white fingers into the cold, blue sky. For an hour we trudged up the frozen mountain road, carrying our skis, and, thereafter, carved sweeping trails in clouds of powder snow, pausing, now and then, for hot soup and coffee. The skiing was warm work for the sunshine glared fiercely off the snow but you could tell it was freezing hard for gloveless fingers stuck to the metal of our skis. We watched the huge, golden orb of the sun sink slowly towards the western hills and then, finally, disappear behind the purpling mountain wall. And, immediately, our warm, sunlit slope was transformed into a cold, shadowed world of tilted ice – slightly menacing where before it had been friendly. Cautiously, we slithered down the frozen mountain road at the darkening to the car and drove home towards the sunset. The sky above the dark line of the fells was a pageant of gold as a savage night of frost gripped a silent countryside. No matter what the forecast tomorrow would be another glorious day in the fell country.

[The lattice masts on the fell-top radio station on Great Dun Fell have now been replaced by a curious structure, looking, especially from a distance, like a gigantic golf ball.]

A Mountain Grandstand

Ten red deer trotted daintily across the rough ground just below the summit, stood for a moment silhouetted against the sky, and then disappeared one by one, over the edge of Grey Crag overlooking the lake. You often see red deer on Place Fell – only two or three miles from their sanctuary in Martindale which has been a deer forest for centuries. Sometimes, in the rutting season, the people of Patterdale, snuggled under the side of the fell, can hear them roaring, and now and again a few deer swim the lake and go adventuring into old Cumberland. They say bad weather is on the way when the Martindale red deer appear over the skyline of Place Fell, but this sunny January

25

morning was a day in a thousand and the barometer was rising. We made straight for the summit from Side Farm, up the steepening grass – steep enough, in places, to need handholds – and through the shattered rocks of Capel Crags, pausing now and again to admire the parallel valleys from Dovedale to Aira Green opening up across the lake. Place Fell is the perfect grandstand – sculptured coves between encircling ridges, the houses, farms and hotels like toys 2,000 feet below, the pleasure cruiser moored for the winter by the jetty and tiny patches of snow clinging like fragments of lace to the rooftree of Helvellyn. We saw nobody on the hill, our car remained the only one parked in Patterdale, three buzzards soared in widening circles above the sunlit slabs and juniper clumps of Grey Crag and, on the way down, we came upon four grazing fell ponies, their long, shaggy tails sweeping the ground.

The Old Goose Bield

We started our winter scramble up the broken rocks of Great How Crags in the Coniston fells from a point immediately behind the goose bield, where we had lunched. I only know of two or three goose bields or fox traps in the fell country and this one, hidden among the tumble of boulders beneath the crag, is the largest and perhaps least easily noticed of them. The trap, cunningly built with rocks into a bee-hive or igloo shape, is nearly ten feet across and might originally have been up to six feet high. A carefully balanced plank would have provided the entrance and at the inner end of this precariously poised highway would have been placed a long-dead and very smelly goose. Once the fox reached the goose the plank would tilt, depositing him within the bee-hive with its inward curving walls and thus unable to escape. A refinement might have been the intended collapse of the delicately balanced dome on to the furiously frustrated and unfortunate fox. Most of the dome has in fact collapsed – whether by design or the years of rough weather, it is impossible to judge – but the construction skill, achieved without mortar or cement, can still be admired, even if we deplore the cruelty.

[Since this was written, 12 years ago, the goose bield has disintegrated and may now be difficult to find.]

Far Horizons

There was one rare morning, sandwiched among weeks of rain and gloom, when the long-hidden fells were suddenly revealed as shining white mountains below deep blue skies. An hour or two later I was treading unmarked snow on Helvellyn – two feet deep in the drifts, wind-crusted or ice elsewhere but, above one thousand feet, a complete white blanket. The views from the top had the astonishing clarity that sometimes occurs after the skies have been washed clean by incessant rain. Great Gable, with its vertical-looking north crag, looked about a mile away, the cliffs of St Sunday Crag, the other side of Grisedale, within throwing distance and the 'golf ball' radio station on Great Dun Fell in the Northern Pennines easily recognised. The hill Criffel, south of Dumfries and beyond the Solway, was clear enough for studying its sculpturing, while far behind it and well to the west was another, obviously higher, hill and it was capped with snow. This, I decided was probably The Merrick, 2,674 feet above sea-level and the highest Scottish mainland hill south of the Highlands. The maximum theoretical distance, under perfect conditions, for a hill of this height to be seen from the top of Helvellyn is something like 140 miles so that this sighting, at about half the distance, was by no means exceptional. It does not, however, compare with the reported sighting by several people, on a remarkably clear day some years ago, of Ben Lomond from Red Pike in the Buttermere fells – a distance of about 120 miles. This wonderful Helvellyn day had clearly been one to seize. The next day we were back to the rain and cloud.

Magic on Fairfield

Through binoculars, from the snowbound summit of Fairfield, you could just pick out people on top of Scafell Pike – nearly ten miles away as the crow flies. Much closer, the crags edging the Helvellyn ridges stood out black against the snow and, with the naked eye, it was easy to spot groups of walkers around the summit shelter. The hills seemed alive with people on this magical day around the turn of the year – a completely cloudless sky, unbroken sunshine on sparkling snow and a blazing clarity that seemed to bring nearby peaks within throwing distance. Only rarely, each winter, do we get days like this in the fells. There had not been enough snow and ice in the Deepdale gullies for climbing but the water-ice on the fellsides, caused by the hard frost following the heavy rains and floods so quickly, was quite

The north crags of Fairfield from Deepdale, with Ern Nest Gill below Link Cove just left of centre.

dramatic. Everywhere, becks were frozen into silent immobility and great sheets of ice, like armour-plating, lay across the slopes or hanging over the crags. In places the glistening boulder-plates on these tilted ice-rinks must have been a foot thick but snow-ice, formed by the successive thaws and frosts of compacted snow, had not yet had time to form in this sudden winter spell. Sheltered by one of the summit cairns it was possible to sit and bask in the sunshine but, on the open fellsides, the north wind was bitingly cold. To the south-west the dazzling waters of Grasmere and Coniston burned and flashed like giant mirrors and, westwards, the familiar shapes of Gable and Pillar bulked dark against the sunset. It should be another good day tomorrow but the forecasters warn that a change is on the way.

Enjoying the Cold

It had been the coldest night of the winter. Rydal Water and Grasmere were frozen right across, the tracks up Tongue Gill sheeted in ice and clouds of spindrift, white against the blue sky, were being blown off the summit of Fairfield in the strong east wind. From the old packhorse trail up Little Tongue the soaring white front of the mountain looked more interesting than the usual way from Grisedale Hause so a bee-line was made for the top. I was too lazy to put on crampons, which remained strapped to the rucksack, so that, in the steeper places, where the snow lay on top of ice, steps had to be cut – an unusual, but pleasant, expedient on a modest afternoon walk. It was sheltered, kicking and cutting up the slope, but the step on to the slippery ice-rink of a summit had something of the breathtaking shock of a winter bathe. The top was being swept by a furious, biting wind that, with the icy, drenching clouds of driven snow, provided a battle all the way to Greatrigg Man where an escape could be made, south-west, out of the maelstrom. Just before turning out of the icy gale I noticed a pair of ravens, beaks into the wind, hanging almost motionless in the sky high above the plunging sweep of Calf Cove, unable to move against the blast. On the trot down there were many pictures – ice-sheeted tarns, snow clouds over Scafell and Gable, the great orb of the sun sinking down to Wrynose Pass and, looking back, a near full moon riding high in the eastern sky.

A Rock Gymnasium

Boulder Valley below Low Water in the Coniston fells, is not marked on maps, but has been known to climbers for more than 80 years. It contains the Pudding Stone, one of the largest boulders in Lakeland, and a scattered collection of other huge chunks of rock, many of them named – a natural gymnasium for the adventurous. Fifty years ago, on off-days when the big crags were out of condition, we would tackle most of the routes. The Pudding Stone alone boasted ten, varying in standard from easy to almost impossible. Recently, to round off a day in the snow, I introduced two young friends to the strenuous delights of Boulder Valley, but slyly avoided personal contact with all but the easiest climbs. The harder routes looked quite frightening. How on earth had we done these things in nailed boots? One of my young companions, with far more strength than I, boldly demonstrated, at a third attempt, that the desperate Overhang on the Pudding Stone – that has always defeated me – is by no means impossible. A walkers' route to Levers Water now passes the Pudding Stone and up through the once-secret valley, while the beck into which you fell if unsuccessful on the Beck Stone is now spanned by a wooden bridge. Many more people pass this way now, although perhaps not to climb. But the fate of the Bowder Stone in Borrowdale – condemned to the Victorian indignities of a ladder to the top, countless postcards, and cups of tea – is unlikely to descend on the Pudding Stone. Perhaps boulder climbing is going out of fashion, for the six routes on the nearby Inaccessible Boulder seem less well known today than they were in the 1930s, and who climbs now on Kentmere's Brock Stone or the Y Boulder in Mosedale?

Christmas Capers

Four outings in Christmas week – much more than my usual ration – illustrated the variety of fell country winter weather. As an appetiser for our Christmas dinner my son and I strolled over Winder and Arant Haw in the Howgill Fells – a lovely, still morning with hazy sunshine, a little cloud on the tops and nobody about except two men walking five couples of hounds, three terriers and a sheepdog. The next day we were in driving sleet and snow with a biting wind on Red Screes, seeing little from the summit except cloud racing across the snow and wasting no time in driving back home for the second appearance of the roast beef. The other days were spent on Wetherlam and Helvellyn – the first, doing a snow and ice climb on the east face of the mountain and the second watching the unveiling of the new summit memorial commemorating the aeroplane landing of sixty years earlier. The east face of Wetherlam had been selected as being likely to be sheltered from the biting north-west gale but the wind must have veered during the day for, at times, it was difficult to avoid being blown off the mountain. By far the best weather, after weeks of incessant rain and high winds and immediately followed by the usual depressing mixture, was on the Helvellyn pilgrimage – a perfect day of sparkling, sunlit snow, a steady north wind and long, clear views. Two miles to the north there was a greater depth of snow in the ski-tow drift on Raise than many of us can remember in previous Decembers but much of this will now have been washed away by the return to the dreary mild, wet weather which, regrettably, seems to have become the norm in these parts.

A Limestone Hill

On a wild day of gale-force winds that would have swept us off the fells or crags, we sought a more sheltered day by a leisurely exploration of Whitbarrow, the thickly wooded limestone fell that stands guard over the reclaimed marshlands of the Kent estuary. We crawled through

Wetherlam's east face showing popular winter snow gullies.

spiky thickets of blackthorn, along adventurous sheep-trods above the beetling cliffs, savouring the remarkable exposure and marvelling how present-day aid-climbers manage to get up these smooth overhangs. Half an hour later we came upon two of them at work on another precipitous face, but found that their modern techniques and athletic skills only made two old climbers feel even older. A little further on, as we squirmed out of a fairy cave, there was a sudden movement in the woods and three roe deer trotted silently and elegantly through the trees and disappeared into the gloom. There must have been plenty of badgers underground for we saw many of their setts, and there are red squirrels, too, in these crowded woodlands where the old yews form an almost impenetrable screen just below the cliffs. From the top of the crags we could study the complicated drainage system that controls the rivers and prevents the flooding of these now fertile mosslands, and look north to the cloud-wreathed Lakeland fells where the tips of the snows reached just below the mists. On the other side of the hill, we looked down on ancient farms and damson orchards cosily nestling within the shelter of the great white cliffs and hardly noticing the gale sweeping the tops.

Fears for the Future

The old year faded away, unseasonally, with mist and drizzle – an unhappy year, in many ways, best forgotten. More rewarding, perhaps, to look forward to 1976 – the Silver Jubilee year of our national park. Something like 570,000 acres of the Lake District were designated as the country's largest national park on January 30, 1951, and the order finally confirmed on May 11. We were nearly 80 years behind the Americans with our national parks for the story began with the great Yellowstone Park in 1872 and many countries followed suit before our National Parks Act of 1949. But there are now ten national parks in England and Wales – although none, as such, in Scotland – and nearly one-tenth of the country now belongs to the nation. It has not been an easy first 25 years in the Lake District Park, although a solid basis has been achieved, and many problems lie ahead. What are needed is a firm government decision that the preservation of the amenities must override the twin aim of recreational provision – already recommended by the Sandford Committee – a properly planned hierarchy of roads, surer safeguards against mineral exploitation and the like, clear-cut policies on caravans, water skiing, second homes and depopulation, and curbs on the more blatant forms of tourism. The Lake District must not be over-commercialised, cheapened, or trivialised, and great things could happen this Silver Jubilee year if many more people come to realise that this very special place can be irrevocably damaged, even by small things, just as a scratch can ruin an Old Master.

[Fifteen years after this was written, in January 1976, one must still feel ever-increasing concern for the future of the Lake District national park which, especially at weekends and holiday periods, more and more closely resembles a national car *park each year. It is deeply regrettable that commercial interests should continue to foster mass tourism so blatantly in an area once mainly appreciated for its peace and quietude.]*

Crampons, Skis and Compasses

FEBRUARY

Step-Ladder to the Skies

Four days after an uncomfortable round of the ice-bound Coniston fells in a bitingly-cold south-west gale, two of us were on Fairfield in alpine picture-postcard conditions of sunlit snows and cloudless blue sky. For added interest, and to avoid possible processions on the Grisedale Hause tourist track, we went straight for the summit from the source of Tongue Gill – about 1,400 feet of, successively, deep powder, compacted wind slab, crusted snow-ice and ordinary ice. And for even more interest, we left our crampons on our rucksacks and kicked and cut our way up the steepening snow dome with the axe. The view from the cairn had the clarity and perfection you can enjoy on many Lake District tops on just two or three days every winter – dazzling sunlight glistening on waves of snow-bound summits reaching to the horizon in all directions. There was nothing to be seen except snow and ice, blinding white or faintly blue in the shadows, and it seemed strange, in that high alpine wonderland, that, in an hour or so, one could trot down to main roads and cars, houses and green grass, all hidden away in unseen depths. For future climbing days we examined the state of the snow-packed gullies dropping into Deepdale, and then crunched down over Greatrigg Man and Stone Arthur to the car. It was freezing hard but the blazing sunshine, reflected off the snow, was strong enough to burn our faces. Down at the foot of Tongue Gill, we looked back at the great snow dome of Fairfield, glowing in the late afternoon sunlight, and there, nearly two miles away but perfectly clear, was our long ladder of steps, arrow-straight to the summit.

A Good Winter

For those who enjoy snow in the hills this winter has, so far, been the best in the fell country for five or six years. The first falls came at the end of November and snow has remained in many parts of the hills since then – sometimes completely blanketing the tops, other days in large snowfields mainly on north-facing slopes, or in straggling drifts and gullies. In places drifts have been up to 20 feet deep and some of these could remain until after Easter – even though, from south and west, the fells might by then appear completely clear of snow. Cornices as wide as a house have built up on some steep, east-facing ridges and there have been avalanches in some of the gullies – one of them engulfing a climbing party. My diary shows that since the first snows I have been fortunate enough to get into the hills 25 times for skiing or snow-climbing. Sometimes we've been in freezing mist, falling snow, or – only once – pouring rain but, generally, the winds have not been so ferocious as in many previous winters and some days have been quite perfect – cloudless, still, and sunny, with views over sparkling snows to Scotland or the sea. On a few of these perfect days it has been possible to make long ski traverses or circuits of the tops – opportunities only rarely feasible in Lakeland and to be seized quickly.

[This was the winter of 1976/77. There had been many winters several years earlier just as good for climbing, skiing or hill walking – or even better. Indeed, during the 1950s and 1960s, we used to count on up to four months of skiing in many winters, although most of the snow would be above 2,500 feet, necessitating long portages of skis and boots. In more recent years winters on the high fells have tended to start later and be compressed into a much shorter duration.]

All Sorts of Snow

Except to the very young, snow in the towns or on the roads is an abomination: on the hills it is either a delight or a death-trap. Several people have been killed on our snow-bound fells this winter and many others injured or guided to safety. In all cases the critical factor has been the changing nature of the snow, often accompanied by lack of experience or proper equipment. The townsman or motorist mostly knows only two types of snow – slushy or drifted – but in the fells we have powder snow; compacted snow; wind-slab; breakable crust; hard, frozen snow that might be polished or ridged; snow-ice, either white or black; snow that might avalanche, either wet or dry; and other variations. Each requires a different technique, and perhaps equipment,

34

The track to Keppel Cove, with Catstycam in the background.

for climbing or skiing – or the experience to know when it should be avoided. On a recent traverse of the Kentmere hills on skis two of us encountered powder snow – up to our knees in places – breakable crust and ice, although from the valley the sunlit fells appeared clothed in an innocuously uniform white carpet. We also finished the day in thick cloud although, under unbroken blue skies from the first summits, we had had views across waves of snow-capped mountains for 30 miles. For much of this month the Lakeland fells have in effect been covered by an ice-cap, topped with loose snow in places, conditions necessitating crampons and ice-axes, even for ordinary walkers. This fact has just not been realised by many visitors who have been beguiled by the sight of smiling sunlit snows and, sadly in a few cases, paid the penalty. When our fells seem most attractive they are often most dangerous.

[There were several days this month – February 1978 – when the snow, because of hard freezing after slight thaws, was rock hard and highly polished in places, resembling tilted ice-rinks. Progress is impossible under these conditions in the usual rubber-soled mountain boots, unless steps are cut with the axe (the slow old-fashioned way) or crampons are worn. Crampons are, of course, a necessary tool for climbers nowadays since nailed boots are no longer worn, and more and more winter mountain walkers are now wisely taking them into the fells too. They weigh very little, and can be easily carried on the rucksack for possible use later, perhaps in steep, icy places on the descent.]

The Winter of '47

Seated around a cosy fire at the Kirkstone Pass Inn, 1,500 feet above sea-level, we discussed the snow. 'The worst we've ever had,' said two holiday motorists, marooned on the summit by deep drifts on the Windermere side. My friend and I, who had reached the inn on skis, by-passing the snow plough and snow blower battling through ten-foot drifts, did not agree. I recalled the early months of 1947 and the telegraph poles along the Shap Fells road sticking up incongruously only a foot or so above huge banks of snow. Then there was the 'lost' railway engine later 'found' completely buried in a snow-filled cutting near Barras station. And the terrible sheep losses – an estimated two million in the country, including 40 per cent of breeding ewes around Lakeland and thousands of lambs. One farmer at Birkdale in north Westmorland had only 45 sheep and seven lambs remaining out of a flock of 700. On Casterton fells a sheepdog called Hemp sniffed out and 'set' more than a hundred sheep to be recovered alive by the shepherd. One old ewe that miraculously survived had been buried for six weeks. Village schools, half-hidden in snow drifts, were closed for weeks. Even the budget meeting of the county council had to be repeatedly postponed. Troops – and German prisoners – were used to dig out the roads over the fells. But this day in February 1979 we were enjoying the snow – sunlit sweeps of hard-packed powder on slopes sheltered from the bitter east wind. Far below, as we skied the powder, we saw the blower break through the last drifts and watched the first cars edge slowly over the pass and down through the dusk to the Woundale gate.

Skiing Delights

Two rather desultory attempts on the Kentmere Horseshoe on skis were defeated by thick cloud. Near 'white-out' conditions on skis are particularly trying for it is difficult to hold a compass course when every turn takes you off route. Our retreat from the summit of Yoke took us south and then east, down long slopes of hard snow, to within 200 yards of the sturdy farmstead of Hartrigg in Kentmere – a glorious run once we had slid beneath the cloud. The second attempt – two days later, in the reverse direction – foundered on the upper snow slopes of Kentmere Pike. When you can't see your companion, or be sure whether the slope goes up or down, it is time to turn back. On both days, once the dale became visible, the rewards came with the descent but, briefly from the Pike, the clouds lifted to the north and Mardale Ill Bell was suddenly revealed – a great, white, corniced dome, sparkling in sunlight and looking like an alpine giant. Then, just as quickly, it was gone. Both days we used climbing skins, simple devices that give the skier the freedom of the fells in winter. With their aid, in reasonable weather, the relaxing ascent and careful route selection, can be almost as enjoyable as the run down, and all the mountains, given sufficient snow, are within your grasp. But most modern downhill skiers do not even possess skins – normal equipment 40 years ago. Two pairs of ravens flew croaking up the valley towards golden eagle country as we curved down the snow towards Brockholes in the evening, and we saw where a fox, with his trailing brush, had climbed the slope before us.

The Troutbeck Round

There is a particularly soothing rhythm in the ascent of snowbound fells on skis fitted with climbing skins. You gain height steadily in easy, ascending traverses, choosing the most comfortable angle, and the motion is so measured and relaxing that all your attention can be directed to the enjoyment of the gradually widening views. If you feel like it you could compose a poem or even a Country Diary; at a pinch you could close your eyes for a time. In ideal conditions it can be the easiest way to get up a mountain – provided you're not in a hurry. Recently, on a perfect day of sunlit snows, just before the 'high' slid away to the east, I enjoyed a lone traverse of the Troutbeck fells on skis, exulting in the contrast between the leisured ascents and the exhilarating, and sometimes rather undignified, downhill swoops and turns. Two walkers, doing the ridge in the opposite direction, found the crusted snow rather tiring. But, using skins, the uphill sections were almost effortless, taken slowly, and the descents, on varied snow surfaces, proved ideal or awkward, but always interesting. As on previous visits to the high fells during this spell of winter perfection the clarity of the views and the complete absence of wind were quite exceptional. You could sunbathe in comfort by the icicle-hung cairns on Ill Bell and look across half of winter Lakeland to the bold dome of Great Gable, 15 miles away. Much closer, to the north, High Street surfaced like a great white whale and, to the south-west, the long length of Windermere reached out to the sparkling sunlit waters of Morecambe Bay. Only two or three times each winter can you capture days like this.

Swindale Memories

My winter round of the Haweswater fells, across miles of new, sunlit snow, started and finished in Swindale – the valley that escaped the flood. There were plans for a 100 foot high dam – the old church had been demolished, years before, in readiness – but then the water engineers changed their minds and built a modest ten-foot weir instead, leaving the dale virtually unspoiled. Few people seek out this remote trough in the hills – a place without even a car park or litter bin, since neither are needed – but it would be difficult to find a more charming retreat. Today there are only three farms, a tumble of crags where we used to climb in the 1950s, scattered woodlands, and a green, sunlit floor of intake fields watered by the winding pools of Swindale Beck.

The dale head is a craggy wall, patterned by waterfalls, with the line of the old corpse road swinging down to the last farm. This was the way Mardale's dead were taken, by horseback, for burial at Shap; the last sad journey was made in 1736. Swindale in more populous days produced its great men and scholars – the farmers, it was said, could sow in Greek and reap in Latin – and about 30 years ago, I found the tiny schoolroom later turned into a temporary church. Clearly, the sheep had taken it over but inside were five dusty pews, the parson's lectern and, in one corner, the organ, less than three feet long, on which, by furious pedalling, I managed to produce three lugubrious notes in the bass. But on my recent visit I could find no trace of the building which must have suffered the same fate as the collapsed farms at the head of the dale. A sad place, Swindale, but a valley of memories and much quiet beauty.

[It would be in the early 1950s when I 'played' on the Swindale church organ.]

Aircraft Crashes

Seeking a snow gully suitable for climbing on Great Carrs in the Coniston fells, I almost stumbled on a large piece of aircraft wreckage. Indeed, the eastern crags of this mountain and an area perhaps 100 yards west of the summit are littered with crash debris – the remains of a Halifax bomber, damaged in a raid on Berlin nearly 50 years ago and limping back to its Yorkshire base. The bomber, approaching from the west, just failed to clear the summit by a few feet. All seven of the crew were killed. This is one of the best-known sites of aircraft wreckage in the Lake District fells but there are up to 20 others, mostly on the higher tops with a total of deaths probably exceeding 50. Many were wartime disasters, unreported at the time – one of them a German bomber that crashed after the blitz on Barrow-in-Furness – but there have also been several peacetime tragedies, including two, on Thornthwaite Crag and Crinkle Crags, during one June weekend in 1937. And I remember a September day many years ago when a light plane crashed near Great End, killing its two occupants, after scraping a rock outcrop. In most of the disasters the aircraft were flying too low either through damage or because the pilots had risked descent to find a way through cloud or had been caught in sudden air currents that had sucked them down. I have sometimes wondered whether some device like a small radio beacon on a suitably high summit might be of any practical help. We have too much paraphernalia already on some

Crinkle Crags above Oxendale.

of our tops – monuments and fancy cairns, for instance – but if one really useful construction could save lives no one would question it.

Avalanche Conditions

Half-way up the north-west ridge of Caudale Moor we could see that the south gully of Dove Crag, two miles away across the trough of Kirkstone Pass, had avalanched so, almost certainly, our own climb would be off because of soft snow. Where, a few days earlier, the steep gully to the left of Dove Crag had been choked with snow it was now a chute of rubble, earth and scree ominously black against the white fellside. We had intended cramponning up and down some of the moderate gullies on Caudale Head, assuming that in this north-facing corrie there might be a chance of decent, hard snow, but the Dove Crag avalanche suggested we were far too optimistic. And, when we reached our gullies, we found them, too, ready to slide and quite unsafe. The crumbling cornices were undermined, there were great cracks and crevasses across the slopes and, in places, whole sections of the gullies had slipped, leaving towers of tottering snow and nasty, dark holes.

Had the snow been frozen hard it would have been fun kicking up through what looked like an alpine ice-fall but it was of the consistency of porridge – newly-made porridge at that. Agag-like we kicked downwards for a few steps but the snow seemed bottomless and there was the feeling that at any moment the whole gully would slide – as South Gully across the valley had done. So, gingerly, we crept out and contented ourselves with a round of the tops in unseasonally warm sunshine. Indeed, we later sprawled on a flat rock in the middle of a melting snowfield and enjoyed a February sunbathe. I can't remember such a poor season for winter climbing. Have the 'good' winters come to an end?

[They seemed to have done, since the next two winters (1988/89 and 1989/90) were no better.]

Dance on Crampons

The ferocity of the gale forced me to exchange a planned solo route up the steep, east face of Coniston Old Man, above Low Water, for a simple round of familiar heights. Snow conditions were perfect for climbing – rock-hard surfaces, ideal for crampons – but it was difficult, in the gusts, to avoid being swept off your feet and, at times, I found myself hanging, almost desperately, on to my implanted axe on slopes that, in summer, are hands-in-pockets places. The descent to Goats Hause, on the lee side, down delectable slopes of glazed snow-ice was almost a running dance on crampons but, without them, would have been impossible – except by step-cutting – so hard and polished was the surface. Peeps down the snow gullies on Dow Crag confirmed excellent conditions for a later visit but care had to be taken to prevent an involuntary exploration of their depths for the gusts made balance quite precarious. The arctic delights of this wild but sunny day were familiar enough – vast slopes of frozen snow, frozen waterfalls, and icicles, 20 feet long and thick as an arm, hanging from the crags – but an unfamiliar sight was the extraordinary patterning of the cracks in the ice on frozen Low Water. I have seen Low Water frozen right across on dozens of occasions and, one severe winter, saw the tarn heaped high with great ice-floes, but this cracked design, looking like a jigsaw puzzle, a spider's web or a shattered windscreen, was something new. The whole surface of the tarn, covered in white snow-ice, was divided by cracks into several hundred parallelograms and triangles of almost equal size as if some artistic giant had been at work with a glass-cutter.

Getting Lost

Getting lost in the fells is surprisingly easy – even if you have been exploring them for half a century. On a short half day in the Coniston fells before the snows came I missed the summit of Swirl How in thick mist and did not realise my mistake until I found myself, off route, on Great How Crags. Cursing my stupidity I steered a compass course through the grey blanket for Grey Friar and at least had the satisfaction of hitting it off exactly, but the experience made me think. Here was I, getting lost, through over-confidence, on fells that I thought I knew as well as my garden. How do others with much less experience get away with difficult conditions and, especially, how do silly people without map or compass manage to cope with visibility restricted to five yards? In unfamiliar country, I suppose, I take adequate precautions whereas in the Lake District, where every feature is familiar, I am careless, not bothering to consult a compass. As a result I have often been lost, temporarily, in my own fells but never in strange country or on bigger mountains. It is all very well having an eye for country but you have got to be very good indeed to avoid going round in circles in a white-out without a compass. Mist, however, provides some of the joys of the hills – the dale, for instance, leaping into focus below your feet through a gap in the cloud, a rocky summit rising above a sea of cotton wool, or, as the other day, Little Langdale Tarn, and the vale of Ambleside, smiling in the sunlight, suddenly spread out like a map as you step down through the clouds.

Trusting the Compass

Hill days of thick cloud and persistent rain – our frequent weather pattern recently – may only be useful for the exercise, but compass work can add satisfaction and even enjoyment. Picking exactly the right line with visibility down to yards makes you forget unpleasant conditions. One firm rule is to trust the compass implicitly even though the direction may seem wildly inaccurate. The only time this blind trust led me astray was a dreadful day on Liathach in the Highlands, many years ago, when my sole guide happened to be a compass I had found in the depths of Walker's Gully on Pillar Rock – clearly discarded by its owner because it didn't work, perhaps because of a fall. In the fell country the Hart Crag-Fairfield area can often provide problems in thick mist and deep snow when it is necessary, with tracks and cairns obliterated, to avoid unseen crags and hit off ridges with some exactitude. I was alone on Hart Crag the other day in fog and snow, with driving rain. The need for careful compass work was obvious but the mental exercise made me oblivious to weather discomforts. In very familiar country nothing was recognisable in the untracked snow and it was curiously rewarding to reach almost-buried summit cairns and plot the next leg of the round. High snows in thick mist can be strangely misleading but at least, if necessary, you can retrace your tracks and work it out again. Towards the end of a circuit that, but for the navigation, would have been a rather miserable plod, it was exhilarating to pick up the first track of the day on Hartsop-above-How and to see the mist rising at last, from the lonely depths of Deepdale far below.

Straight-Line Walks

Crossing the fells in a straight line can be an entertaining but strenuous exercise. Due west across the national park on Grid 09 avoids the necessity of swimming lakes or tarns but is pretty tough and takes two days. A far easier stroll is to walk from Clappersgate along, roughly, bearing 300 degrees, until you reach High Raise, the apex of the central dome of the Lakeland fells and a magnificent viewpoint. My own version of this exercise is to seek out all the little summits in turn – there must be nearly a score, Loughrigg alone has half a dozen – and then, on the return journey, miss them all out, taking the easiest line. On a recent traverse and return I felt justified in cheating a little, here and there, since the snow made slower going, but it still filled in a longish day. The views, on a rare, windless day with sunshine glinting on the snow, were varied and impressive with the Langdale Pikes and Crinkle Crags rearing like alpine peaks and, from High Raise, the whole of the northern fells reaching in white waves to the horizon. Far below, on one side, the green sunlit trough of Langdale provided contrast with the dazzle of the higher snows and, on the other, the pools of Rydal Water and Grasmere and the shadowed curve of Far Easdale were restful pictures. Loughrigg, Silver How, Blea Rigg and Sergeant Man, evocative names, were passed in turn and many a frozen tarn. It is a splendid high road, with many dips, well tracked in summer but, this day, a switchback of unmarked snowfields along which I trod my straight lines over every little height. And the return, avoiding all the tops, with the shadows lengthening across the snow, was kindly to tiring legs.

[Close study of maps can reveal many of these straight-line walks. An excellent one, straightforward except for the final scramble, is to go north-west from Cockley Beck to the top of Scafell Pike, without cheating, that is to say, keeping exactly to the same compass bearing all the way.]

Skating Memories

Low Water in the Coniston fells, frozen right across with smooth, black ice and fairly sheltered from the biting wind, looked quite tempting to an old ice skater. There was a time many years ago when we used to take our boots and skates into the fells, and I remember pleasant afternoons on Goats Water or Stickle Tarn as well as scores of days on the rather less adventurous ice of Rydal Water or Tarn Hows. We don't seem to get regular winters like that nowadays but, testing the ice on Ratherhead Tarn the other day and listening to forecasts of even colder weather, it looked as if this winter might well prove a return to the old pattern. Boyhood memories of moonlight skating on Tarn Hows, reached after a 20-mile cycle ride, are fading now but a recollection of a sunny Christmas Day spent on skates on the same idyllic sheet of ice is less than twenty years old. We kept our skates on at lunchtime as we lolled in the trees at the edge of the ice, munching pork sandwiches and mince pies, washed down with a bottle of wine and skated until the encircling, snow-bound fells turned purple in the dusk as the frosty silence of night reached down to grip the earth in its iron fist. A more dramatic memory is of the great frost of 1928 or 1929 when I skated a mile or two along the length of Windermere, frozen over from end to end and then, cheeks glowing with sun and frost, faced the long bicycle ride home in the darkness. Hundreds of cars were parked on the ice at Lakeside that winter and there were braziers to keep you warm, refreshment stalls and dense crowds of people, many of them brought to Lakeland by special trains from London and the South to see the 'great ice carnival'.

[I wrote this in February 1986 but my hopes for a return to the hard, skating winters of earlier years have not been fulfilled. This, in fact, proved to be my last skating day, not only because later winters have yielded little ice, but also because my changed feet can no longer be thrust into my old skating boots, even when wearing the thinnest socks possible.]

Fox and Foxhound

My only encounters all day were with a fox and, later, a foxhound. I was walking up Wetherlam on a sad, anniversary mission when, on the edge of a quarry above Tilberthwaite, I saw the fox, less than 50 yards ahead, outlined against the sky. Strangely, for a fox, he was walking, his long brush almost sweeping the ground – apparently sure of his safety on his home ground. A quarter of an hour later a lone foxhound bounded across my path and up into the misty crags, baying as he went. There was no sight nor sound of a hunt and I wondered whether he had lost the pack or was on some private business. But he was clearly following a definite line with great determination – probably the scent of the fox I had seen earlier – and I watched him working his way up through the crags and the snow and baying all the time, until I lost him in the mist. The day worsened and I wondered whether the fox had escaped in the white-out and, later, whether the foxhound had found his way home easier than I had done. I had map and compass to guide me over the summit and down the steep, snow-bound crags of Wetherlam Edge but found it awkward, even on familiar ground. The hound had only his nose and his sense of direction but I am sure they sufficed. I must have been over Wetherlam a hundred times but, with visibility down to nil and deep snow masking every feature, it was not even straightforward locating the summit while the way down steep gullies and crags had to be plotted with great care. On such a day, I hope they *both* got home safely.

A Memorial Mountain

The great whale-backed hump of Wetherlam, soaring above the Brathay, has been described as the most industrialised of Lakeland mountains, the 'mountain of a hundred holes'. But the caves, shafts, and quarries, mostly disused, are no more than insignificant scratches on the armour of a noble mountain. Centuries of burrowing by miners and quarrymen have only underlined the superiority of nature over man's puny assaults. For 50 years Wetherlam has been a treasured reminder of youthful adventures, but the familiar fell has now become a memorial. On a recent day of sunlight and snow, the cloud shadows racing across white-capped contours, two of us scattered the mortal remains of a deeply-loved comrade – my brother – from the summit rocks. We felt sure he could not have chosen a more splendid resting place. Far below, the sunlit trough of Little Langdale and the Romans' highway over the passes; to the east, dark woodlands and many sparkling waters; westward, the well-loved crags of the Coniston fells, and north-west, like ramparts across the horizon, the jagged turrets of the highest land in England. There was little wind, no sound to disturb the quietude, nobody in sight within half a county and the only movement in a vast, hushed landscape a pair of ravens quartering the upper recesses of Greenburn. Silently we contemplated the scene – on such a day, surely the finest view in the country – and, thinking of happier days, paid our silent tribute.

[Wetherlam has now been a memorial mountain for me for 15 years.]

Hunting by Motor Car

Little groups of cloth-capped men along the Coniston Old Man quarry road, searching the fells through field-glasses, showed the hounds were out. Parking my car at the fell-gate, I could hear their furious yelping, the so-called 'mountain music' of the foxhunters. Suddenly, I saw them, a long string of brownish-white dots, twisting and turning round the outcrops and streaming at great speed across the fellside. They came to the top of The Bell, the craggy knoll high above Church Beck, and immediately slithered down grooves and gullies in the cliff, each one exactly behind another, like a pouring of quicksilver. Then in a flash they were across the rough road just ahead and up the rocky, east face of the Old Man, the dots getting smaller and smaller until you could not pick them out against the snow, with the noise and the excitement gradually fading away. I never saw the fox but hoped, after such an arduous chase, he had got clean away. Following fox hunts by car, as nine-tenths appear to do nowadays, seems a curiously unrewarding 'sport'. Several followers drove up the quarry road as far as the zigzags on the mountain track in a variety of vehicles – the first time in 60 years I had seen this – but none saw more of the hunt than I did, which was no more than an eye-straining minute or two. There seemed to be only two people following the hunt on foot and they were at least a hard mile behind. The water-ice on the upper slopes above Low Water was too thin and brittle for climbing, needing much more frost, and there wasn't nearly enough good snow-ice; so I cramponned an easy, wandering route up among the crags to the ridge and came down the side of Raven Tor as the late afternoon shadows lengthened across the snow.

The 'Magic' Boots

Towards the end of the wettest four months in the fells for years it was a new experience to emerge from yet another squelching day hardly even damp and completely dry-shod. We were in driving snow in the Langdale fells testing boots and clothing designed by the former Olympic gold medallist and now marathon organiser, Chris Brasher – and, in my case, as an old mountaineer set in my ways, re-thinking ancient prejudices and traditions. The boots were the biggest surprise – especially their lightness and comfort. My usual mountain walking boots weigh just over four pounds the pair, my winter climbing boots about five pounds and my ski-mountaineering boots an uncomfortable eight pounds. Multiplying these weights by thousands of steps on every outing I now realise the vast tonnage I have been lifting over fells and rocks for a lifetime – perhaps unnecessarily. For these new 'magic' boots weighed precisely two pounds. Further, they were half-sprung, something like a shepherd's boot, and this new springiness, combined with the lightness, almost gave the impression of being gently pushed uphill. Mind you, these are not boots for the all-round mountaineer. They do not take crampons and I would not like to climb difficult rocks in them but for an ordinary walk over the fells – the activity of most people in the hills – they seem a significant step forward. The soles are interesting too, the rubber cleats so designed that you don't pick up stones and earth, making the surface smooth and slippy – a small contribution to the environment. I must make further tests in more difficult terrain to reach a final decision but this first trudge over the Langdale fells in snow was surprisingly satisfying.

[This 'Country Diary' in February 1983 attracted dozens of requests from readers wanting further information about the 'magic' boots and, especially, where they could be bought. (Incidentally, I would have been less out of pocket had more of them enclosed stamped addressed envelopes!) My considered verdict on the boots after years of use of various pairs is that they are splendid for walking up or down grassy fells, but lack stability on rough ground, especially traversing. Sideways to the slope the stockinged foot tends to slide inside the boot. Perhaps later models have been strengthened at the sides; if not, I suggest that they are.]

New Window Views

Since the town hall clock is in full view from the windows of my new eyrie I could, I suppose, dispense with a wrist watch when in residence but, scenically, much has been sacrificed by the move from country to

The Derwent Fells from Eel Crags.

town. Buildings are rising daily on the development site around me, increasingly blocking the view, but at least I can see the thousand-foot bulk of Benson Knott to the east of the town, and the ruins of Kendal Castle, birthplace of Henry VIII's Katherine Parr, peep prominently over the town roofs. Straight ahead from my study window is the town's artificial ski slope, floodlit at night, and through binoculars, individual skiers can almost be identified. There is talk of the castle being floodlit and this could be a splendid sight. A short section of the Whinfell ridge can be picked out from my bedroom window when the sun is shining and the shoulder of Bannisdale's White Howe, beyond Whiteside Pike, is just visible. At first I thought it might be Great Yarlside but this seems doubtful. I'll work it out some day with map and compass. On poor days, when the rain is streaming down the town roofs and the clouds low down on the fells, the view is perhaps best at night, with the building scars hidden and the lights of the town glittering brightly through the dark so that I might be looking down on a fairyland. Sadly, most of the green vastness of the views I have left, familiar fells crowding the horizon, is no more but there are some advantages – especially the barely three-minute downhill stroll to shops and pubs. I am only two miles further from the hills and now, without my huge garden, there may be a little more time to devote to them.

[White Howe is, indeed, the fell seen from the upper windows of the maisonette into which I moved in January 1989, a hill often traversed in familiar rounds of the Bannisdale fells. And Kendal Castle was floodlit for the town's 800 years charter celebrations. It was a fine sight from my bedroom, but not nearly so splendid as that from my earlier home of the moonlit summit snows on Red Screes.]

Furthest East

By map and ruler I discover that the nearest two-thousander to my new home is Grey Crag, a remote height above Longsleddale about four miles west of the road over Shap Fells. As the crow flies it is just nine miles away and the top easily attainable, by car and on foot, within two hours. Sadly, its summit is not in view, even from my upper windows, although the head of Bannisdale, a mile from the top, is clearly visible. But, from many visits over the years, I can picture it easily enough – a lonely, grassy hump at the head of a cluster of desolate valleys reaching eastwards towards the Eden and the long line of the Pennines. At the cairn, looking southwards at Morecambe Bay silvering the horizon all the way round to the dark bulk of Black Combe, you are immediately aware you are on the verge of Lakeland. This is where the moorlands, rising from the former main road to Scotland, end and the mountains begin. For Grey Crag has the signal distinction of being the most easterly of the 200 summits over 2,000 feet high in the Lake District. It is a splendid viewpoint, not so much of the Lakeland fells but of wider horizons – the sprawling foothills sloping down through woodlands and villages to the coast, distant ranges crowding the skyline and the long length of Windermere and miles of sea glittering, if you are lucky, in the sunshine. On a recent visit, starting from the splendid packhorse bridge at Sadgill in Longsleddale, there was new snow on the tops, making the bastions of High Street, High Raise and Harter Fell seem far higher and more spectacular than they look in summertime. It was good to be alone up there.

Clouds and Cornices

MARCH

Return to Black Combe

It was a sort of jubilee pilgrimage – a walk up a little mountain I had first climbed about 65 years ago. Black Combe is perhaps the most familiar hill in Lakeland to thousands of people who can see it from their sitting rooms in Morecambe or the front at Blackpool, but not many bother to go up there. We saw nobody on our walk in 1926 and nobody the other day, just the sheep cropping the new grass in the intake fields below the fell and the ravens quartering the summit. On our first visit, knowing no better, we had just ploughed straight up from the Whicham Valley road until there was nowhere higher to go. From the top we had looked down on the Furness peninsula spread out below us like a map and at the then not-very-familiar Lake District mountains. We did not know then that Wordsworth had been up there and had claimed that the view from the top was the best and the longest in Britain. To a boy it just seemed a very big mountain with an elusive summit. But the other morning, sunny, fresh, and a good drying day, it was just an easy upland walk – except for the furious east wind that, at times, nearly blew us off our feet. There were white horses on the breakers along the coast and ice on the pools, while the last few yards to the circular cairn, right in the teeth of the gale, were as tough as any treadmill. There was no encouragement to admire Wordsworth's view – sadly restricted by cloud – but good fun to scamper down, ears tingling and cheeks burning, to the comfort of a favourite inn, a delight we had been too young to enjoy in the 1920s.

Crampons or Nails?

For half a mile to the left of Dove Crag – as viewed from Kirkstone foot – are four or five steepish snow slopes, sometimes with small cornices, reaching up to the summit ridge. Pottering about alone in winters I had climbed all but one of them and, the other day, managed to collect the last – not without some trepidation at times. Conditions were perfect for crampons but would have been extremely hazardous for anybody without them and an ice-axe. The snow was frozen hard as rock and glazed with ice so that, without crampons, progress would only have been possible by step-cutting – the traditional way of ascent before the introduction of moulded rubber soles, replacing nails, forced the general adoption of crampons. There was nobody about and I had the vast, unmarked ice-fields of Dove Crag and Hart Crag, dazzling in the sunlight, to myself. The snow-ice was so hard that the crampons left little impression and on the steeper places, the front points had to be kicked in hard to take hold. I see that a member of the Alpine Club, following the sad death of a member of the Guinness family through a slip on snow, is recommending the use of nailed boots for walkers on British hills in winter. The high, frozen snows were clearly out of bounds to inadequately equipped walkers the other day but I would have been happy with my pre-war 'iron boots', shod with Stubai waisted clinkers and tricounis – now consigned to the attic. Incidentally, an effective, non-climbing use for crampons is, round about now, for aerating the lawns by walking up and down them for a few hours with the things strapped on to your boots.

[*My pre-war 'iron boots' now decorate the premises of a Lake District mountain equipment dealer – as a curio!*]

In the Clouds

Nothing to be seen in Deepdale the other day except the swollen beck and sodden lower slopes reaching up into the thick cloud blanket. We squelched and felt our way below unseen crags into Sleet Cove and found the snow we had been seeking – a white, untrodden highway rising steeply between black rock walls towards a grey void. Would the snow gully reach the Fairfield ridge without undue difficulties? We couldn't be sure for we were uncertain to a few hundred yards of our exact position but the snow, after loose scree and wet boulders, was a welcome change. Crampons biting nicely into the hard snow we mounted steadily pausing now and again to secure each other on the steeper sections. Every 50 feet or so we could see a little farther ahead through the gloom but the white ribbon continued unbroken. So much snow seemed unbelievable after all the rain and the knowledge that the south-facing slopes were completely bare. On we climbed, the cloud getting thicker until we could see only a few feet ahead, and then, after a final steep section where hand-holds had to be cut, the gully flattened out and we found ourselves on an icy ridge. I never cease to marvel about the extraordinary difference between north and south-facing slopes in our Lakeland winters. We must have ascended nearly 1,000 feet on unbroken snow on a day when motorists might have doubted the existence of even a pocket handkerchief of the stuff. A quick compass bearing in an icy wind for the summit of Fairfield and we cramponned across level ice to a familiar cairn and a decision on the best way down out of the clouds.

Seeking the Snows

If I can detect from my house even a pocket handkerchief of snow on the fells I know there will be great drifts of it on the north and east faces of the mountains. To the casual sight of the motorist driving north through the district the other day the fells would have appeared completely clear of snow, but if he had climbed into the hills and looked south or west he would have seen a different picture – snow on all the heights. Winter, therefore, appears to last longer in the fells if you live at Penrith or Keswick than if your home is at, say, Kendal or along the Cumbrian coast. Since I live in the south of the national park I need some scale for assessing the likelihood of snow for skiing or winter mountaineering, and I find that with only one tiny patch visible from my windows – normally in Hall Cove underneath High Street – there will be a sufficiency of the stuff in the right places. Whether the snow will be frozen enough for gully climbing normally requires investigation on the spot, but you can generally ski on material with the consistency of porridge or wet sugar. From the apparently snow-free Kirkstone fells the other day – as seen from the south – the westward view showed Bowfell and the Scafells liberally covered in large white drifts, suggesting ample opportunities for winter adventure. Even close at hand the effect of the orientation of the fells could be seen at a glance. The south-east corrie of Red Screes – useful in early winter for easy snow climbing – was completely bare but the north-east corrie, facing away from the sun, was full of snow: from spring to winter within one mile.

53

The south-east corrie of Red Screes in summer.

Wild Weather

To emerge out of a steep, shadowed snow gully on to a sunlit mountain ridge is one of the great moments of winter in the fells. One minute, chilled despite the exercise, you are coping with problems of balance and – if there is a cornice – verticality; the next, you are suddenly in the sunshine, treading easy snows and looking out over smiling hills. It was like this the other day, stepping out of a Deepdale gully on to the Fairfield summit ridge – except that the wind, not felt in the sheltered snow couloir, hit us like a battering ram, making it difficult to stand, let alone advance. But, our climb behind us, we eventually struggled, between gusts, to make our token summit visit before escaping from the gale down the steep snow of Flinty Graves into the sheltered moraines of a dale flooded with afternoon sunlight. The previous day, while a Force 7 gale pounded the Cumbrian coast, we had been less fortunate. An attempt on the long gully leading from Brown Cove to Helvellyn Low Man had had to be abandoned because we could not even stand on the crusted snow in the boisterous gusts and, more than once, were bowled over. So we traversed on to White

Side and Raise and allowed ourselves to be blown home down the tourist route. The general public does not associate avalanches with the winter scene in the Lake District but they happen all the same. Our Brown Cove gully was piled with avalanche snow – you could see where the cornice had collapsed – and other snow gullies on the east side of Helvellyn were the same. We hoped that nobody had been in the way when the huge accumulations of a long winter crashed down the mountainside.

The Lost Foxhound

The foxhound, dirty and dejected, was mournfully casting about in the snow near the summit of Fairfield, tail tightly curled between his legs. Visibility was down to five yards and the hound's aimless footprints, in all directions, showed he was completely lost. I had climbed a snow gully out of Deepdale and the hound watched me take off my crampons and then, when I moved off, attached himself to me for the rest of the day. Which pack he belonged to – the Ullswater or the Coniston – I could not guess, but at least I could get him below the cloud. We steered by compass over Hart Crag and across the shoulder of Hartsop-above-How, the hound almost walking to heel. Then down the side of a rocky ravine until suddenly we came below the mist, and there was the long length of Deepdale, curving down to Patterdale far below. I noticed my companion's tail was now jaunty and erect; did he now know he was safe and on his way home? But were his kennels at Glenridding or at Ambleside, on the other side of the fells? An Ullswater hound, I thought, would have bounded ahead down Deepdale, surely on familiar ground, but this one just kept plodding behind me. Perhaps he came from the Coniston after all, or perhaps foxhounds don't remember scenery but merely rely on scent and instinct. I didn't know. Surprisingly, he had great difficulty in crossing Deepdale Beck – not liking water or sore pads? – but soon he was sniffing around the Deepdale farms and by a subterfuge, I managed to lose him, before reaching the car. Later I was conscience-stricken. Should I have taken him to the kennels or handed him over to the police?

Over the Cornice

A depressing fortnight of rain, with cloud-wreathed fells, and then, suddenly, a perfect day. Alone below the white wall of Helvellyn, beside the icy waste of Red Tarn, it was hard to credit there had been such a tremendous thaw, that so many millions of tons of snow had washed down the becks. Cornices overhung the face that sloped, an unbroken white curtain, to the frozen tarn and, on either side of the corrie, the snows reached up to the rock turrets of Striding and Swirral edges. Warm sunshine flooded the cove, not a whisper of wind and hardly a sound except an occasional distant voice from the tiny black specks creeping along the ridge. The frozen snow was perfect for crampons and ice-axe, and a ladder of steps up the centre of the face eased the work. You run the gauntlet on this ascent of spectators critically observing, or photographing, your progress, or lack of it, and they were there again that day. But this did not lessen the familiar thrill of pulling over the shadowed cornice and stepping on to the sunlit summit ridge, with views across mountain Lakeland to the Scafells and beyond. Still no wind, even above 3,000 feet, and not a cloud between Helvellyn and Scotland. Two days earlier from my home I could only see across two sodden fields. Descending the Lower Man snow couloir into Brown Cove, I came upon grim evidence of the rapid thaw – a recent avalanche of parts of the cornice that had swept thousands of tons of snow, piled in huge, frozen blocks, into the cove. This is one of the dangers of the snow-bound hills to the inexperienced or ill-equipped, and Easter visitors should be aware that smiling, sunlit fells – as seen from the valleys – can still be lethal.

Above Red Tarn

It was tempting, on this superb March day, to spend the whole afternoon lazily sunbathing in the snow on the shore of Red Tarn below Helvellyn's east wall. After a week of rain, cloud or high winds, this was a day in a thousand – warm alpine sunshine, snow-plastered fells against a cloudless, blue sky and not enough wind to flicker a match. I sat on the edge of the frozen tarn to eat my lunch and to savour the sight of encircling walls of snow and rock with their clean-cut cornices – always one of the most dramatic winter scenes in the Lake District. There were two distant, matchstick figures on the rock towers of Striding Edge but no footprints in the new snow except my own and the quietude of the scene was complete. The only movements in a stilled, frozen world were the aerobatics of three pairs of ravens circling the summit and the slowly lengthening vapour trails of unseen aircraft. Having found the perfect sanctuary why go any further? I could doze in the sunshine another two hours before the shadows crept down into the corrie. But conscience pricked and, after half an hour, I had to bestir myself. The steepening snows of the east wall, through an outcrop of crag, went well although the new snow demanded care in making secure steps. But conditions improved below the cornice – a double affair with a convenient ledge for the final pull over the top – and then the sudden reward: waves of snow-bound peaks reaching to the horizon, with the Scafells probing the western sky. Two people eating in the wall-shelter were the only others enjoying the superb view from a mountain top that has attracted up to a thousand people on some far less rewarding summer days.

What's in a Name?

Who, I have often wondered, was Kilnshaw whose eponymous Chimney is a particularly striking feature of Red Screes above Kirkstone Pass? The names of pioneer climbers have sometimes been given to rock chimneys on our crags but Kilnshaw's (or Kilnshaw) Chimney has been a name on the maps for much more than 100 years so he can't have been a climber. Nor can I trace the name among the various owners or tenants of Kirkstone Pass Inn since Parson Sewell of Troutbeck first opened the place – formerly The Travellers Rest – in 1840. The Chimney is a steep scree gully with rock walls cleaving the craggy eastern slopes of the fell like a giant sabre slash. In summertime there is only one slightly awkward pitch, generally either wet or greasy, but in winter this is often hidden under many feet of snow, making the climb a straightforward ascent. Two of us, to salve our consciences on a bitterly cold day with a furious north-east gale, recently clawed our way up the Chimney – thinking, most of the time, of the blazing fire and warming drinks at the inn. Snow goggles were necessary because of the spindrift that poured and gusted down the gully but these were soon frozen over so that we saw very little. The thickly-clouded summit on which it was difficult to stand was a howling wilderness of snow but the descent into the south-east corrie by an easy snow gully was sheltered from the worst of the blizzard. Back down at the inn we decided that Parson Sewell, the vicar-innkeeper, would have been expertly authoritative about the weather. Once asked to pray for rain for the crops he sensibly replied from the pulpit: 'It's no use praying for rain while t'wind's i' this quarter.'

Unconsolidated Snow

The snow in the couloir at the side of Dove Crag was so soft and unconsolidated that sometimes I was up to the waist in it and, for every step, at least to the knees. My ice-axe was quite useless and upward progress only achieved at the steepening top by punching in the arms to the shoulder and hauling mightily. It felt like clawing oneself out of a crevasse – on a modest winter walk over Dove Crag and Hart Crag from lovely Dovedale. Rarely have I found the fells so sodden below 1,000 feet – eroded tracks turned into becks and morasses of mud everywhere – and, above that height, miles of sunlit snow fields that flattered to deceive – a beautiful, glistening and completely untracked carpet that proved immensely tiring to traverse. I thought of scrambling for a brew-up into the cave among the overhangs on Dove Crag where, if you are not a somnambulist, you may pleasantly spend the night – and record it in the visitors' book – but the snow seemed too treacherous and I contented myself with the exhausting trudge over the two summits. Even the unseen snow-filled becks had to be treated like alpine crevasses although the only risk was of dropping through the waist-deep snow into the water and not into icy depths. Seen from Hart Crag the Helvellyn range was blanketed in thick black cloud, already advancing on Fairfield, and, a couple of hours later, there were snow flurries as I drove home over Kirkstone. Dovedale, crowded with cliffs and tumbling becks, has always been a favourite corner – desperate summer climbs on the crags, winter excitements in the gullies, Dovedale Slabs, unroped in nailed boots, half a lifetime ago, the buzzards soaring above the screes and the tasty hazel nuts in the woods every October.

Spring in Borrowdale

Borrowdale basked in early spring sunshine, savouring its midweek, out-of-season quietude. Nobody watched the flooded Derwent swirling through the birches. Sheepdogs lazed, undisturbed, in farmhouse porches. Seatoller carpark was empty, and only two cars defined the Seathwaite road end. Sunlit fells, sprouting woodlands, the sparkling cascade of Sourmilk Gill, and morning birdsong in the hedgerows suggested spring but there was ice on the Grains Gill track and the shadowed, north face of Great End was still in winter's grip. The transformation took an hour – blue skies and shirt-sleeves sunshine in the dale; steeply soaring snows and ice reaching into grey, boiling clouds on the great crag above the Esk Hause track. Being alone, a modest route was taken up the crag on frozen snow, perfect for crampons. It had been balmy and windless below but, towards the top of the crag, the north wind was sweeping spindrift up the gully ahead of me. On the arctic wilderness of the summit visibility was down to yards but back down on Esk Hause, half an hour later, the sun was gilding the snow and Great Gable had been clear all day. Some Outward Bound students – the only people met on the round – were sliding about on top of the pass on short, plastic skis. Near the head of Ruddy Gill the snow drifts were ten feet deep and I had seen icicles like giant stalactites hanging from the crag. The Styhead track was deserted and Taylor Gill Force in lonely, surging spate. In a hard winter this great weight of falling water has been frozen into immobility and climbed as an ice route. 'More snow to come,' said the farmer, Stan Edmondson, down at Seathwaite and, three days later, the passes were blocked again by new falls.

Magnetic Variations

Two readers' letters seem to query the general advice in my last diary note to trust the compass implicitly in thick mist on the fells. One warns that a compass held in a hand on which an analogue quartz watch is worn could produce inaccuracies; the answer here might be to hold the compass in the other hand. With regard to the other warning that iron in the rock might affect compasses, the results of a detailed survey carried out in the Bowfell area some years ago by the Brathay Exploration Group may be helpful. One of the few things that some old guidebooks said about Bowfell was that magnetic rock on the summit made compasses unreliable, but the survey showed that deviations only occurred if the compass was actually placed on certain rocks or held very close to them. Minor deviations could be detected at several points between Crinkle Crags and Esk Pike – about three degrees near Shelter Crags, for instance – but not if the compass was held in the hand, well away from the rocks. However, on the north-west side of Ore Gap, between Bowfell and Esk Pike, deviations of up to 170 degrees could be contrived with the compass laid on the rock, sending the walker back the way he had come if he resorted to this unusual practice. The group's conclusion was that to avoid being misled on Bowfell you should not place your compass on or near rocks. There are haematite deposits on the appropriately named Ore Gap and iron ore used to be taken from here to bloomeries in Eskdale or Langstrath. This pass has been in use for at least 2,000 years, and stone axes from the Pike

Walkers on Great Carrs, with the Scafells to the left and Crinkle Crags and Bowfell to the right.

o'Stickle 'factory' might even have gone this way and down to the coast for export.

Enjoying Navigation

The most unlikely looking day for the fells can often bring its quiet rewards. It was a depressing morning – car headlights probing the fog and a persistent drizzle. Reaching Low Tilberthwaite there was nothing but streaming fellsides, sodden sheep, and thick mist, but the familiar scent of woodsmoke that has always marked this sleepy corner for me, seemed to cheer the gloom. Steel Edge, the fine, rocky spur plunging north-east from Wetherlam's summit ridge would, I thought, make an interesting ascent. Everything was hidden in mist, but I knew its direction. Wet snow underfoot soon changed to a crisp or frozen surface, and the rain had now given way to thickly falling snow, swirling in the wind. As height was gained the mist thickened, necessitating careful compass work. Somewhere to the right would be the snow gullies of Hen Tor, so often climbed on bright, winter days. But my little world that afternoon was just a few yards of steep snow ladders through ice-spattered crags, with unseen depths on either side. It was the fascination of the work that brought the reward: keeping the right line, kicking or cutting steps in the now perfect snow; balancing up the rocks; and the quiet satisfaction of snatching a moderately challenging route out of what, away from the heights, was a miserable day. Just to judge the right moment, on Swallow Scar, for a 90-degree swing to the east to hit the summit ridge, seemed an achievement that made everything worthwhile. Nothing and nobody had been seen all afternoon, since leaving the smoking chimneys in the valley, apart from a few yards of rock and snow and the whirling flakes; but it felt good, on one's own, to have been pleasantly stretched for an hour or two.

Winter Came Late

What a strange winter so far in the fell country – biting winds and swirling snow flurries one day, perhaps thick fog and drizzle the next, and then a sunless day or two of almost eerie stillness and quietude. We seem poised in a limbo before the expected snows, with nature unable to settle into its accustomed pattern. The middle of March and no skiing or snow-climbing to speak of yet for the first time in many years – and little snow in the Cairngorms, either, and none in Glencoe. Three days ago the edge of the world, a blanket of grey fog, was at the bottom of my garden; this morning I could pick out the profile of Great End which must be 15 miles away. Yesterday, it was difficult to move in places on the tops against a furious north wind; today, not a twig moves in the sleeping landscape. An hour ago a shaft of wintry sunlight, viewed from my study window, briefly illuminated a dusting of snow on High Street but, as I write, the mists are creeping across the tops and even the Troutbeck fells have disappeared. Now it has started to snow again and only the nearest fields are visible. Two recent trips to the heights to try out an expensive cagoule in the new 'magic' material that is claimed to defeat condensation, are remembered. From lonely Grey Crag, the nearest two-thousand footer to my home, there was the reward of clouds suddenly torn apart to reveal a quick vista of Yorkshire summits and the distant, silvered fringe of Morecambe Bay. Another day a frozen tarn on Sergeant Man was crossed with ease before the descent of the grey tors and heathery rock-gardens on Tarn Crag to the sheltered peace of Easdale. More log-splitting this afternoon in preparation for the real winter which, surely, will soon be here.

[Winter did finally arrive that year, 1980, but it was late and short, the pattern for several subsequent years.]

High Above Low Water

The craggy fellside above Low Water in the Coniston fells is transformed in a hard winter into a 900-foot wall of snow, ice and rock threaded by gleaming white gullies and topped by a saucer-rim of cornices. On one recent visit the scene might have been a colour picture of the Alps – the tarn frozen right across, the sunshine sparkling on the soaring snows and bright blue sky throwing the sculptured cornices into bold relief. I chose a shallow gully line to the right of the main crag but found a little ice pitch, high up, a bit too precarious for a lone climber and had to pick an easier way. Neither of my two axes could make much impression on the six-inch-thick ice, hard as concrete, although, with a companion, the place would not have seemed nearly so formidable. But there were no further difficulties, the cornice was easy and I stepped out of the sheltered corrie on to the Old Man ridge to meet a biting wind, despite the blazing sun. People met on the ridge bemoaned their lack of crampons for, that day, even the ordinary tourist tracks were sheeted in ice and the whole mountain encrusted in frozen snow – potentially dangerous for ill-equipped walkers. Indeed, I had had to put on my own crampons before reaching Low Water on the quarry track and kept them on for the steep descent of Gill Cove to Levers Water. These conditions occur during part of most Lakeland winters and, on such occasions, safety can only be assured by the use of crampons – even by ordinary fell walkers – and, of course, ice-axes. Yet I rarely see walkers with crampons and I even meet people in winter on places like Striding Edge, when they're plastered in ice, without ice-axes.

A Nameless Tarn

The tarn, bigger than a rugger field but still without a name and not even marked on large-scale maps until about 15 years ago, sparkled in the morning sunlight. We were walking the pleasant heights around the shy dale of Greenburn – Steel Fell, Calf Crag, Gibson Knott and Helm Crag – and, as usual, the tarn surprised us by its size for an innominate one which, despite a longish period of dry weather, looked as expansive as ever. The shallow tarn lies on the rather boggy ridge between Steel Fell and Calf Crag immediately above the even boggier valley of Wythburn into which, I suppose, it drains. Nearly 30 years ago Heaton Cooper, the Lakeland artist, reporting that the tarn, up till then, had never appeared on any map, suggested the name of Steel Fell Tarn and hoped it would have 'a place on the maps of the future'. At one time, long before the fusion of the Lakeland counties, I suggested the name Boundary Tarn since the pool lay exactly on the then boundary between Cumberland and Westmorland while, among a few close friends, the tarn is sometimes jokingly called Griffin's Tarn because I'm 'always going on about it'. Anyway, it has been shown on· the maps for some years now but is still without a name – possibly the largest of dozens of tarns in the district unnamed. The delightful stroll up the south-east ridge of Steel Fell, although so close to the Dunmail Raise highway, is clearly not often used and the sunny bowl of Greenburn, with its pools and waterfalls, is unknown to many visitors and usually quite empty of people.

Exploring the Underground

On one of the wonderful alpine days in our best outdoors winter for years three of us deserted the sunlit snows to go underground-exploring in the long-abandoned Coniston copper mines. My guide was Colin Thornton who, although living in distant Ilfracombe, seemed as familiar with the bowels of these fells, the dark, flooded levels, shafts, holes and rusted machinery, as I am with crags and outcrops on the surface. Fifty-odd years ago some of us, with candles for light and only our balaclavas for protection, used to poke about in these old workings, not knowing what we were doing. Now, with modern equipment and a knowledgeable leader, some of the exciting, 400 years story of mining in these fells became clearer and I could only marvel at the courage, strength and determination of those who gouged out these vast caverns and awesome depths. The 'old men' they were called – although few lived beyond their forties – and they drove in the early tunnels and shafts, in the days before gunpowder, with nothing better than hammers and wedges. Eventually the workings reached a depth of 1,200 feet with, in places, another 600 feet of shaft to the roof, and some of the levels drove nearly a quarter of a mile into the fellsides. As we splashed through the winding drifts the beams from our headlights showed us old ladders reaching vertically up to unseen heights or dropping down through flooded shafts to frightening, dark depths. Here, in the dust that killed so many of them, in terribly constricted places, laboured the 'old men' whose initials can be found, here and there, chiselled out of rock. These unsung men, Austrians, Irishmen or Cumbrians, must have been a race apart.

Deepdale Delights

The high corrie of Link Cove, almost completely ringed with snow-bound crags, sparkled and danced on this bright spring morning – the sunlight glinting on the snows soaring steeply to the summit ridge and the tiny becks tripping, sliding and tinkling down through the mosses to the dale a thousand feet below. My gateway to the hanging valley had been 'Ern Nest Gill' – my name for the steep ravine beside Ern Nest Crag – but this time, although I had climbed it several times, summer and winter, I couldn't get past the big waterfall pitch because of the weight of water coming down and had to escape, very wet, up the side. The snows reached down to the floor of the corrie and the steep snow gully immediately to the right of Scrubby Crag was selected as the longest ladder to the heights. Full in the sun the snow, however, proved too soft for enjoyment, with axes and crampons quite useless, as steps, even after several kicks, kept breaking away. But, at least, it was a sunny way to the top and a round of the snow-bound, Deepdale summits – a change from the usual cold, shadowed interiors of winter gullies. Summit views across most of mountain Lakeland were needle sharp – a common enough feature on bright days following heavy downpours, as this one proved to be. Near the Hart Crag col two foxhounds, probably stragglers from some Ullswater hunt, were casting round in circles, clearly lost, and I was reminded of a lost foxhound, encountered once as I emerged from Black Tippet on a misty snow day that had followed me, thankfully, trotting to heel, all the compass-found way down to Patterdale. But nothing else that moved was seen all day – except for two buzzards slowly soaring above Deepdale and two pairs of ravens energetically quartering the skies.

The Bowfell Hut

The mysterious stone hut near the top of Bowfell, plastered in snow so that its shape merged into the crags, was even more difficult than usual to find. Twice I passed it before the regular masonry of the walls gave it away. Presumably it is a shepherd's shelter but why he built it here, high up in rough crags facing east across the trough of Mickleden, is difficult to determine. Could it have been some sort of look-out? The shepherd, like those who used the miniature shelters near Small Water, must have been a very small man, careless of his comfort. I can only just squeeze inside by taking off my rucksack and wriggling in backwards. The hut is on about the 2,800 feet contour – at a similar height to the former 'smuggler's hut' near the top of Central Gully on Gable Crag. Fifty years ago you could just pick out the shape of the remains of the low walls of the Gable hut; now all the stones have disappeared down the gully. But the Bowfell hut is completely intact, including its stone roof. Inexperienced walkers should not try to find it, especially in winter conditions, for it is sited among crags in a steep place just to the north of the north gully of Bowfell Buttress. Its discomforts could hardly commend it even to the hardiest of mountaineers. Their idea of five-star accommodation among the crags might be the splendid cave on Dove Crag where a dozen people could bed down in comparative comfort. But a few steps from this 'bedroom' is a 300-foot vertical drop to the screes so this is hardly a safe howff for somnambulists.

The Hills of Youth

Sixty years ago this summer I cycled the 18 miles from my home to Water Yeat, south of Coniston, had a bathe in Beacon Tarn, went up Torver Beacon and then climbed the craggy, little hill above High Nibthwaite, on the other side of the lake, and built a tall, rickety cairn on top. It was the first, and the last, time I had built a cairn on a hill or mountain and I remember stopping a mile or so down the road on my ride back home and looking back with pride at the little, dark matchstick high in the sky. The other day, not without nostalgia, I repeated the round, using a car this time and omitting any cairn building and, of course, any bathing since my appreciation of winter dips has long since disappeared. Memories of that day in the 1920s came back as I tramped again over these lovely, little fells but I had forgotten about the magnificence of the view from the Beacon – and its special significance. For, straight ahead on this recent bright, frosty morning, filling the sky to the west and north, stretched the fells that meant most to me in my youth. Leftwards was the rocky spike of Stickle Pike, my very first hill as a 12-year-old schoolboy, and, further left, the great bulk of Black Combe on the edge of the sea, my first mountain a year or two later. And, four miles away, beyond Little Arrow Moor, the gullies and buttresses of Dow Crag where, from a hut on the shore of the lake, half a dozen of us had gone climbing almost every weekend

Dow Crag near Coniston.

for many years. The happy hills and crags of youth and still, after all those years, barely changed.

[This sixtieth anniversary round was done in March 1987. I should have done it years earlier and kept on doing it for this is a lovely, unspoiled area.]

Spring in the Air

APRIL

Daffodils and Damson Blossom

Daffodils, damson blossom, flaming forsythia, and purple aubretia hanging over cottage walls – all, with the hawthorn, ash, and rowan bursting into leaf, part of our April glory. As foreground to the spring snow still cloaking the heights, the new colour along the lanes, in gardens, and orchards, seems to light the way towards the hills. Wordsworth's 'host of golden daffodils' grew along the shore of Ullswater near Gowbarrow Park, but Dora's Field – properly The Rashfield – adjoining Rydal Mount where he died, is perhaps better known today for its spring display of daffodils and narcissi. The blooms are often at their best around the poet's birthday, April 7. My own daffodils are already beginning to yellow and so, too, are the thousands of blooms along the roadside all the way to the lake. And Brigsteer Woods could be carpeted in yellow very soon. The famous Lyth Valley damson blossom will be at least a week later – in an average year April 18 is about the date to see it at its best. For the best effect of the clouds of white on a thousand trees, the blossom should come before the leaf but, after a savage winter, the leaf sometimes comes with the blossom or even before it, making the picture not quite so fine. There is no lovelier route to the Lakes from the south in spring than through the sleepy dale where grows, in almost every garden and orchard, the damson that some people consider the best in the world – oval, not round, in shape, with a perfect dusty bloom and sharp nutty flavour. And the dale, nowadays, has another distinction – a certain hostelry with more than 60 malt whiskys on offer and a most erudite barman. You can do them all in a short day – the daffodils, the damson blossom, and a dram or two of your favourite malt.

[Regretfully, the hostelry is not the place it was in 1984 and Reg Jackson, the erudite barman who knew his malts, has now retired.

A Wasdale Transformation

It's not often, nowadays, when better days can be seized at any time, that I take to the hills in thick mist and rain but it seemed very feeble to slink back from Wasdale just because of bad weather. Besides, there's always the chance, even on the worst days, of one of those great moments in the fells when the clouds are suddenly torn aside and the

Wastwater Screes.

sunlit dale, far below, leaps up at you in a flash. Navigation along the top of the Wastwater Screes in the swirling cloud and relentless drizzle merely involved keeping to the crumbling edge above the gullies and shattered crags, and what, in fine weather, is an airy tramp above yawning depths with dramatic views, could only be pleasurably remembered. But, half-way down the curious crater of Greathall Gill, with its crumbling rock pinnacles, the rain suddenly stopped and, as I drew closer to the toe of Wastwater, the cloud slowly thinned and the valley started to reveal itself like a photograph in a developing tank. First, the lake, as the clouds floated away towards the far shore, and, then, gradually, the background of the fells – Buckbarrow, Middle Fell and Yewbarrow – each one quickly taking shape and colour as, remarkably, the sun came out. And the miracle was not yet over for, minutes later, on this still, windless day, as the last ripples faded across the lake, Wastwater, often so black and stormy, became a perfect mirror with the far crags and sunlit fellsides beautifully revealed, upside-down, and the now-bright blue sky reached across, in the picture, to the foot of the screes and the lake shore path winding interestingly, across the boulders.

The Old Corpse Road

A wild morning with the tops hidden in cloud and a biting nor'easter sweeping flurries of sleet across a brimming Haweswater weakened an earlier resolve to do a worthy round and I found myself, shamefacedly, crawling along the Old Corpse Road inventing excuses for my lack of moral fibre. This was the way – until about 1736 when a graveyard was provided at Mardale chapel – the dead were carried, strapped on the backs of ponies, for burial at Shap. Walking the lonely fell track to Swindale, about a third of the way, this dark morning it was easy to imagine those long, sad journeys – sometimes, no doubt, in worse weather than this. To brighten the way, though, there was the tumult of the plunging necklace of falls in Hopgill Beck and, for a while, the almost unmistakable merry, yelping sound of a fox hunt on the far, mist-laden shore. For some time I searched the fellsides, below the cloud, with binoculars for the streaming hounds – until I realised the yelps were the squawking of gulls fighting over possession of the little island beyond The Rigg. The Old Corpse Road is barely the width of a sheep-trod in places but the steepish start had been carefully graded with zigzags to ease the way for the laden ponies. It is still a green road – unlike the grossly-eroded tourist tracks; clearly not many people go this way to enjoy the sudden vista of lovely, unspoiled Swindale opening out far below. I came back through the clouds over Selside Pike, seeing nothing. The tramp across the lonely moor, alone with my thoughts, had been the best part of the morning.

Mardale Waters

The lovely name, Mardale Waters, is printed by the map-makers across the crags and contours that make up the fell land between the superb mountain tarns of Blea Water and Small Water. Perhaps the name was originally given by the Mardale shepherds to the twin tarns at the head of their dale, but I have always taken it to embrace the becks that scurry down the fellside towards the lake in shining necklaces of pools and waterfalls. The other day these dancing becks, freed from the ice that earlier had encased them in winter silence and swollen by melting snowfields, were merrily splashing down to the flooded dale in a hundred sounds of hurrying waters. Appropriate, perhaps, that this strange, evocative name – unique in Lakeland – should be applied to the dale head more influenced by water than any other. Mardale is the valley they drowned – its lake doubled in size to become the biggest reservoir in England – and its waters now reach to the dale head, thus halving the journey to the great basin of the surging Mardale Waters and quickening their conversion from musical mountain becks to so many million gallons of water storage. My round of the tops that circle the dale head was a snow walk in the clouds, with a compass helpful, but the mist cleared below the Nan Bield, with splendid views of all the Mardale Waters and a well-filled Haweswater – far finer than when the lake is drawn down. There was a dead sheep in one of the tiny rock shelters by Small Water – had it crawled in there to die? – and, at the end of the dale road, photographers scanning the skies and the crags for a sight of golden eagles.

A New Way Up

The steepish east face of Wetherlam is a useful place – especially in winter and spring – for ancient mountaineers anxious to convince themselves they are not yet completely 'past it'. Besides the tourist ascent of Wetherlam Edge which can be interesting when plastered in ice there are the straightforward snow gullies on either side of Hen Tor, the slightly intimidating crag itself, easy snow gullies to the south, the pleasant rock arete of Steel Edge and several other scrambles that may involve avoiding – or even exploring – old mine shafts or levels. The other day the snow in the gullies was too soft and sparse for climbing but an interesting way up the fell was found by taking a direct line from a derelict mine just above the old mines road that leads over the shoulder to Coniston. A rather wet wriggle up the side of a little

Yew Tree Farm near Coniston, with Wetherlam behind.

buttress led to a broad grass ledge below a pleasant line of cliffs that the 1:25,000 map suggests is called Swallow Scar – not to be confused with Swallow Scarth, the east-facing crag between Helvellyn and Nethermost Pike. Swallow Scar has everything the geriatric climber requires – nice, clean rock set at an accommodating angle, nothing difficult and plenty of good holds. There are three buttresses, all providing easy, airy scrambling and just over the top there's a lovely little tarn, set among rock outcrops, where, for many years, I've eaten my sandwiches, sheltered from the east wind. A stroll across to the summit and then pleasantly down the rocks of Steel Edge – curiously unnoticed by Wainwright and, therefore, trackless until quite recent years.

Aeroplane Crashes

We came upon the wrecked aeroplane during a snow walk on Scafell Pike – a crumbled mass of wreckage jammed among boulders 800 feet below the summit. How the three occupants survived such a crash seemed a miracle. Wheels, jagged pieces of metal and sodden cushions

71

lay scattered in the snow. Two officials were recovering instruments from the shattered cockpit. I recalled a similar plane crash two miles away on the slopes of Great End 12 years ago; both the occupants were killed. The remains of perhaps 20 aircraft still litter our fells, with complete engines in some cases, and elsewhere only twisted bits of metal. Some of the planes were wartime bombers, perhaps limping home, damaged after action, and losing height. Two or three crashed on the Scafell range, one of them a Whitley bomber with, miraculously, three survivors, one of whom, the Canadian navigator, later told me of their remarkable escape. A minimum of 3,300 feet would clear every peak in England but presumably some pilots have risked coming lower to find a way through mist, or have been caught in air currents. I have often wondered whether some echo-sounding device or radio beacon on the highest summit, Scafell Pike, would be practical. There is too much paraphernalia – monuments, triangulation columns, fancy cairns, and so on – on several of our summits, but such an extra one could, perhaps, save lives.

[The Scafell Pike plane crash with its miraculous escapes was in April 1978. Nothing came of my echo-sounding/radio beacon suggestion and there have been fatal aircraft crashes in the Lake District fells since then.]

Crowds on Helvellyn

Helvellyn at holiday time is the lodestar for a remarkable cross-section of the genus tourist. On Easter Monday there were hundreds up there – possibly up to 1,000 visited the summit during the day. They came from all parts of the country and were of all ages, with or without experience, suitably equipped or ridiculously dressed as if for beach or promenade. The most popular mountain in England attracts them all – some people making their first and only ascent, in a lifetime, of a mountain. This day all the gullies were packed with snow, the east face hung with white curtains, and Red Tarn still frozen right across, but the tourists followed, single file, along well-trodden tracks enjoying the sunshine and the views, peeped over the cornices and generally retreated down the edges in good order. There was nobody else on the east face when I cramponned up the wall although a family party was in camp by the frozen tarn. One of the national park rangers, checking the processions on Striding Edge, told me he had had to turn back one visitor, trembling with fear, on one of the rock steps. Now and again he spoke by radio with his base – 'weather perfect, snow soft, no problems'. Together we glissaded down to Red Tarn. A lone climber was on the face, following my steps up to the cornice. Black specks were moving along the edges, but the corrie – unchanged, in its snow and ice, since January – was deserted. In the early evening sunlight Red Tarn Beck, flooded with melted snows, was a tumult of white waterfalls and churning pools. Ullswater was gay with small boats and playing children.

Overhanging Cornices

The fell country has been packed with visitors this holiday weekend and, no matter what the weather, large numbers – some of them on their first outing of the year – will be out in the hills today. Not all of them will be alive to the conditions which may well be the exact opposite of those in the valleys. A day or two ago, for instance, the snow cornices along the Helvellyn summit ridge were 20 feet thick, overhanging or vertical and the snow wall on the east face up to 800 feet high. Nothing of this could be seen from any road – indeed, motorists would hardly be aware there was snow in the mountains – and other east and north-facing slopes were also still in winter garb. Two or three days before Easter while ascending the snow couloir out of Brown Cove on to Helvellyn Lower Man I met two people coming down – without ice-axes or crampons. They explained they had been unable to get off the summit ridge and down any of the tourist routes because of the cornices and had been forced to attempt the descent of the gully. The snow was steep and icy in places, it was snowing slightly and the summit ridge, when I reached it, was arctic – cold and windy, with swirling mists and acres of hard-packed snow. As it happened, they got down all right, but they should not have been on Helvellyn, intending a descent to the east, without ice-axes and, over the years many accidents have occurred in just these circumstances – some of them fatal. One hopes that the mountain rescue teams have had a quiet holiday weekend but, judging by the past sorry records and the repeated evidence of much stupidity and foolhardiness, this may be a forlorn hope.

An Airy Rooftree

The holiday crowds had gone but there was a gentle trickle of walkers along the airy rooftree of Crinkle Crags and on to Bowfell on a glorious midweek day of unbroken blue skies with views across several counties.

Over the burnished sea we could see the Isle of Man and across the Solway Firth, the dim shape of the Scottish lowland hills. On the pointed peak of Bowfell – from many angles the most distinctive summit in Lakeland – a national park ranger, with splendid Alsatian in attendance, was collecting litter in a huge plastic bag. 'Not so bad up here this holiday,' he confided, 'but Helvellyn was appalling the other day. Sacks of the stuff.' We discussed the shortcomings of some outdoor folk, the eroded conditions of the tourist track up The Band and the growing nuisance of transistor sets on mountain summits. I told him that the rocks behind the chock-stone on the so-called 'Bad Step' on the Crinkles had collapsed and there was now a new 'through' route for those too timid to tackle the little ten-foot wall. But footgear and equipment used on the tops this Easter, he said, had generally been good. The message, he thought, was at last getting through to the jeans and gum boots brigade. Snow patches still clung to the upper rocks of the Scafells and I could just pick out the last of the snow on Blencathra's Sharp Edge, 13 miles to the north-east.

Secret Cove

Ruthwaite Cove, almost secretly cradled beneath the long summit ridge of the Helvellyn range, is the perfect retreat on a lovely April day or, indeed, on any day. Crowds stream along the ridge to the most popular summit in England but hardly anybody ever goes into the cove – only a steep half-mile below the tourist track – and the other five coves flanking the range to the east are, fortunately, equally neglected. A week after the Easter invasion I went up into the cove to climb a snow gully, later descending into the neighbouring, and equally splendid, Nethermost Cove and, apart from the walkers on the summit ridge, I saw nobody all day. The morning sun blazed down on the long curtains of snow but the top 200 feet of my climb was hard snow-ice and the bulging eight-foot cornice ideal for the axe. Before my careful ascent I had sat, shirtless, in the sunshine on the edge of the snow, eating my sandwiches and marvelling at the complete absence of wind. Three days before I had almost been blown off Helvellyn in a gale of driving rain. The sun glinted on the mirrored waters of Hard Tarn a short distance away – a perfect jewel caught on its rocky shelf – and almost the only sound was the murmur of the beck splashing down the contours. Two miles away across the valley the farmer from Braesteads was bringing down his sheep off St Sunday Crag and, now and again, I could just hear the barking of his dogs. Nethermost Cove, on my return from the summit, was just as idyllic – a hanging valley of crashing waterfalls and placid pools.

An Avalanche Climb

Winter climbing conditions were poor but my friend from the south had looked forward to a day in the snow and this was the only opportunity. Massive cornices of wet snow, ready to fall, hung like bulging ice-cream cornets over the east face of the Helvellyn range and many of the gullies had avalanched already. It was obviously too risky to tackle a climb that might avalanche at any moment so we selected one where the cornice had already collapsed – one of the Tarn Crag gullies on Dollywaggon Pike – and kicked up the avalanche debris to

Grisedale Tarn, with the crags of Dollywaggon Pike on the right.

the top. Belaying in the soft snow, even with a 'dead-man' plate, proved unsatisfactory so we climbed unroped, taking extra care to consolidate our steps and hoping they would hold. Although the overhanging part of the cornice had collapsed a great deal more loose snow had to be cleared from the top – on to the long-suffering second man – before we could haul ourselves on to the sunlit upper slopes of the mountain.

Five minutes later we were in a blizzard – one of the 'wintry showers, heavy in places' of the weather forecast – with visibility about two yards. Two young people, crouching near the summit cairn and uncertain of the way, asked us whether we could guide them down to the Helvellyn track which avoids the top of Dollywaggon so that most of the pilgrims to the most popular mountain summit in England never visit this worthwhile outlier. We put them on their way and then examined the top of the Nethermost Pike gullies to satisfy ourselves that we had been right to leave them alone. We had been; it looked as if a touch or a shout would have collapsed some of the more pendulous snow balconies, ten feet thick. The sun was out again, glinting on snows reaching to the Scafells, and we trotted happily down to Raise Beck in our shirtsleeves.

The 'Back of Skiddaw'

The ten 'two-thousanders' in the spacious, rolling country at the 'back' of Skiddaw can be collected in a round starting and finishing at Carrock Mine that can be done, by steady plodding, in six hours. You rarely meet people in these lonely, untracked fells with their long-deserted mines, high heather-covered sheep pastures and occasional glimpses of distant sea but, remarkable on a Lakeland fell walk, this modest round now boasts two mountain huts. One of these – if you include the Skiddaw outlier of Sale How – is part of Skiddaw House where the shepherd, Pearson Dalton, lived alone, at 1,500 feet, with his dogs, his goats and his cat, for 47 years – the loneliest house, you could say, in England. The room where Pearson had his comfortable old sofa, radio set, oil lamp and cosy coal fire was taken over as a shelter for walkers by the Mountain Bothies Association several years ago and now the old shooting box on Great Lingy Hill has been made wind and weather-proof by national park rangers. On a recent visit I found water in a plastic container, matches and methylated spirit, a little food of doubtful quality and a fairly new hut log-book with an already-long list of visitors. You could sleep there if you don't mind roughing it but the place is hardly remote enough for a real mountain hut since you could trot down to Carrock Mine and the mine road to Mosedale in a quarter of an hour. Useful, though, as a shelter for eating your sandwiches out of the rain as I found on this wet March day when a compass was needed to locate some of the tops. Perhaps vandals don't read this newspaper but I hope they'll leave the Lingy Hut alone.

[Seven years after this was written in the early 1980s the Lingy Hut was still unvandalised.]

Circling the Crinkles

Crinkle Crags is unusual among our fells in that it carries crags on both its eastern and western slopes and not just to the east which is more usual. Indeed, its western slopes, high above Lingcove Beck and facing across the upper Esk to the Scafells, must be among the roughest and rockiest in the district and, therefore, since this complicated fellside is completely untracked, a good place for an adventurous scramble. I often go this way after traversing the Crinkles and Bowfell – if my car is on Wrynose – to avoid going over the five tops and Shelter Crags twice. From Three Tarns I steer south-west, cross Long Top into Adam-a-Cove, traverse Ray Crag, Stonesty Pike and Little Stand, wander up and round the delightful little crags and tarns of Gaitkins and finish off with Cold Pike. The other day the Crinkles and Bowfell were crowded with processions but I saw nobody from Three Tarns to the car. Weather-wise, it could not have been a more perfect day – really cloudless blue skies, hardly a breath of wind and plenty of snow on north and east faces to whet the appetite. (Two days later, on Helvellyn, I estimated the cornices above Red Tarn were nearly 20 feet wide.) Green Hole and Great Moss, far below me, smiled in the afternoon sunshine and I studied a snow gully above Little Narrowcove in the Scafells for a future visit. Now and again I spotted tiny match-sticks of people wandering along the Crinkles track seven or eight hundred feet above me but there was no sound, not even from the foaming Lingcove Beck far below. An even more amusing ploy which I commend is to do a complete circumnavigation of Crinkle Crags, including the eastern gills, along perhaps the 1,900-foot contour – quite a roughish day.

Steep Grass

As youngsters we thought the Wasdale flank of Kirk Fell the steepest grass slope in Lakeland although more than half a century of widespread exploration has since yielded steeper places. But I don't think there are any grassy fellsides in the national park as steep as several in the soaring Howgill Fells, just across the Lune and the motorway. Of course, there are Lakeland fellsides of rock and scree at punishing angles – the east face of Helvellyn or the top of the Blencathra hills among dozens of examples – but grass slopes where hands as well as feet are needed for upward progress are rare. Whereas, in the smoothly-domed Howgills, bare of crags except at their Black Force and Cautley corners and even unmarked by dry-stone walls, the ascent of many of the towering grass slopes that sweep above a score of becks could demand rock-climbing postures. No point, though, in clawing up grass clumps when the ridges leading to the rounded tops are all straightforward walking, but the adventurous Rough Fell sheep, seeking sweeter herbs, cross these precipitous places on nine-inch trods with the aplomb of Alpine chamois. An afternoon over The Calf and other heights, enlivened by a bitter east wind and brief showers of horizontal snow, had me traversing some of these places and calculating, for example, the length of a fall from a slippery snow-hold, to Calf Beck, looking almost vertically below my boots. There's nothing like this in the Lake District – nor even on those steep bits in the Brecon Beacons – and, under the right lighting, these hanging velvet draperies of mountainsides, sleek as sealskins in the evening sunshine, give to these lonely fells a rare beauty not even seen in more famous places.

Potter Fell Pottering

It must have been 30 years since I had last been on Potter Fell, the great sprawl of soaring moorland, two or three miles away to the north, that fills our windows. We used to take the children there, playing around the tarns and exploring the becks but, with so many far more exciting corners within easy reach, seem to have neglected, of late, places on our doorstep. Almost shamefacedly, therefore, two of us went back there the other day – to find many changes. There seemed to be more tarns than we remembered – at least ten of them, including the reservoirs – and enough barbed wire, three or four strands thick in places, to enclose a prison camp. Clearly, the access situation has changed. Further north towards Skeggles Water, with the land rising to the Longsleddale heights, the way was more straightforward and we could enjoy the open views, the song of skylark and curlew and, a couple of times, the distant scurryings of mountain hares. This broad wedge of land running south from Harter Fell is not nearly so well defined as the parallel ridges to the east that reach up towards Grey Crag from the Shap Fells road but all are equally lonely, trackless, unvisited and therefore highly desirable to the few seeking to escape the hordes. Tourists don't know these ridges – and seem less welcome today on Potter Fell – but the birds, seabirds especially, seem very much at home there. There must have been two or three hundred black-headed gulls on one of the tarns the other day, as well as several varieties of duck.

The Whinfell Ridge

Six miles north-east from our windows – but, sunlit on a clear day and, especially under snow, looking almost within shouting distance – lies a shapely switchback line of little fells which we usually call the Whinfell ridge. There are five hills in the row, all about 1,600 feet high; the ridge is five miles long, but seems much longer when you walk it. To avoid backtracking the whole way, the traverse of the ridge can be combined with a return walk through the quiet, unspoiled valley of Borrowdale – the Borrowdale of Old Westmorland that has nothing in common, except beauty, with its tourist-ridden cousin south of Keswick. Sometimes I do a circumnavigation by returning along the heights to the north of the dale; on a recent visit, however, I walked from High Borrow Bridge to Low Borrow Bridge by way of the switchback ridge, returning up the dale, through the woodlands, past the pools in the beck and, farther on, the derelict farm buildings that speak, sadly, of better days. The ridge, still untracked, is an easy walk with splendid views, especially at this time, of the snow-streaked Lakeland heights, but half-way along, on a saddle, is the obscene monstrosity of a radio-repeater station looking like something out of science fiction. About half a mile short of this apparition is the almost equally incongruous but far more pleasing sight of a larch plantation, perhaps 100 feet below the summit of Whinfell Beacon. Five hundred years ago Whinfell was one of the beacon hills of Westmorland warning of raids from across the Border, and the larches were doubtless planted so that a ready supply of good firewood would always be available.

[There is now a second radio-repeater station on the ridge, perhaps not quite so monstrous as the first one but an additional intrusion on a formerly unspoiled horizon.]

Greenburn Occasions

Among our several dales still littered with the debris of centuries of mineral exploitation is the shy valley of Greenburn, curving into the Coniston fells from the fort of Wrynose Pass. Threaded by a chain of pools and waterfalls and with the fine cliffs of Great Carrs as headwall, the perfection of the dale is only spoiled by the ruins of the old copper mines, the scattered spoil heaps and the ugly reservoir that was once a secluded tarn. In 1,000 years only two events have touched the peace of Greenburn. One was the coming of the miners; the other – much more recent – the crash of an aircraft on the crags. You can still see the remains of the plane, and the mess the miners left behind will still be there when the twisted metal has sunk into the ground or been carried off by trophy hunters. Whether Greenburn was part of the activities of the Mines Royal under the first Queen Elizabeth I have never been sure, but it was still very active over 100 years ago. But when the long haul to railhead made it uneconomic it was simply abandoned, like a dozen other mines in Lakeland, leaving a grievously scarred dale and an air of sad desolation. On my way to climb a snow gully on Great Carrs I pottered about the ruins, trying to picture the hard life of the miners in that lonely place, and reflecting on the greed for wealth that has disfigured so much of our fell country. At least it couldn't happen today. Farther up the dale the aircraft remains were hidden in deep snow, and signs of recent avalanches down the gullies called for a cautious ascent. But the cornice was firmly frozen and from the sunlit snows the dale still seemed a scene of unspoiled solitude.

Messing up Mickleden

The most beautiful turf in Lakeland – Mickleden's mile-long lawn of the greenest sheep-cropped grass – is now scarred by a road that, from the top of Rossett Pike, looks like a long, ugly strip of toothpaste. This is the price we have had to pay for the new paved way up the lower reaches of Rossett Gill that many of us could readily have done without. Land Rovers had been used to transport Manpower Services Commission workers and their tools to the sheepfold at the foot of the gill, churning up the floor of this lovely dale into a mess of rutted tracks. Presumably the road of beck-washed pebbles was laid down to cover the mud and the mutilated turf – and perhaps also, thoughtlessly, to provide a firm surface for those walkers who, strangely, seem to prefer stony roads to untracked ways. Two of us discovered this latest abomination on a recent round of the head of the dale, avoiding tracks, that took us from Troughton Beck to the snows of Bowfell and down by grassy moraines to the glorious pools of Mickleden Beck. We were shocked and irate at this insensitive treatment of a treasured corner that we have known all our lives but relieved to learn that the National Trust intend to do something about it. The stones, we understand, are to be scooped up or dispersed, the line of the road covered with soil and the area reseeded with the same fine strain of fescue grasses. One can hardly expect that the wonderful green carpet I have known for more than sixty years will be restored but, hopefully, the present intrusive highway will disappear and the floor of the dale become, once again, a delight to the eye.

[Still, lovely Mickleden will never be the same again.]

An Untracked Ravine

There must have been a hundred people milling around the top and the ridges of Helvellyn – including two mountain bike riders bumping along the rocky track – but I had seen nobody, not even in the distance, on my way up. The steep, untracked ravine of Whelpside Gill, where cataracts crash down the three-tiered crags just above the forest, is a favourite ascent of mine for I have always had the place to myself – a pleasing circumstance hardly likely on any of the other dozen or so popular routes to the summit. Admittedly, the lower reaches through the forest is hard work – reminiscent of jungle bashing in Burma 45 years ago – but the rest, especially the scramble through the crags on clean, dry rock, avoiding the waterfalls, is a delight on a sunny morning. And, on hot summer days, you can dawdle your way up, taking an occasional dip in the pools – without bothering with a bathing costume for there'll be nobody around. High up the gill bifurcates and the left fork leads you to the almost secret spring of Brownrigg Well, just below the summit but rarely visited for the way is untracked. At more than 2,800 feet this must be the highest spring in England – a tiny gurgle of icy water bubbling out of the mosses in a little hollow that, a mile or two lower down, becomes a foaming torrent. The other day the final hundred yards bed of the gill was covered in two feet of snow, the beck flowing unseen below my feet but its murmur dimly heard and the spring itself buried in a deep drift. Mine were the only tracks in the snow which would have made a nice little ski run. The cornices on top were twenty feet wide, reaching the vertical in places, and, far below, Red Tarn was a dark shimmer of purest ultramarine.

A Superb Winter

No sign yet of spring on our bleak fellside. There are still masses of snow on the tops, great drifts of it in places, the fields and hedges are still brown, and hardly anything has started moving yet in our garden – except new molehills almost every day. For skiers it has been – and still is – the best winter for years, for ice-climbers conditions were, earlier, quite superb, and mountain walkers have been enjoying outstanding distant views for weeks. In our exposed corner, however, the weather feature with greatest impact so far this year has been the wind, both in its persistence and in its ferocity. The biting east winds at the beginning of the winter did more damage in my garden than in any previous year, with dozens of plants and shrubs destroyed, and, within the past weeks, the winds have been back again, whistling round the house, roaring in the wood higher up the fellside, scattering tree branches across the drive and, one day, cutting off our electricity for eight hours. But it was not these scourging east winds that did the most damage for, in February, one particularly furious gust of a swirling westerly gale tore down the roof of our rear porch, smashing windows and putting out all the lights. And it's still far too windy for workmen to put it all back again. Earlier this year I heard or read that the British Isles wind speed record of 144 miles an hour, measured in the Cairngorms in 1967, had been broken and, if this is true, I'm not surprised. Perhaps, too, the England and Wales record gust of 134 mph recorded on Great Dun Fell in January 1968 has also gone in this windiest of winters.

[This was the April of 1986, probably the best outdoors winter of recent years, and the windiest.]

Heralds of Summer

MAY

Safely Grazing Sheep

The great bowl of the dale was filled with noise – the pleasant, homely noise of hundreds of sheep and their newly-born lambs. First, perhaps, a deep-throated 'baa' from close at hand, answered by a plaintive note in a higher key from across the intake fields, and then a few rather mournful chords, a peremptory command to the offspring from some impatient, old ewe and, all the time, a high-pitched bleating from the lambs. As the evening shadows crept across the lovely, green turf the clamour grew more insistent and the lambs became more frisky – enjoying their last hour before sleep, just like youngsters, with games on the grass or 'follow my leader' through the gap in the old stone wall. With enviable energy the little, clumsy bundles of wool fought and jostled one another, sometimes struggling for possession of a little mound of turf or trying out the new-found springs in their wobbly legs with high jumps and somersaults. Meanwhile, the ewes stolidly cropped the turf, keeping an eye on their excited charges and now and again replying to a frightened bleat with a reassuring grumble. Something like 200,000 of these cuddlesome creatures will have been born this spring in central Lakeland when lambing time is over – all of them unrecognisable from their fellows by you and me but immediately identifiable by their proud mothers and even, in many cases, by the farmers. Here is the biggest and most important crop in the fell country – thousands of baby Herdwicks, Swaledales, Roughs, and crosses, the first-named 'heafed' to the same stretch of fellside that their ancestors have occupied for generations.

A Langdale Round

New lambs, cuddly bundles of black and white – an average of one and a half to each ewe – neatly patterned the floor of Mickleden and the familiar dale was loud with their cries. Far too bright a morning to last, with every crag on the Crinkles sharply focused in blazing sunlight, and, sure enough, heavy showers punctuated my zigzag progress up the Stake. The reward came on the topmost rocks of Pike o'Stickle – clouds sweeping off the summit of Bowfell, great blue rents in the darkened sky, and, in a moment, the rocks steaming in the sunshine and, far below, Langdale reaching brightly towards sparkling waters. Three snow patches still clinging to the north slopes of Esk Pike, and the remains of a distant cornice on Great End; otherwise, summer had reached the dales, suddenly lush and green, and spring embraced the heights. Nobody on Harrison Stickle or Pavey Ark – this was a midweek walk – but, after the descent of Jack's Rake, blue tents by Stickle Tarn and young adventurers waiting for the rocks to dry, skimming pebbles across the glass-calm pool. I came down to the valley by grassy ledges, avoiding the sadly eroded screes and sat on a sunlit terrace drinking beer and watching a shepherd, with his dog, slowly quartering the fellside, counting his lambs. There were a thousand people in the bar over Easter, the proprietor told me; today, apart from four footsore tourists treating their feet, I had the place to myself. The car park was deserted – except for grazing sheep – as the sun crept down behind Bowfell and the hills turned purple in the afterglow.

May Snow

Between the rain clouds sweeping across Mardale Ill Bell I can see from my study window the snow patches in Hall Cove and there is much more of it, unseen from here, on the north and east slopes of the fells – half-way through May. But this is nothing unusual. Sixteen years ago there were two inches of new May snow on my lawns one morning and the following evening, as we were trooping into the Mary Wakefield Festival concert, the blizzard returned, quickly coating the Kendal pavements with three inches of wet slush, so that some of us sat through the music with damp feet. The festival is with us again this week and the farmers' weather forecast has already hinted at snow showers in the north. Snow is my perennial delight – but not new snow in May or June when we expect dry, sunlit fells and warm rocks. I remember June 1975, when there were quite heavy snowfalls so that it looked high

The Langdale Pikes, with Bowfell behind.

summer across the green fields, the blossoming hedges and the thick woodlands but mid-winter on the backcloth of the fells with snow down to 1,500 feet and the summits more alpine than in December. Earlier that month I had kicked steps in hard snow up Cust's Gully on Great End and the previous September seen visitors snowballing each other on the top of Helvellyn. We have had a lot of snow on the fells this winter, with an excellent skiing and winter climbing season, but also a great deal of rain and miserable, cloudy weather. Indeed, since our return from Canada last September we have had more rain in these parts than I can remember in any other year and the fells have never been more persistently saturated. Perhaps all this foreshadows a blazing summer.

[This was the May of 1983 and the window view was, of course, from my previous fellside home.]

'New' Way Up Pillar

There are several ways up Pillar – Black Sail, the High Level Route, Wind Gap, White Pike from Ennerdale and so on – but for an inveterate scrambler a 'new' line, first spotted years ago, seemed worth trying out. The idea was to take a direct line from the Y-boulder in Mosedale to the summit, using a rocky ridge on the left side of Wistow Crags and a final stretch of slabs leading to the cairn – perhaps 1,500 feet of scrambling. It would avoid the long detour to Black Sail or the scree trudge to Wind Gap and should provide both energetic exercise and interesting route-finding. On a day that began with a hailstorm on Hardknott and ended with a thunderstorm on the return journey everything went well, for the south-facing crags on the Mosedale breast of Pillar quickly dried in the midday sun and I could make my staircase to the heights as easy or as difficult as I pleased. Half-way up I stopped for a breather, for the lovely, rough rock, although not technically difficult, was steep enough to be tiring for a geriatric septuagenarian. Far below my boots, Mosedale Beck meandered in pools and shingle beds all down the long dale to Wasdale Head and, straight ahead, the Scafells, still patched with snow, filled the southern view. Even Lord's Rake on Scafell looked choked with snow, but Great Gable, peeping over Kirk Fell like an atomic explosion, and the other heights were bare, sunlit and summery. Only the shadowed ridge of Red Pike and Yewbarrow, curving in dark towers to the unseen lake, looked faintly hostile. A quick peep at Pillar Rock and the snow gullies in Great Doup and the trot down the tourist track to the Wasdale intake fields, loud with the sound of new-born lambs, rounded off an exhilarating short day in what had almost seemed a 'new' corner of the fells.

Above the Esk

After weeks without rain Great Moss could almost be crossed dry-shod and Little Narrowcove beyond the dwindling upper Esk was easily entered without the need for boulder-hopping. Above the foot of the cove the precipitous face of Ill Crag rose for 1,600 feet in a soaring wilderness of crag and scree to the sixth highest summit in Lakeland. The sun blazed down on stony wastes but, high above the rocky peak of Pen to the left of the cove, the last snows of the winter still hung in the gullies below the roof of England. A few years ago two of us had made a scrambling route up the face of Ill Crag; I had returned alone to try another line, and to enjoy an hour or so of leisured progress up steep, sun-warmed but undemanding rock. There are no tracks, scratches, or recorded climbs on this impressive face which is split into three crags, each probing higher towards the tiny, pointed summit, but the smooth, grey face of the highest crag, which I avoided, could yield a couple of worthy routes to a more determined attack. I tried to keep on rock all the way, avoiding the screes and, by working leftwards from crag to crag managed to achieve this except for the last bit to the cairn. The route was airy without being frightening and the silence and solitude, the exciting depths, and the sunlit views to increasingly distant horizons all added to the delights of neat progress up an easy ladder to the heights. From the Esk to the summit rocks, there had been no sight or sound of others, but, from the cairn, the Scafell Pike processions came into view. These I joined for the trot down to Esk Hause, but the long walk back to Hardknott was a silent trudge in the evening sunshine.

Getting to Grips

After an absence of several years from anything approaching serious climbing a recent day on Dow Crag near Coniston clearly showed how old skills can disappear with advancing years. I first climbed on this superb crag 54 years ago, continuing with almost weekly visits for many years, but now was alarmed to discover that holds seemed to have grown smaller and moved farther apart. Agility, after an active life, was not greatly impaired but there were new psychological problems – the fear, for instance, of stepping up on sloping holds in exposed places where, years ago, there would have been no hesitation. The crag has changed, too. Most of the grass ledges on which we used to dawdle between pitches had disappeared, huge chunks of rock had fallen from the cliff, the gullies were badly eroded, there seemed more loose rock on the climbs and the screes at the foot of the crag had become an ugly wasteland. But most of the old delights and the glorious views were still there – the sight of the Scafells and the long length of Dunnerdale, for example, from the top of the crag or the long-remembered thrill of looking down on the black pool of Goats Water from half-way up the face. I have skated, bathed and fished for char in or on this perfect mountain tarn and, on wild winter days, seen its spray hurled half the height of the crag. But, the other day, the pool was glass-calm with the white figures of two early bathers looking, from high on the cliff, like tiny frogs. And the descent to Coniston in the evening sunshine was the same as scores I have enjoyed over the years – the shadows lengthening across the turf and the old, familiar crag stern and dark against the sunset.

[Since I wrote this in 1982 my climbing skills have continued to deteriorate but I still like to get my fingers on a bit of good rock now and again and the almost sensuous delight of careful, balanced movement in steepish places – provided the holds are good enough – is, fortunately, still there.]

Bliss in Buttermere

My mountain diary shows that the only noticeable rain in the fells during April fell on the second of the month. On that day I went up Helvellyn from The Swirls in a heavy shower, climbing a snow gully on Browncove Crags on the way, and came down in a minor snowstorm. During the rest of the month the fells basked in sunshine, with clear, frosty nights, while the snows retreated, the becks dwindled to trickles, and you could even cross the Great Moss in upper Eskdale dry-shod. Perhaps the most perfect day for weather of many superb April mountain days came at the very end of the month – cloudless skies, hardly a whisper of wind on the tops, embracing views that derided distances, and warm enough for sunbathing. Two of us lazed among the Buttermere fells, finding any excuse for dawdling, dozing, smoking, or restful contemplation of the miles of still, silent Lakeland that stretched to hazy horizons below our feet. From the vast, green amphitheatre of Birkness Combe, threaded by its winding, musical beck, we reached our first grandstand on High Stile by a scramble up Grey Crag – just in time to admire a solo ascent of Oxford and Cambridge Direct by a girl climber in far better form than ourselves. Sleepily, we discussed the curious anomaly that although the snows had almost disappeared from the north and east faces of Great End and Helvellyn the sunlit, north-west slopes of Scafell Pike were still plastered in white. Idly we identified every distant top and crag, recalling half-forgotten adventures, before continuing our leisurely round of the smiling fells and then down to the Gatesgarth lake-shore intake fields, loud with the murmurings of sheep.

Blue Remembered Hills

It was one of those hazy, lifeless days when the high fells might have been no more than palely-painted scenery in vague, washed-out colours like a Chinese picture, without sculpturing or depth. There were no features, no crags, screes or fellsides, just the familiar shapes, with the nearer ranges like Causey Pike and Maiden Moor an indeterminate grey, Grasmere and the Buttermere fells with a bit of blue in them and Pillar

Robinson from Rannerdale Knotts.

and the Gables an entirely light blue wash. Walking the Robinson-Hindscarth-Dale Head round seemed, for a change, curiously unrewarding – no sunshine, no wind, no shadows, almost a walk through flat cardboard scenery. No cloud or mist but nothing to see except well-remembered outlines. Back down in lovely Newlands and closer to the scenery there seemed more to admire – the tiny reservoir in Little Dale, caught below dark crags, that always looks the perfect mountain pool, and the green, zigzag tracks among the long-disused mines, where, in the sixteenth century, men toiled in their hundreds for the riches of copper, silver and even a little gold. It is difficult to believe that this most peaceful dale, still completely unspoiled by the scars of tourism, was once one of the most industrialised parts of the north of England, loud with the clamour of a dozen rich and active mines. Today, the mines, long since grown over and part of the scenery, have to be sought out and the only sound in the dale the other day was the call of a cuckoo high in the crags, the only movement in the landscape a distant, creeping tractor in a tilted field.

Alone on Scafell

Only three people on Scafell Pike – the fewest I have seen there, except on wild winter days. They had come from Mickledore out of Eskdale and, on their first visit to the roof of England, questioned me about their proposed return route from the source of the Esk. As the thin mists cleared they stood spellbound by the sudden appearance of the soaring precipice of Scafell Crag with the dark pool of Wastwater far

The Scafells reflected in Wastwater, England's deepest lake.

below. Our tracks in the new snow, otherwise unmarked, took us in opposite directions for I preferred a scramble up Pulpit Rock on Pike's Crag – one of the most dramatic viewpoints in Lakeland. Scafell Crag was lightly etched in snow which seemed to heighten the ferocious appearance of the great, dark cliff. Had I really climbed up those steep walls in more active years? The Great Flake on Central Buttress seemed even more overhanging than in reality while Botterill's Slab and Moss Ghyll Grooves looked as holdless and precarious as church steeples. Only close-up views of Pillar Rock can compare – in England – with this scene of savage, mountain grandeur which is even more dramatic under snow and ice. But, this day, the new snow was melting quickly in the warm sunshine and the familiar luncheon-place in Hollow Stones, reached later, was the ideal place for a snooze, with the tinkling sounds of the beck for music. Still not a soul about, although a weekend, and not even a climber on the warm, sunlit rocks of Pike's Crag. Several times I was almost startled by the 'horse and man' on the summit of the crag of that name, although I have known the rock formation for fifty years. The trot down Brown Tongue was easier than the upward toil but, this time, the bathing pool in Lingmell Beck, despite the sunshine, could not tempt me.

Descending the Dungeon

Six weeks of drought had reduced the final waterfall in Dungeon Ghyll to little more than a trickle, encouraging a solo descent of the mile-long ravine to complete a scrambling round of the Langdale Pikes. Despite many ascents of the gill under varying conditions I could not remember ever climbing down it before, but it looked the most interesting way home. (The Ordnance Survey correctly use the Old Norse name 'gill' for Lake District ravines in general but stick to the Victorian poetic affectation of 'ghyll' in Dungeon Ghyll and Stock Ghyll – no doubt because of long-established usage – although it still looks wrong.) Ruskin thought Dungeon Ghyll more rewarding than any ravine he had seen in Switzerland – 'the loveliest rock scenery, chased with silver waterfalls, that I ever set foot or heart upon' – but he was only describing the lower, tourist-ridden section. The higher, largely unvisited parts of the dog-leg ravine with more spectacular falls, pools and beetling rock are far more worthy, and the weight of water coming down determines the severity of the many obstacles. Once down the upper fall, just below the tourist track, you might almost be in a Himalayan gorge – a hidden world of soaring rock and dark pools, with only a narrow strip of sky and the sound of falling waters. An open middle section follows and then you are in the lower ravine with one or two quite exposed places – if you attempt a direct descent. One particularly beautiful fall, through steep woodland into a superb pool,

Waterfalls in Dungeon Ghyll.

has few rivals for dramatic and colourful setting in the fell country. It was unusual to complete the climb and emerge on the popular Pikes track reasonably dry; previous ascents had always been sportingly aquatic.

An Oxendale Scramble

We have always called the place Browney Gill although the Ordnance Survey, curiously, insist on Brown Gill – the most easterly of the wonderful trinity of ravines that cleave the Oxendale slopes of Crinkle Crags, nearly a mile long with 1,400 feet of scrambling. For those addicted to the slightly eccentric sport of gill climbing, the difficulties, as always, depend on the volume of water present. Melting snows and quite a lot of rain have flooded the becks recently so that the other day Browney Gill was satisfyingly aquatic. The dozen or more waterfalls and waterslides all presented interesting water management problems and the passage of the pools was often mildly adventurous so that one finally emerged on the busy Crinkle Crags track impressively soaked. The gill has three contrasted sections – a narrow, wooded ravine, choked with fallen trees; a long necklace of pools, more open to the fell; and a final, steep ladder of waterslides below the cliffs of Great Knott. This day the sun was streaming down the gorge, burnishing the rowans and the holly, sparkling on the pools and, occasionally, shining through the waterfalls above my head so that they looked like avalanches of snow. In fifty years exploring these places I've rarely seen anybody in a Lake District gill – unless I had a companion. Corners, you might say, for the connoisseur – wonderfully devoid of scratches, orange peel and beer cans and awkward enough to deter the masses. Rewards are the seclusion, the joy of the pools on a hot day, the thunder of the falls, the unconventional exercise, and the pleasantly tingling fear of an unexpected ducking.

[Written twelve years ago. Since then – a book of mine on Lakeland adventuring might have been partly to blame – the gills have become better known to scramblers and you can't count on having them to yourself.]

High Above Coniston

Fifty years ago we knew it as the White Lady – the long waterslide, just north of Coniston above the Ambleside road, that looks in spate like a lace curtain draped down the fellside. It makes a good scramble on to the Yewdale fells, the main entertainment being the athletics necessary to keep fairly dry. On top is a curiously neglected corner, cheek by jowl with the almost over-popular Coniston fells – a trackless, heather-spattered plateau dotted with little rocky summits that provide perfect grandstands for viewing the southern fells and the whole length of Coniston Water. Two of us, alone except for adventurous sheep exploring the crags, watched the processions along the snow cornices of the Old Man and Swirl How two miles away. The fells seemed 'wick wi' fwoak' but, in fifty years, I've never seen anybody on these little hills that, from some directions, almost seem to overhang the village. Perhaps, with its craggy escarpment to the east, it is hardly walkers' country although there is an easy approach from Wetherlam. Tempting ways off to the main road may require climbing techniques. Throughout a short day we used our hands almost as much as feet, seeking out the most interesting ways up the rocks and finishing off down a craggy staircase that required some care. But the absence of tracks, cairns, beer cans, and orange peel took me back to the early 1930s when we used to go up here for a scramble on an off-day. Nothing seemed to have changed except for the view, far below, of Coniston Old Hall where we had our own hut. This was a lonely farm in the old days; today it is a bustling centre for caravans and sailing craft.

Blatant Peak Bagging

Five summits in the Blencathra area, collected on a short May day of sunshine and storm, were the start of a modest but blatant peak-bagging challenge. The aim is to traverse all the 203 listed tops of more than 2,000 feet in the district within six months – a suitably pointless but conceivably enjoyable task for an old-age pensioner. All the ground has long been familiar but seeking new ways up and linking summits together into horseshoe rounds might require a little ingenuity. An unconventional ascent of Blencathra by ravine and crag with a final scramble up the patchy snow, still hanging like a tattered lace collar below the summit, was an encouraging start with close-up views of sheep clinging to the rocky upper slopes like the seabirds on St Bees Head. Not a breath of wind on top, dazzling sunshine on the snow patches, and unrestricted views for 30 miles but, five minutes later, a great black pall crept over the mountains and I was in a thunderstorm of driving rain and hail. Ahead, visibility shortened to yards but, curiously, through a bright gap below the black cloud to the south I could see the sun still shining on the High Street snow gullies. But the rigours of my new game meant a trudge across featureless moors to collect undistinguished tops around the desolate valley of Bannerdale before winding back along the skirts of the mountain wall to Threlkeld. Few people nowadays go into these lonely dales in the corner of the national park, but, 100 years ago, Bowscale Tarn, with its legend of two undying fish, was a big tourist attraction for Victorians.

[The two hundred-odd summits were easily re-collected within three months in 1977. With better planning and more dedication the job could have been done, I think, within a month. The outings were described in 'Freeman of the Hills' *(Robert Hale, 1978).]*

The Gadarene Club

The heartening sight of schoolboys on a scrambling trip – they had a rope – actually demolishing cairns, rather than stupidly piling them up, enlivened a morning stroll along the pleasantly undulating track to Blea Rigg. In charge of the dozen lads was a master who, now and again, would point to a cairn which, within seconds, would be flattened by willing workers, the stones adding to the scattered millions on the fellside. He was also quietly supervising the collection of litter as they went along. Curiously, this welcome destruction of unnecessary cairns occurred on the same ridge where, about twenty years ago, I discovered one day that scores of new cairns had been built at the side of the well-known trail – presumably by youth parties under indifferent leadership, with nothing better to do. Sixty years ago P.J.H. Unna, who gave thousands of acres of wild Scotland to the nation – providing they were kept unspoiled – was writing of the unfortunately fictitious Gadarene Club – 'formed for the sole purpose of destroying unnecessary cairns'. Within eighteen months, he reported, he had levelled between 300 and 400 ugly piles from only half a dozen Lakeland fells and commended others to complete the work. But, despite the efforts of these lads on Blea Rigg and others, like myself, who delight in cairn-wrecking – only some of the unnecessary thousands alongside the eroded tracks, not the relatively few important ones – their proliferation goes on. Not only are most of these new cairns unnecessary and unsightly; they can also, in the wrong places in bad weather, be a danger, causing confusion over routes.

Avoiding the Bogs

One of the boggiest places in the fells – worse than any of the Mosedales, Great Moss at the head of Eskdale or the High Tove to Bleaberry Fell traverse above Thirlmere – has always seemed to me to be the Wyth Burn valley reaching south-west to High Raise. You come down it, since it is on the direct line from the Scafells to Helvellyn, when you are doing the round of the Lakeland 'three-thousanders' – and probably avoid the place thereafter for there's at least a mile of bog and morass to wade through. Indeed, right in the middle of the dale, is a huge swamp, marked succinctly on the map The Bog, which seems, especially in mist and heavy rain, just as evil and menacing as Christian's Slough of Despond must have been. How many sheep, tempted on to the morass by the sight of sprouting reeds and grasses, have had to be rescued by shepherds with ropes and poles and how many have sunk through the slime, with mournful gurgles, to their unseen deaths, it is impossible to say. Probably no human beings have been lost here without trace but several, perhaps in cloud or darkness, must have spent anxious and struggling minutes before feeling dry land beneath their feet once again. And yet, the other day, after a fortnight of warm, dry weather, two of us, on a High Raise–Steel Fell round, passed this way dry-shod by the simple expedient of avoiding the usual track to the south of the beck and wandering round the contours on the other side. It seemed an excellent, easy way to Greenup Edge – full in the morning sun, with the silvery chain of pools and waterfalls below the moraines to admire, the song of the larks and, for company, those stolidly browsing Herdwicks that had, so far, avoided a wet and sticky end.

Greenburn Delights

The great bowl of Greenburn below the sweep of Wetherlam has always been a favourite corner, perhaps for the rock pools in the beck that remind me of a well-loved corrie in Skye, or the bold sculpturing of the Great Carrs Crags; but mostly, I think, because it is a quiet, lonely place well away from popular tracks. There is no direct public path into the dale from Fell Foot and the old mines track along the valley floor ends at the tarn, dammed up in the mid-1800s to provide water power for the new copper mines there. The derelict buildings of the long-abandoned mines, the breached dam, and the rather ugly reservoir with its stagnant pools give an air of desolation to the middle of the dale but, below and above the mine workings, the steeply enclosed valley can be a magical place. The first lambs were trying out their tottering legs in the intake fields at the entrance to the dale, the hedges and the rowans were tardily bursting into leaf, and the sunlight glistened on the pools in the beck, shining through the spray from the little waterfalls, as I walked up Greenburn the other day to its craggy headwall. Three snow gullies dropped through the crags, straight as plumb-lines – steep but uncomplicated winter routes under good conditions. The snow, however, was far too soft and insecure for pleasant climbing or safety, and after a few feet up the central gully I retreated, reaching the summit over the disintegrating cornice of a nearby couloir. Five miles away, north-west across the Duddon, the Scafells were still plastered with snow, but the winter climbing season was over and spring – a very late spring – was just round the corner. Down from the fells, it had already arrived with a blaze of daffodils and forsythia lighting the way home.

Circling Glencoynedale

It might have been Lakeland fifty years ago – hardly a vehicle on the roads, nobody in the fells, no tracks for most of the way and Lady of the Lake quietly chugging a ruler-straight line down the middle of Ullswater. Daffodils still brightened greening hedgerows crowded with cherry and blackthorn blossom but on Raise, north of the shrinking Helvellyn cornice, there was just enough snow for skiing. Two of us slowly strolled round the fells that enclose the quiet side-valley of Glencoynedale starting with the curiously named Sheffield Pike and finishing with the aptly named Birkett Fell – formerly Nameless Fell but renamed in the early 1960s in honour of the late Lord Birkett who fought so hard in high places for the Lakeland he loved. Neatly chiselled into a stone plaque set into the summit cairn is the name of the fell, so that the fell that used to have no name is now the only fell in Lakeland to have its name on top. The hills stood up proudly in the afternoon sunshine as sharp as if cut out of cardboard and the smoke rose straight from the chimneys of the farm in the dale far below where I was once invited in for a gigantic meal with the men, hungry from sheep shearing. I remember especially the piping hot blackcurrant pie – nearly the size of a dustbin lid and cut into four. We came down by the lovely track across Brown Hills with its superb views of the three reaches of Ullswater – surely one of the most delightful paths in the district and so little known. There were two tiny yachts, one with a white sail, the other red, slowly drifting like butterflies on the southern reach below Place Fell but nothing else moved and there was no sound.

Looking for Eagles

Patient people with binoculars trained on a remote crag in the High Street area were perched in the morning sunshine on summits and outcrops hoping for a sight of golden eagles. Perhaps they were looking in the wrong place but most of them saw nothing and the eagles did not take to the air during the hours we spent traversing much of the length of the old Roman 'road' that followed the heights between their forts at Brougham and Ambleside. Down in one of the dales carved into the east flank of High Street, concealed in a hide, devoted wardens appointed by the Royal Society for the Protection of Birds were still maintaining their 24-hour watch on the eyrie, after several weeks, and gently diverting people who might get too close. Some of the ridges were swarming with walkers but, from above, the dale looked empty. One day, many years ago, walking up this rough side valley, I saw an eagle slowly circling the heights, four red deer working their way through the head of the corrie and, in the meadows near the lake, fifteen fell ponies quietly grazing. But, on this recent day, even the deer and the ponies seemed to be in hiding. The remains of snow cornices still clung to the Helvellyn ridge and there were huge snow patches above the wild steeps of Blea Water Crag. Hayeswater, Penrith's water supply, was a mirror for the surrounding fells and its beck, tumbling down to Hartsop, a sparkling string of pools and waterfalls. Later I heard that at least one eaglet had been hatched – another success in a story that goes back for twenty years when, after 200 years of absence, golden eagles returned to Lakeland.

[Some weeks later I watched, through binoculars, the eaglet in its nest, its little beak opening in anticipation for the food for which the parent bird – unseen by us – was no doubt searching from the sky. The huge, untidy nest of twigs and branches was not in its usual place but nearly half a mile away, perched on top of a ten-foot wall of crag.]

A Lonely Dale

There's no signpost pointing the way to Bannisdale and you can't see the long trough of the valley from the Shap Fells road. A winding lane takes you over a fellside and down to the floor of the dale where the surfaced road ends, and only a rough pot-holed track leads to the farthest of the two farms nestling under the headwall of the high fells. Bannisdale mercifully is spared the turmoil of tourism since it is a dead-end valley, so there are no car-parks, caravan sites, petrol pumps, public conveniences, road signs, or litter. Besides the two farms, two lonely miles apart, you could say there is nothing there except a long strath of meadows – loud with the cries of sheep and lambs the other day – the winding beck, a rash of woodlands and crags and, all round the bowl, the sweep of the surrounding fells. Seven or eight grassy summits, none of them reaching 2,000 feet, are huddled around the dale and traversing the ten miles round these lonely fells took less than five hours. The way is completely untracked and uncairned – a rare delight in over-used Lakeland – and the views unusually extensive – the Lakeland fells from a 'new' angle to some: the great sweep of the Pennines, Whernside, Ingleborough and the Howgill Fells, and the silvered seascape of Morecambe Bay. There was still some snow on the Scafells, much more on Cross Fell. The sun glittered far below on the meandering courses – past scattered hamlets – of the rivers Kent, Sprint and Mint. Apart from a man rebuilding a stone wall 100 yards from my car – he was still at it, about two feet higher, on my return – I met nobody all day, and saw no one even in the distance.

My First Hill

Sixty-two years ago I had looked out from this little rocky summit with unseeing eyes, barely noticing the tangle of scenery spread out below: a long, wooded valley, grey rocks crouching in the bracken and, in the distance, the blue-grey hills. Today, revisiting my very first hill, every part of the picture, every fellside, crag, wood or farmhouse was well known and, after a lifetime of hills, lovingly remembered. The little rock peak, an elegant cone stuck on the end of the long ridge leading to the Coniston fells, was Stickle Pike and we had climbed it, as a school party, after walking from Foxfield railway station and through Broughton Mills. I still have the faded, yellowing photograph of the summit party – all of us in school uniform with distinctive caps, blue blazers with badges, and shorts. Before the final summit bid the geography master issued two orders: 'Don't drink from streams, it will spoil your wind'; and 'Don't roll boulders down the fellside'. Ever since that far-off summer's day in 1923 I've always obeyed his second, sensible command and consistently ignored his first. We finished off that first real hill day wolfing down a huge meal of scones and cakes in

Stickle Pike in Dunnerdale – my very first hill.

a cool, farmhouse kitchen. But the very special memory was of the wonderful scent of woodsmoke – sniffed perhaps as we walked back along the lanes in the evening. Indeed, whenever I smell woodsmoke today I am back in a flash to early days in the thickly wooded country east of the Duddon. And Stickle Pike, the other day, was almost as magical as I had remembered it.

[Since this was written in 1985 it is now 68 years since my introduction to the hills. I will always be grateful to my old geography master, the late H.M. Sawtell, for first opening my eyes to their beauty.]

Long, Sunlit Days

JUNE

Above Crummock Water

The summit of Mellbreak proved a delightful vantage point from which to view the ring of surrounding fells on a perfect summer's morning. We had decided on an easy, dawdling day and the ascent of the rocky prow of the north top from the Kirkstile Inn – with a drink there beforehand or afterwards or both – and a return from the south top along the shore of lovely Crummock Water seemed to fit the bill. From the inn this curious wedge of fell between the lake and the wettest of the Mosedales, towers steeply from its skirts of scree like a pyramid of crags but the ascent, zigzagging through the outcrops, goes easily enough – especially after a pint. 'New Year's Day Hunt at Kirkstile' is one of the more tuneful of the hunting songs but the Melbreak Fox-hounds that hunt these parts spell their name, for some reason, with only one 'l'. (Bets can easily be won among otherwise knowledgeable hill-folk by asking how Mellbreak, the fell, is spelled. Further money might also be made by querying the spelling of Criffel, the distinctive Scottish peak just across the Solway.) Outstanding in the panorama of the Buttermere fells from the top is the craggy front of Grasmoor with the splendid scrambling route of Lorton Gully in full view every yard of the way. Great Gable and Pillar can also be picked out and, far to the east, the wavy line of the Helvellyn range. The descent from the south top, nearly a mile away, was down short-cropped grass steep enough to jolt the thighs if taken at the trot – the only time we went hard at it on this lazy day – and the stroll along the shore of the glass-calm lake pure delight.

Buttermere, with Great Gable on the skyline.

Disintegrating Crags

On my last hill day before the welcome rains unadventurous visits were paid to two crags which, although among the biggest in the fell country, are largely eschewed by climbers – in one case completely so. The spurned crag is Hobcarton, the massive, disintegrating cluster of cliffs just below the summit of Hopegill Head, and the rarely visited one the splendid ring of precipices, just across the dividing trench of Gasgale Gill, known as Dove Crags. This huge cirque – a great bite out of the sprawling dome of Grasmoor – is a good place for hard icemen in winter but, apart from a couple of routes, is mostly ignored in summer because of the unreliable nature of the rock. Hobcarton's rock, however, is far worse – not only loose but shattered and splintering – and no climbers go there although the crag must be 500 feet high along much of its curving length of nearly a mile. This is the Skiddaw Slates country of rounded fells and collapsing crags but the crumbling scree and soil is very fertile for many plants. Grasmoor must be the largest natural rock-garden in the district and the red alpine catchfly grows on Hobcarton – and only in one other place in Britain. Skiddaw Slates is the rock for producing our best mountain heathers and nowhere does the

102

Hopegill Head and Hobcarton Crags. The rare alpine catchfly grows in one of these gullies.

bilberry grow with greater abandon than on Hobcarton where the sheep can't get at it.

Discovering Blencathra

The soaring southern front of Blencathra – so exciting to photographers near the Thirlmere dam – is one of the biggest mountain walls in the fell country, rising nearly 2,500 feet in just over a mile. Five steep buttresses of grass or heather are cleft by four wild ravines, each threaded by plunging waterfalls and necklaces of pools. Ways up the buttresses, attractively rocky in their upper reaches, are deservedly popular, but few people explore the trackless ravines or swarm up the gills although these are the most rewarding features of the mountain. Blease Gill, Gate Gill, Doddick Gill and Scaley Beck are all wonderful, rough places, each with its own individuality and full of surprises round every corner – unscratched, without litter or any evidence of man, save for the old mine levels low down in Gate Gill. You can scramble up one ravine and down another, with diversions on to the more interesting sections of the ridges and, in this way, easily explore the whole mountain wall in two visits. I was there again the other day in brilliant sunshine – between the hail showers – scrabbling about among the pools and waterfalls and marvelling at the dexterity of the mountain sheep. Seen from a distance, at some angles, they looked not unlike the kittiwakes perched on the ledges of St Bees Head. As mountaineers they must command respect. The scrambler finds a profusion of hand-holds on rocks or heather; these experts, on crumbling ledges above steep drops, do just as well with tiny feet alone – their lambs as well. Nor do they scatter at your approach, as might other sheep, but, precariously balanced, bravely stand their ground.

Fleeing from Flies

Grey Friar is the lovely name of a lovely, lonely hill in the Coniston fells that bulks for miles, in craggy steeps, high above the Duddon. I planned to lie up there on the two summit outcrops throughout a long, hot afternoon idly admiring the twin views, so familiar for a lifetime, sunbathing and, probably, sleeping. From one cairn there is the sweep of the Coniston fells from Great Carrs to White Maiden and Caw with Dow Crag, from this angle, like a miniature Matterhorn; from the other, across the trench of Mosedale, the superb thrust of the Scafells, the highest land in England. But it was not to be. The flies were there in busy thousands, crawling over the rocks, swarming over my body and dropping in my coffee. Swirling a handkerchief about my head I escaped to the prow of Great Carrs where I thought the uprush of air from the Greenburn gullies might blow them away but there were more thousands of them there, in sole command of even this rocky eyrie. Why do flies swarm on summits? Two of us once encountered a black cloud of millions of them hanging around the Hart Crag summit cairn and refusing to disperse, despite spraying and frantic towel waving. Eventually, on this recent day, I found a fly-free, sunny ledge on a little crag high above Cockley Beck and here, between snoozes, enjoyed several modest rock routes, watched the cars inching over Hardknott Pass, studied the sunlit symmetry of Harter Fell and admired the blue curve of Slight Side rising over shadowed crags to Scafell top. Nothing moved except the cars on the passes and the ravens. There was nobody about and the fells – the becks stilled by drought – slept in the afternoon sunshine.

A Mountain Grandstand

From the top of Place Fell, when sunshine and chasing cloud shadows sculpture the Helvellyn ridges, the western view can be outstanding. The fell is the only height I can recall from which you get a close-up picture of parallel valleys climbing to high mountains, the dales scooped into saucer-like hollows below circling ridges. All these side-valleys, from Dovedale to Gowbarrow, are seen across the curving reaches of Ullswater with the houses, farms and hotels of Patterdale and Glen-ridding looking like toys 2,000 feet below. The other day, from the summit, you could watch the motor cars going through the villages, the lake 'steamer' pulling into the pier and white sails of yachts dotted across the water like drowsy butterflies. Tiny handkerchiefs of snow – the last of the long winter – still clung to the high east faces of Lower Man and Nethermost Pike. By making a bee-line for the top from the toe of Ullswater – barely half the distance of the usual Boardale Hause route but much steeper – the summit was reached, without stopping, in one hour. The four miles of beautiful shore-path from near Sandwick to Patterdale can also be covered, if necessary, in the hour so that the complete round, including the traverse of the Place Fell skyline and the descent by the waterfalls of Scalehow Beck, can even be achieved by active septuagenarians in an afternoon or summer evening. Sometimes, high up on Place Fell I have come upon herds of red deer crossing the ridge from their sanctuary in Martindale – but not on this evening.

They say in Patterdale that when the deer appear over the shoulder of the fell bad weather is on the way.

Piel Island Memories

On a day of low cloud and squally showers, we fled the fell country and for a change had a look at Piel Island – the lonely lump of land, 400 yards wide, mid-way between the southern tip of Walney and the end of the Furness peninsula. The twin features of Piel Island are the castle, built about 650 years ago, and the sprawling pub of rather later origin. Sixty-odd years ago, as boys, we used to scramble on the crumbling walls of the castle ruins. An old fisherman would row us, for a few pence, across the half-mile channel from the lifeboat station; today a ferry of sorts with an engine is rather haphazardly available. The island pub used to have no licensing hours – police surveillance being difficult, if not impossible – and for all I know you may still be able to drink there at all hours. But on this recent visit the place did not appeal. After 60 years, the castle ruins looked quite unchanged although much more of the eight-feet-thick walls must have tumbled down in the wild weather. The castle was built by the abbots of Furness as a stronghold and look-out against the raiding Scots; there is said to have been a watch-tower near the abbey in 'the Vale of the Deadly Nightshade' for picking up signals from the distant castle when pirates were astir. Five hundred years ago, in the reign of Henry VII, Lambert Simnel was brought from Germany as claimant to the throne of England and landed on Piel Island, with the pretender holding his first court in the castle. In this outlandish place, loud with the cries of seagulls but within easy sight of the great cranes of Barrow shipyard, a little bit of English history was made.

Coledale Merry-Go-Round

For easy going, vast changing views across the tops to the Scottish hills and switchback walking all the way there's nothing better in the fell country than the cluster of mountain ridges around Coledale Hause. You can do a lengthy round of thirteen summits from Braithwaite or Buttermere – on the map more the shape of a squashed spider than a circle – and finish, breezily, at the trot almost ready, if really necessary, to go round again. I last did that a couple of years ago and, the other day, ambled round Grisedale Pike, Grasmoor and Crag Hill (or Eel Crag, as we all know it), without stopping, in such a ridiculously short

106

time that I was back home again, half-way through the afternoon, hours before opening time. Fitness has little to do with these scamperings; it is the easy terrain, the springy turf and peat smoothly carpeting these roller-coaster ridges of Skiddaw slate that allow you to stride the miles, after the initial pull from the valley, in almost-slippered ease. For me these are the heather and bilberry fells but the slate that weathers down to the fine scree, encouraging the abundant growth of these colourful plants, does not produce much rock for climbing. Crags there are in plenty and the flanks of the ridges are often pleasantly precipitous but most of the cliffs, of crumbling, shattered rock, although of spectacular appearance, are scansorially disappointing. No, this is fell walking country *par excellence*.

Fell Ponies

There is a lonely dale in the eastern fells where your chances of seeing golden eagles, red deer and Fell ponies – possibly all at once – are probably greater than anywhere else. On almost every visit I have seen at least one of the three and the other day I encountered both red deer and Fells there – about a mile apart. There were no eagles about that day but I have seen them there on previous occasions for I know the sites of their eyries. In the crag the great bird is normally invisible – except perhaps to experts with binoculars, but its powerful, sweeping flight, so different from the aerobatics of the raven or the soaring circles of the buzzard, is unmistakable. The native Fell ponies of Cumbria are increasing in numbers and in popularity and a few still run 'wild' – untamed, unbroken and unkempt but gloriously free. Their tails almost sweep the ground, their manes are long and matted and, in the winter, they grow thick shaggy coats to keep out the weather. The biggest stand between 13 and 14 hands high and nearly all are black or brown, with little or no white on faces and legs. Encountered in the fells they sometimes seem rather fierce but, tamed, they become the most docile of creatures – ideal as children's riding ponies. Most Fells are registered and named and many are the descendants of the very first in these parts to be given a name – a saddled pony, with trailing rein, found cropping the heather on the slopes of Stainmore after the retreating remnants of the '45 had straggled northwards through Westmorland. Nobody knew whether he had been ridden by Englishman or Scot but they took him down to one of the farms and called him 'Ling Cropper' – a name still persisting in the breed today.

[Today, all Fell ponies are under ownership – none run 'wild'.]

Spy-Glass Hill

The dramatically sculptured wall of the Scafells, the highest land in England, rising in crags and scree above the wilderness of the upper Esk, must be one of the great views in the fell country. And it is best seen in close-up from barely three miles away – ideally when thrown into relief by morning sunlight – from the little summit of Border End, just above the top of Hardknott Pass, perhaps ten minutes' walk from the car. The splendid panorama was again enjoyed the other day during an afternoon's traverse of the heights surrounding the lonely trough of Mosedale, and I wondered how many of the thousands of motorists crawling over the pass each summer bother to seek out this sudden and quite breath-taking view, so very easily attained. Border End is only 1,700 feet high but, from its rocky crest, you can pick out every detail of the Scafells from Slight Side to Ill Crag, with all the east-facing crags, and study the five miles' winding progress of the upper Esk and its superb string of pools and waterfalls. Here, at a glance, is the very best of wild Lakeland – falling water, cliffs and a soaring ridge-line. Turn leftwards and you can trace the Esk all through its long dale to the coast, so that you have the unusual sight of a lovely river from its source to the sea, and, farther round, there is the view of the long miles of wooded Dunnerdale and the 'back' of the Coniston fells. While, westwards, a few hundred feet below the crags at your feet, is a bird's eye view of the Roman fort of Hardknott, with the commandant's house, the granaries, the bath-houses and the parade ground laid out, as if on a map. All this for ten minutes' exercise – but most people can't be bothered.

Above Wastwater

The simple, airy walk along the top of the Wastwater Screes is best savoured in clear weather when the dramatic views down the gullies and shattered crags, as well as the splendid panorama of peaks at the head of the dale, can be seen in close-up. A recent traverse, however, in heavy rain and thick mist, cut down visibility to yards, but the bonus for setting out in such weather came on the return journey along the foot of the screes. The rain stopped as I was descending to the toe of Wastwater down the curious crater of Greathall Gill with its crumbling rock pinnacles, and the clouds suddenly lifted to reveal the deepest lake in England smiling in the afternoon sunlight. So smooth was the surface, so blue the sky, and so bright the sunshine that the crags and fellsides of Buckbarrow, Middle Fell and Yewbarrow were accurately reflected in the mirrored waters – a restful colour picture of absolute perfection. Three browsing goats at the foot of Great Gully disturbed my lunch – only blows would shoo them away. A patient fly-fisherman on the far shore, the only figure in sight, served to underline the serenity of the scene. The small pumping station at the foot of the lake, no more intrusive than a farm building, seemed innocuous enough – for the time being. Already the sun had dried the piled boulders on the screes, making their crossing no more than a pleasant balancing exercise, although, further on, a father with his young family – the youngest slung in a rucksack – was having difficulties. A slightly adventurous walk for the inexperienced but the gradual unfolding of our finest dale head is more than ample reward.

Avoiding the Bogs

To arrive with dry feet at the foot of Cam Spout Crag on Scafell from Cockley Beck in the wet season – which can be any time – requires guile and agility. Mosedale is always wet – as are all the Lakeland Mosedales – and to avoid the bogs it is necessary to eschew the cairned track and steer a dry course up the higher slopes to the west. Once, before discovering this trick, I tried out plastic bags tied over my leaky boots, thinking these might be the answer. The bags, however, were each pierced with aeration holes, making them worse than useless. Freezer bags, though, might work. But, having traversed Mosedale dry-shod, the crossing of Lingcove Beck and the upper Esk, with both in lively spate, can add additional flavour to the day, for athletic leaps across slippery boulders and churning waters necessitate some confidence and dexterity. By steering a course through delightful, untracked country it is then possible, however, to avoid altogether the formidable – in really wet weather – crossing of Great Moss and arrive with dry feet for a sheltered lunch-break among the conveniently tilted Sampson's Stones. The last time I went this way was on a very wet day when a projected rock scramble up the edge of Cam Spout and on to Scafell had to be abandoned for a more pedestrian route up the steep grass to the right. In drier weather the rock route can be very pleasant. Untracked routes above the upper Esk take one into some of the roughest and wildest country in England. These are our best and highest mountains and this is their best side. Whether you are walking in good weather or bad, with wet or dry feet, this is always a corner to uplift the spirit.

Perfection on the Scafells

It was stiflingly hot in the great oven of Grains Gill but the cooling sight of a patch of old, hard snow half-way up the dark recesses of Central Gully on Great End helped a little. This was the first day of June in the middle of a heat wave but I remembered climbing the gully – to escape the blazing sun – early one July, many years ago, and

The Scafells from Bowfell.

having to kick steps up a steep snow drift that was almost ice-hard. There must have been 60 more-or-less-recumbent people around the summit cairn on Scafell Pike but complete solitude and quietude was found on a rocky knoll perhaps 300 yards to the north where the unobstructed views were startlingly clear. The nearer Scottish hills could be picked out just to the left of the huge bulk of Grasmoor – although not, this time, the Isle of Man – but much more interesting were the close-up pictures of Great Gable and especially the Napes ridges, needle-sharp in the brilliant, afternoon sunlight, with Naples Needle itself easily identifiable without binoculars. Just to the right of

Tophet Wall was the only dark, shadowed part of the mountain or its crags – the spectacular overhangs above Great Hell Gate up which, that very evening on Channel Four, I was to watch two leading climbers putting up a desperate, new route. But the most colourful picture on this most beautiful summer afternoon – enough to pull me up dead in my trot down the Corridor Route – was a striking juxtaposition of dark, yawning depths and sunlit crags with the soaring fellsides of Gable for backcloth and, in the foreground, a superb mountain pool that had caught the cloudless sky in its mirror and reflected it back in matchless royal blue. Was this, when we look back, to be the best day this summer?

[I can't now remember whether there were any better days than this in the summer of 1985 but I doubt it.]

Heather Tracks in Newlands

There is no more delightful descent from the high fells on a summer's evening than down the long north ridge of Hindscarth into the perfect vale of Newlands. From the Buttermere Fells earlier the mountain horizon had been blurred by heat haze, the hills mere purple shapes against the westering sun, but towards evening the peaks leaped into sharp focus and the colours shouted to be seen. The Causey Pike range, for instance – grey crags tipped with gold and the blue shadows of the ravines setting off the bright green turf – while, opposite, the long line of Eel Crags was a brown wall of rock thrusting through the contrasting greens of bracken, bilberry and heather. 'By heather tracks wi' heaven in their wiles' goes the route down the Hindscarth ridge and through the Scope End crags to Little Town on the floor of the dale. Winding through the rock outcrops the heather tracks lay above a bright green carpet of bilberry spread above the lush turf of Goldscope where the German miners worked in the reign of the first Elizabeth. Down to the west the beck slid through the contours in Little Dale in a silver chain of pools and waterfalls and, ahead, scattered woodlands divided the trim fields. In the morning I had heard the cuckoo in the High Snab woods and there he was again, this time somewhere high in the crags of Maiden Moor. And dropping nearer to the dale, suddenly after the quiet of the heights, an orchestra of sound – the cries of lambs, the barking of sheepdogs, the rattle of farm tractors, and the clatter of pails in a dairy. Then, through leafy lanes aflame with gorse, to the car and, a few miles further on, to the noise and bustle of Lakeland on holiday.

111

The Glaramara Tarns

On a bright June morning with a southerly breeze blowing white billowing clouds off the Scafells the hummocky summit ridge of Glaramara seemed a promenade for the gods. Great Gable and the Buttermere fells rose, blue and massive, through the heat haze, sunlight bathed the nearer crags, insects worked in the dry grass and larks sang unseen overhead. Most rewarding of all were the tarns. There are about ten on Glaramara, each one mirroring the white-flecked blue sky, and the best is one of the smallest – Lincomb Tarn, cradled in rough grey crags with the shapely peak of Bowfell framed in its southern gateway. This perfect jewel of a tarn has long been one of my favourites among the hundreds of smaller Lake District mountain tarns. Others would include the tarns on Haystacks, Lambfoot Dub above the Corridor Route to Scafell Pike, Hard Tarn below the Helvellyn ridge, and Blind Tarn in the Coniston fells. Goats Water, Small Water and Bleaberry Tarn, among several others, are dramatically sited but lack the intimacy of the smaller mountain pools. Heaton Cooper, the Lake District painter, finds Sprinkling Tarn 'the most completely satisfying of all the tarns of Lakeland'. But the adjoining Esk Hause highway, for me, robs this fine pool of some of its magic. A more secluded rock tarn on Seathwaite Fell, a few hundred yards away to the north, has rather more appeal. Ideally, the perfect mountain tarn should be a pool among rocks, remote from tracks and suddenly encountered, a balm to the spirit, as you scramble round a corner.

A Rocky Staircase

Old climbers, probably unable even to get off the ground on modern routes, still like to get their hands on a bit of rock now and then – provided, in my case, it's not too steep and there are plenty of good holds. Two of us had scrambled up Low Water Beck in the Coniston fells, carefully avoiding the two waterfall pitches, and, lunching by the tarn, decided to continue our modest pottering by taking to the splendid rough slabs on the far side of the pool. This fine corrie is better known to us for its winter climbing but the slabs, most bountifully fashioned with the sort of holds we require nowadays, led us in a delightful summer scramble of several hundred feet almost to the top of Brim Fell. From our airy staircase, mounting with unaccustomed ease, we watched the sunlit tarn, below our boots, grow gradually smaller and more ultramarine in colour and, across the combe, the pilgrims making their dusty way up the stones and screes of the tourist route through the quarries. We felt almost sorry for them as they toiled up the over-cairned zigzags while we idled up our step-ladder, exulting in the 'jug handles' that always appeared when needed, the comforting roughness of the rock, the happy continuity of the little rock cliffs, the airiness of the situations and the aerobatics of the ravens circling overhead. In winter this steep wall of the corrie, ringed with cornices, can sometimes, for me, be a slightly intimidating place but this day, clear and sunlit, it could not have been more welcoming. Fingers and toes well satiated, we slid down the rocks of Raven Tor to the valley.

Remembering Mardale Green

The fells that so nobly ring the head of Mardale – Harter Fell, Mardale Ill Bell, High Street and Kidsty Pike – provide one of the easiest of mountain rounds as well as the chance to see red deer, Fell ponies and perhaps, if you are especially fortunate, a golden eagle. Almost everywhere along the traverse you are treading springy turf on still-uneroded tracks and trotting along so fast and comfortably that, looking back from, say, Kidsty Pike, you may be surprised at the distance covered. Here is still – in spite of the reservoir and its ugly, white shoreline – one of the finest dale-heads in the national park, for all the crags on these otherwise-grassy fells are crowded above this lonely corner with its superb mountain tarns giving it a wild, rugged beauty. Fortunately, the dead-end of the valley road remains without tourist facilities so that it is still avoided by the hordes but increasingly sought out by those connoisseurs of quietude and unspoiled scenery who can shut out the sight of reservoir and dam. Some of us remember Mardale Green before the war and the flood – a particularly peaceful corner of old Lakeland where time seemed to have stood still. And the other day, following a round of the heights, I could recall the scene as I looked down on the remains of the lost hamlet, newly exposed by the drawn-down waters after the long drought. There were the old farm lanes, the walls of the intake fields and the rocky site of the old Dun Bull while round the wooded headland used to stand the little church. A sad scene, looking at these old bones of a drowned countryside, but, up the fellside towards the tarns, Mardale Waters still splashed, glittered and danced down to the lake just as they did in those remembered days before the flood.

113

Skiddaw House Shepherd

Nine years ago old Pearson Dalton locked up Skiddaw House, 'the loneliest house in England', for the last time and walked over the fells, with his five dogs, into retirement. For nearly half a century he had lived there alone, with his five dogs, cats and goats – 1,600 feet up and four rough mountain miles from the nearest habitation – looking after 1,000 sheep roaming the northern slopes of Skiddaw. But every Saturday he walked seven trackless miles over the fells to his sister's home at Fellside for a weekend in 'civilization' and every Monday, no matter what the weather, he walked back to the bleak house on the moors and his workaday week. When he retired at 75 – he had gone to Skiddaw House at 28, on a month's trial, and stayed on for 47 years – they thought the place would be closed down and become a ghost house, but for some time now, the building, once a shooting lodge, has been used by young people as a base for outdoor activities. And one room is kept open, as a mountain bothy, for travellers spending a night in the wilds. The other day the old man's room, now in use for courses, was locked. Here, for recreation on wild, lonely nights, he had his old sofa covered with sacking, a few tattered books, and an old battery radio. Lighting was by oil lamp but he always kept a good fire. I heard he was still alive last year. His little vegetable garden is now overgrown and the shelter trees, the only ones left in Skiddaw Forest, looked more windswept than ever. But the view of soaring fells, grass, heather and sheep, but nothing else except the sky, was just the same.

[This was written in June 1978 – nine years after Pearson's retirement at the age of 75. Whether or not the old shepherd is still alive – at the age of 96 – I have not been able to find out.]

Wonderful Dunnerdale

Wordsworth, in 34 sonnets about its beauty, thought the Duddon the loveliest river in Lakeland and therefore, perhaps, in all England, and many might agree with him. All the fifteen miles from the Three Shires Stone to the sea, the Duddon dances down the dale through constantly varying scenery of crags and woodland – a twisting, knobbly valley that, save for the afforestation on Harter Fell, has hardly changed since his day. In its upper reaches the road is still, mercifully, too narrow for coaches and too winding and humpbacked for speed. I don't think there's an advertisement or a knick-knack shop or even a cafe along its length – although, no doubt, you could get tea in one of the charming

Birks Bridge in Dunnerdale.

little cottages with roses growing over the porch. Nearly 70 years ago the Duddon was the first river I explored as a child – but not very carefully for I used to think, like thousands of present-day tourists, that it was the Duddon that accompanied the road through Seathwaite. In fact, it is its tributary, Tarn Beck, that splashes down beside the road for a long mile while the Duddon is carving its way, unseen by most visitors, through Wallowbarrow Gorge, far to the west. The other day I explored Tarn Beck right to its source in Seathwaite Tarn, continuing the round over Dow Crag and the Coniston fells. Here is a little-known valley, boggy in its lower reaches, but a glorious necklace of pools and little waterfalls as it nears the tarn. Dunnerdale itself, for a lifetime, has always meant shadowed pools on hot summer days, the spring glory of birches and daffodils, the autumn scent of woodsmoke, the chatter of the river among the rocks, and the blue hills of evening standing high all round the compass.

Magic on Harter Fell

The forecast, the TV map a mass of black spots, had been for cloud and rain, heavy in places, everywhere but the sun shone all day on Dunnerdale's Harter Fell and the only clouds to be seen were a few billowing white ones high above the highest tops. It was warm enough to walk up stripped to the waist and, once through the forest, there was the fragrant scent of herbs and a delightful carpet of tormentil and eyebright clustered among the turf. Here is one of the most splendid summits in Lakeland – three towers of grey, welcoming rock commanding grandstand views, across the Esk, of the highest land in England and, down the winding, wooded Duddon, the sea glittering in the sunshine. We first came to know the fell nearly 60 years ago – walking across its shoulder, laden with tent, food and blankets, on our way from Foxfield station to the sanctuary of Wasdale Head. It was a completely different little mountain in those days – long before the Forestry Commission began planting its eastern and southern slopes below the 1,500 feet contour in 1936. Before they put up their fences and thick conifer screen you could wander at will over this craggy, little fell and sometimes we would try to link up the many outcrops into a more or less continuous rock route to the summit. You can't do that today, with just a few way-marked trails through the jungle, but, at least, there are plenty of birches and rowans – and even some beech, red oak, Scots pine and Norway maple – to break up the conifer blanket – far more sympathetic afforestation than in some other parts of the fell country.

Sensitive Afforestation

The forests of dark conifers planted among the fells during the last 50 years are not usually regarded as places of special beauty. We tend to criticize this invasion of 'foreign' woodlands, their regimented lines, blanket coverage and sharp edges against the soaring, green fellsides. Even so, delightful forest tracks of changing, colourful beauty, shadowed or sunlit, may be found in the Lorton fells, on the slopes of Skiddaw, around the shores of Thirlmere, and especially in the Forestry Commission woodlands above the Duddon. Here, on the rocky slopes of Harter Fell, is the nearest approach on a commercial scale to a forest garden – straight lines largely avoided by circling the contours, broad-leaved hardwoods among the conifers, larches and pines between the spruce and everywhere the bright, welcome green of birch and rowan. With the crags exposed and special features, including the becks, left

116

Summit crags of Harter Fell, Dunnerdale.

clear, here is a giant's rock garden designed with taste and devotion. Here, surely, is the Lakeland forest by which the Commission will prefer to be remembered rather than by their widely criticised adventures at Ennerdale and Whinlatter. For years we have known that the Dunnerdale forest will not be further extended and that the central dale heads will never be planted with conifers, and have grown accustomed to the restricted, although reasonably generous, access to Harter Fell. Now comes encouraging news that the Commission is to break up the worst of the sharp lines in Ennerdale by limited felling and replanting under the supervision of a landscape architect. I hope his blueprint will be Dunnerdale.

Summer Scrambles

JULY

Beyond the Caldew

Only one person – a distant matchstick figure crossing the col between Great Sca Fell and Knott nearly a mile away – was seen on a round of the two-thousanders at the 'back' of Skiddaw on a fine July day – the tourist month. But, usually, you don't see anybody in these pleasant, rolling hills that, centuries ago, were 'wick wi' fwoak' and alive with mining activities in a score of shafts and holes. This is splendid, lonely country, most nobly innocent of car parks, caravan sites, public conveniences, cairns or even, in many cases, tracks. The going is easy although rather featureless but the views of the Lakeland fells to the south are refreshingly different and those northwards, of the great Cumberland plain reaching out, below a vast sky, to the Solway Firth and the Scottish hills, impressively spacious. There are seven or eight tops in the round – with a couple more if you diverge to Great Cockup and the lovely cleft of Trusmadoor. We had our lunch in the unlocked bothy – formerly a shooting-box – on Great Lingy Fell and our afternoon siesta sprawled in the shelter of rocks on our last summit, Great Calva. This is the hill that suddenly, after an unknown history, first became important in the 1920s when Eustace Thomas, successfully attacking Dr A.W. Wakefield's record round of the Lakeland fells, decided to include this northern outlier in his bid. Nowadays, being included in the Bob Graham round, it is quite well known. From the summit eyrie we looked back along the seemingly long way we had come and then south to the Lakeland fells along the remarkably natural fault of the Glenderatera valley, the Vale of St John's and the trough of Thirlmere, glittering in the sunlight.

Our Last Big Game

A leisurely round of the heights enclosing Martindale deer forest yielded neither sight nor sound of England's last big game, the lordly red deer. It is said there are up to 300 of them centred on these fells and around Helvellyn, but they had all gone to ground in hidden corners on this sunny afternoon – or my eyesight is not what it was. Far too early, of course, to hear the roaring sound of the stags. It sounded like the 'revving' of a motorcycle the last time I heard that rather frightening noise high above the head of Rampsgill during the autumn rut. Unable at first to place the sudden sound, I then spotted, a thousand feet below me, a huge stag crossing the screes towards some anticipatory hinds, and bellowing as he went. The deer forest – there are few trees there, nowadays – is within and around the valleys of Bannerdale Beck and Rampsgill Beck and the heart of the sanctuary is the steep-sided fell between them known as The Nab. Walking on this remote spur is discouraged by notices, barbed wire and, to the south, a quagmire of peat-bogs, so that the deer thrive undisturbed – so well, in fact, that the stags can scale 25 stone as against the average 15 stone of the less-pampered red deer in the Highlands. This corner of lonely fells has been maintained as a deer sanctuary by the Hasell family for 300 years. At one time the late Lord Lonsdale, 'the sporting Earl', enjoyed the shooting rights and one of his guests, the Kaiser, was said to have been one of the few to have bagged a 'royal' at Martindale. But on this sleepy afternoon the home of the red deer seemed, from the heights, just an empty dale, quiet as a tomb and shimmering in the heat.

A Favourite Gill

Many of the more worthy gills in the fell country – dark, rock-girt ravines noisily flooded with waterfalls and pools – are clearly shown and named on large-scale maps, examples being the Oxendale gills and those on the northern slopes of the Scafell range. But one of my favourites – unnamed and unidentified as a ravine on the map – is hardly even recognizable as an adventurous place from a short distance away, and only yields its secrets when you get inside it. My private name for the place is Ern Nest Gill – a good enough clue for informed mountain folk – and competent scramblers with a taste for steepish rock, superb water cascades, glorious pools and exciting caverns will find it well matches the better-known gills. None are less obvious, more hidden away, than this one; hundreds of people pass close by without noticing it. In fairly dry weather I have climbed it two or three times but have often been defeated, sometimes by snow and ice, and, the other day, by the sheer volume of water coming down. Instead, on this recent visit, two of us avoided the worst of the crashing water by escaping up the right wall which is a pleasant enough scramble. I often use the gill as a route up the best side of Fairfield, traversing from its head to the splendid rough rocks that lead directly to The Step and then, across Black Tippet and Flinty Graves, to the summit. On a sunny day you quickly dry out on these warm, friendly rocks after your immersions, voluntary or otherwise, in the gill. From the crags we looked across at the cave on Dove Crag, wondered whether anybody was climbing there, spotted a circling helicopter and, later in the valley, heard that the steepest crag in Lakeland had sadly claimed another victim.

[Link Cove Gill could be another name for this delectable place.]

Up and Down the Pinnacle

There's nearly a mile of cliff just below the St Sunday Crag summit plateau on the steep Grisedale face of the fell, but for 50 years climbers failed to spot its possibilities. It was not until 1954 that undergraduates from Sheffield University first explored the long line of ridge, gullies and slabs, and discovered a new climbing ground. Crags that had always, viewed from the valley, seemed insignificant proved on close examination to be quite steep, sound and satisfying, and a score of routes were quickly pioneered. The easiest of these, Pinnacle Ridge, provides an exhilarating approach to the summit for an adventurous scrambler with the necessary rock-climbing experience. It is 600 feet long, only moderate in grading, not unlike an easy rock ridge in the Alps and, on a good day, a bracing ladder to the heights in walking boots and rucksack. The other day, in glorious sunshine with a refreshing breeze, I went this way to the summit and then, having enjoyed it so much, climbed down the same way without getting too scared. From the top of the pinnacle the views of the Helvellyn ridges were surprisingly dramatic and I could just pick out the blue of Hard Tarn, one of the most secluded mountain pools in the district. Two thousand feet below my boots I could see shepherds collecting sheep in a fold by Grisedale Beck, and hear the barking of their dogs. The only snags had been the steep, tiring trudge up the Elm How zigzags, long disused, and the rough scramble across unstable screes to the foot of the ridge.

But a satisfying day ended with the lovely walk down the north-east ridge to Patterdale; below lay the long length of Ullswater, its tiny islands riding like yachts at anchor, and the smoke rising slow and straight from cottage chimneys.

Lonely Fells

Seatallan is only two rough miles from Wasdale, and Caw Fell perhaps another two very lonely miles farther on, yet few people bother to go over these fells nowadays. Indeed, you could say they were probably better known 2,000 years ago. The western slopes of both hills are littered with the relics of primitive settlements – circles, burial cairns, tumuli, and many unidentified mounds – and the huge summit cairn on Seatallan is probably early British and could be thousands of years old. When the early tourists 'discovered' the popular peaks of Scafell, Great Gable, and Pillar 200 years ago these lonelier, grassy fells, not far away, had been the home of ancient peoples for at least a millenium. On a recent walk it seemed rewarding to traverse first these quiet, remote hills to get the full flavour of the switchback progression towards the great cliffs of the Pillar range – miles of grass with backward views towards the coast and then rocky heights, great caverns, and the sound of falling waters, far below. There were five minutes, though, on the summit of Haycock when there was no sound at all – not even the hum of unseen aircraft which increasingly disturbs the quiet of the hills nowadays. The perfect silence of a summer evening on a lonely summit, nobody within miles, and smiling, sunlit fells all round the horizon. Much later I came down to the late evening magic of Nether Beck, the pools and waterfalls getting bigger and better with every half-mile and the sunlight still gilding the new bracken carpet. It lighted, too, the dark cliffs of The Screes and the grey rocks of Pike's Crag while a solitary white sail glided across the sparkling blue of Wastwater.

Contouring the Crinkles

Few of our fells have more routes to the summit than Bowfell, the splendid pyramid that mounts guard over Langdale, Eskdale, and Langstrath. All of them – about a dozen, with variations – are very familiar so it seemed an interesting ploy to seek out a new way, avoiding all tracks and intermediate summits, and returning by a different route. The exercise, from the Three Shires Stone, took me across Cold Pike and Crinkle Crags, missing all the many tops and even keeping out of sight of paths, with a final section up the rocks of Bowfell Links to the piled summit blocks, where I met the only people seen all day. Returning, I kept to the Eskdale side, traversing Crinkle Crags low down above Lingcove Beck, and contouring Red How and Gaitkins to the pass. One revelation was the amount of unclimbed rock on these rough, trackless slopes – little cliffs of firm, clean crag at least worthy of exploration on outdoor pursuits courses. The great sunny bowl of Adam-a-Cove with its superb view of the Eskdale wall of the Scafells, was the only considerable grassy area encountered – a perfect belvedere for a summer evening, alive with the sounds of sheep and the murmuring of distant becks. Another rewarding Bowfell round, avoiding tracks, is the circumnavigation of the mountain, embracing Three Tarns, Ore Gap, Hanging Knotts, and the east-facing crags – a perambulation interesting in either direction. The value of these unconventional scrambles is they take you into 'new' country, rarely visited except by the occasional shepherd or foxhunter. There is the quiet thrill of navigation, even in clear weather, and the satisfaction of working out a steadily unfolding route round the contours.

[Much of the worthy rock on this round – done 12 years ago – is still unclimbed, or at least, not climbed regularly.]

Mardale Green Remembered

By the law of averages we could be due for a lot of rain in the fell country during the coming months. Rainfall in an area which has often claimed national records for wetness has been only 30 per cent of average since 1 April and precipitation totals tend to even themselves out. Recent rains restored the mountain becks and patterned the fell sides with fresher green but made little or no difference to the appearance of Haweswater, England's largest reservoir, which, a week ago, was drawn down 11 metres or about 35 feet. During the 1976 drought the level sank by 15 metres but in July of that year it was only $8\frac{1}{2}$ metres down so that, if the comparatively dry weather continues, new denudation records could be set up. The other day I came down from a round of the High Street fells to find much of the once-idyllic hamlet of Mardale Green, drowned by the water engineers 40 years ago, almost indecently exposed to public view. I sat, at the entrance to Riggindale, on the tumbled ruins of Mardale Hall and tried to bring this lovely corner, dimly remembered, back to life – the little, yew-shaded church on the side of The Rigg, the old Dun Bull on the farther shore, the farms, the winding lanes and, always, the air of peace and quietude. All gone, now so long ago – just the old walls showing above the mud, the sheep grazing on the former intake fields, and the ugly white shoreline reaching round the contours. It could never happen today, this rape of a lovely valley and the destruction of an ancient community.

[This was in July, 1978 and Mardale Green has been similarly exposed to public view on later occasions.]

The Best Pools

There are about 500 mountain tarns in the fell country but nobody has counted the multitude of pools in the becks and gills – 1,000 at least, or perhaps thousands? In warmer summers one has bathed or lazed in many of them, often under waterfalls, but so far this cloudy year the appeal of immersion has been limited. Where is the best pool? In the Esk, the Lingcove, the Duddon, the Derwent, the Sprint, or in one of the gills? One of my favourites has always been Blackmer Pot in Langstrath Beck, with its streaming vertical walls, pellucid depths, dimly seen shingle floor and always the roar of the fall in your ears. But I can think of scores of others, overhung with rowans or girt with polished rock, where a dip towards the end of a mountain day has been the perfect reviver. Among the very finest of these treasures must be the large, circular pool at the foot of the glistening wall of Whorneyside Force in Hell Gill, Oxendale. The other day I climbed the gill, keeping near (or in) the water all the way, and found the ascent of the Force, just to the right of the torrent, mildly adventurous in its exposure. This is one of our biggest waterfalls and when you have pulled over the lip, through the spray, you find a second, smaller fall with a matching smaller pool. Higher up the gill is the main ravine, shut in by vertical crags and overhanging trees – as dark and cavernous a place as anywhere in Lakeland. But the pool below the Force is an idyllic corner – perfect for swimming or a shallow dive when flooded by morning sunlight. Sometimes there is hardly a ripple on the glittering surface as the fall slides, curiously quietly, into the depths.

The 'Back' of Place Fell

Seen from the northern extension of the High Street range – or, in close-up, from Beda Fell – the eastern flank of Place Fell, scored by several deep-cut ravines, looks a very exciting place. Indeed, with the

Hell Gill in Oxendale.

shadows in the right places, these great clefts slicing through the cliffs of Hawk Crag are the most spectacular feature of the western view across Lakeland – far more impressive than anything seen around Helvellyn, and almost as dramatic as the view of Pier's Gill from Great Gable. Yet there are no recorded climbs in these ravines, no mention of them in any guidebook, and no tracks in the area or on the map. The 1:25,000 map shows nearly a mile of crag and clearly indicates the ravines, but only one of them, Redgate Gill, is named. Two exploratory visits, before and after heavy rain, showed, however, that the ravines, so impressive from a distance, merely flatter to deceive. All the gills were climbed, either up or down, but proved to be little better than steep, scree gullies, broken up, here and there, by small pools, a few waterfalls, and short pitches of an undemanding nature. In places, the water disappears underground, sometimes reappearing lower down, and another curious feature is that some of the gills split into two and join elsewhere. An unusual hazard, rarely encountered in our best gills, is the occasional presence of great beds of extremely virulent nettles, and Nettleslack happens to be the name of one of the nearby farms in lonely Boardale. But, although these rarely visited ravines are technically, and even aesthetically, unrewarding, the 'back' of Place Fell is a good place for escaping the holiday crowds and discovering a different, rather strange landscape.

Hardknott Hazards

Two youngsters spent much of a long, summer's day struggling on mountain bikes, straining on the pedals, up the Eskdale side of Hardknott Pass, tearing down at breakneck speed and then doing it all over again, many times. 'You should be riding those things on the fells, not on the road,' I told them and they agreed but thought the exercise good training for their mountain legs. Tanks, Bren gun-carriers and secret prototypes of new cars have also been tested and exercised on Hardknott, the most formidable bit of tilted highway in the country, far more demanding than the highest and roughest passes in the Highlands. Much more of a test than, for instance, the famous Bealach nam Ba ('Pass of the Cattle') between Tornapress and Applecross, even before it was resurfaced. As a result, holiday and weekend motorists, unused to our steep mountain roads, are always finding difficulties on Hardknott and the farm tractor at Cockley Beck is often in demand when vehicles have gone over the edge and careered down the fellside. But the smallest car can be driven over the pass if handled properly. I've often driven over at night when the main hazard is that of the sheep sleeping on the tarmac. Even hearses go over regularly. Visitors to the area, however, unpractised in steep motoring, should be aware of the unwritten rule about the negotiation of the steep, zigzag mountain passes in the Alps. It is the vehicle *ascending* that has the right of way; descending vehicles should pull in to allow them through. If everybody followed this rule on Hardknott and Wrynose there would be far less confusion and far fewer accidents.

Furthest East

The ascent of Grey Crag, the most easterly two-thousander in Lakeland, from the Shap Fells road, combined with the circumnavigation of Bannisdale, makes a lonely, if unexciting, 12 miles round. On a recent visit I saw nobody, not even distant specks, all day, nothing moved save the occasional flurry underfoot of startled grouse and the only sounds were the twittering of larks and peewits and the sad call of the curlew. The round is mostly untracked for there are no signs to point the way – nor even to indicate the entrance to the hidden valley of Bannisdale. But along the grassy fells near the head of the dale there are occasional tracks of motorcycles – clearly those of local farm lads since stone walls prevent machines tackling the round from off the main road. The narrow valley road – once threatened with flooding – is unfenced and unsurfaced and ends suddenly, high up the contours, so no tourists go there and the sheep wander along it undisturbed. For most of the way around the heights you can walk with hands in pockets if you wish, so easy and gentle the terrain – except where you have to climb walls, using the 'throughs' if you can find them. The rewards – but only for the connoisseur used to desolate country – are the loneliness, the quietude, the vast horizons and skyscapes, the views stretching from Great Gable to Ingleborough and, far to the south, the sun glinting on Morecambe Bay. But go, if you must, when the bogs are burned dry and, ideally, when the familiar fells to the west are too crowded for comfort.

Our Roughest Summit

Broad Crag, one of Lakeland's seven three-thousanders and the fourth highest mountain in England, is the roughest summit in the district – a tumble of huge, heaped boulders – and the least visited. Not one in a thousand of the pilgrims to Scafell Pike less than a half a mile away

126

turn from the scratched, stony highway to the shrine to scramble on to Broad Crag, although the three-thousander's round should include it as well as the much more accessible Ill Crag. On a recent visit to the Pike I traversed Broad Crag for a change, reaching the summit rocks by way of the splendid, unnamed corrie well above the grossly eroded Corridor Route. This rocky mountain combe, untracked and secluded, with the bold, grey thrust of Broad Crag straight ahead, is not unlike any one of a score of remote Scottish corries. Scattered along a rising grass shelf between the crags are two or three tiny tarns, and seated at the edge of an old favourite pool of mine – the aptly named Lambfoot Dub – I had my sandwiches and coffee. From the rocks around the tarn the great sweep of Great Gable and its soaring rock ridges, with Napes Needle and Tophet Wall most prominent, looked as close and sharp as if viewed through a zoom lens – barely, it seemed, a stone's throw away. The sight of a hang-glider slowly descending from the summit of the Pike, nearly a mile away, and apparently dropping into the depths of Pier's Gill – although I'm sure the pilot must have avoided this fate – enlivened my lonely lunch. Then a final scramble over the deserted Broad Crag and on to the populous Pike on which a score of more or less exhausted pedestrians lay prostrate in the humid heat.

Threefooted Brandreth

It's not often that I go to Threefooted Brandreth, The Pewits or Shivery Man but, with the bogs reasonably negotiable after the long drought, it seemed the best time for wandering the heights between Thirlmere and Borrowdale. The three place names are unnoticed features on a largely untracked traverse of these not very exciting hills. But Bleaberry Fell, a lovely heather-carpeted summit, is a superb viewpoint with glimpses of the Scottish hills on a clear day, while High Seat, the highest of these little fells, has, above the surrounding swamps, the luxury of neat summit rocks from which to spy out a 360-degree vista of the finest mountains in Lakeland. It was the driest traverse of these under-standably neglected tops I have ever made; almost dryshod even in the 'carpet slippers' I use for undemanding summer tramps. And the sunshine, unbroken blue skies, the sound of the larks, and the sight of circling ravens made an enjoyable change of scene. To add a little flavour to the day, the two of us made a scrambling exploration of Goat Crag and its scattered outcrops and, on the way back, pottered about round Raven Crag, Castle Crag and The Benn, several times getting lost in the forest which I always manage to do in these parts.

Thirlmere, naturally, was well drawn down but not offensively so, and the pools in Shoulthwaite Gill were not quite as magnificent as usual. But surprisingly, after the long heat wave, even the smallest becks were still lazily trickling down the contours. Incidentally, what exactly, I again asked myself, is Threefooted Brandreth; and why?

[Brandreth, the fell near Great Gable, is mentioned in an 1805 reference as 'the three-footed Brandreth' and the name is derived from the Old Norse 'brand-reith', a fire-place or grate, but, more specifically, a grid-iron or trivet, probably with three feet. Perhaps a beacon once burned on this summit. (Lake District Place Names by Robert Gambles.) Maybe this obscure place on High Seat above Thirlmere was also once a beacon site.]

A Climbing Centenary

Scores, possibly hundreds, of people climbed Napes Needle on Great Gable during the weekend celebrations of its lone, first ascent exactly 100 years earlier by W.P. Haskett Smith, the esteemed Father of British climbing. Many others, perched on nearby rock ledges, watched the celebratory ascenders – flimsily dressed girls, club elders, 'tigers' hung about with clanking ironmongery and at least one small boy. But the gallery for the official champagne-popping rope did not match that for the 50-year anniversary ascent on Easter Sunday 1936, when the old master himself repeated his brave 1886 adventure before an estimated crowd of 300. Once perched on the top block, Haskett Smith was asked for a story; rarely at a loss for words, the old man replied in an instant: 'There is no other story. This is the top storey.' The sweltering heat in the valley during the centenary weekend was somewhat relieved, above 2,000 feet, by light breezes blowing gently through the crags. Half-way up the ridge behind the Needle, it was interesting to look down on the top block and see no fewer than four climbers sprawled precariously on the top – sunbathing. Several times in the past I have shared the top block with two others and found it crowded; to squeeze four on to the sloping kitchen-table top must have needed some dexterity. Doing the climb in 1931 with G.S. Sansom, who had been on the first ascent of Scafell's Central Buttress in 1914, he recommended me, first, to share with him a stick of barley sugar; the resultant sticky fingers, he explained, would prove useful on the slightly sloping holds. Modern climbers with 'magic boots' but without sticky fingers, however, find it easy.

Great Gable from Esk Hause track.

[This centenary was celebrated in July 1986 and I still remember the sweltering heat.]

Helvellyn – with a Difference

A scramble up the waterfalls of Birkside Gill to reach the Helvellyn ridge followed by the descent of Whelpside Gill seemed a useful way of avoiding the crowds on the most-visited mountain in England. Both gills are rough, untracked and unvisited and we linked them by contouring round the upper rims of Ruthwaite Cove and Nethermost Cove, seeing nobody all afternoon apart from processions of matchstick figures in distant tourist tracks. Only the flies in Birkside Gill spoiled our contentment. The seething swarms were the most numerous and persistent that either of us could remember and the slippery climbing up the waterfalls with a swirling handkerchief in one hand bordered on the perilous at times. A little later, the flies mercifully blown away by a fresh breeze, we perched in a rocky corner admiring, just below us on a lower ledge of Ruthwaite Cove, the superb mountain pool of Hard Tarn, which is certainly among my favourites. Hard Tarn, cradled by crags, is warmed by the early morning sun but I remember an icy pre-breakfast bathe in the sunshine there many years ago. The source of Whelpside Gill is Brownrigg Well at 2,825 feet above sea-level – surely the highest running water in England. And in winter, nearby, is perhaps the longest-lasting snow patch on west-facing slopes in the district. The spring never dries up and it is interesting, working down the gill, to see how the first tiny trickle oozing out of the ground gradually gains in strength, first receiving a tributary half a mile down, then splashing over boulders and collecting a chain of pools and, finally, before entering the forest ravine, plunging over sizeable crags in splendid cascades and foaming waterfalls.

Another Intrusion

You can usually pick out rogue motorcyclists on the fells. They are the ones who have taken off their number plates to escape identification. There was one of these careering up and down the Mardale side of Gatescarth Pass the other day, not only shattering the quietude of the craggy side of Harter Fell but causing more damage to the track than dozens of tramping boots. Motorcyclists – regrettably, in my opinion – are allowed to use the 'green roads' in the fells and, if they have the special permission of the landowner, certain other places, but never common land. But it is all a rather complicated business and 'green roads' are not so easily defined. For instance, the Longsleddale side of Gatescarth Pass is, I understand, a 'green road' but not the Mardale side up and down which this youngster was rough-riding the other day. You usually hear these often-unsilenced machines before you see them and I seem to be meeting them increasingly in the fells – sometimes, illegally, on walkers' tracks and, occasionally, even on bare fellsides or summit ridges. Once, about 40 years ago, before the proliferation of these practices became a nuisance, I met a one-legged motorcyclist, with his machine, beside the cairn on Coniston Old Man and openly admired the skill and determination that had got him up there. But the present-day illegal motorcyclists in the fells, as distinct from the trail club riders who, no doubt, keep to permitted ways, are a regrettable development and flagrant cases should be reported, with the necessary details, to the planning authorities. Surely the heights and the lonely places should be free from the roar and screech of motorcycle engines. They are trying enough on our country lanes.

[Regrettably, the Mardale side of Gatescarth Pass is now, I understand, a 'green road', with the result that the pass is more eroded than ever.]

Days on Pillar Rock

Pillar Rock, notoriously greasy after rain, has been bone-dry for months during the longest drought I can remember. Rain is sorely needed in gardens, fields and reservoirs – and to bring back the music of the becks. But this has been the best summer in memory for climbers and I've no doubt many new and, to me, desperate routes have been made on Pillar and elsewhere. Right at the other end of the scale of difficulty, you come down to my recent lone ascent of the Rock by the ambulatory Old West Route with descent by the despised Slab and Notch, which seemed a fair day for a scrambler of declining years. The climbing, if you can call it that, was easy but the long slog to the Rock over Scarth Gap and the return trudge up and round the shoulder of the Buttermere fells made a tiring round. Wasdale is a far more convenient base. When I first climbed Pillar Rock more than 50 years ago, you could sit on top and look down Ennerdale without seeing a tree. Nowadays, there are millions of them – a vast, dark-green carpet laid for miles down the dale – and from the summit, on weekdays, you can usually hear the harsh sound of chain-saws in the forest 2,500 feet below your boots. Apart from the drowning of Mardale Green 40-odd years ago, this blanket afforestation of the bare trough of Ennerdale has been the greatest change in any Lakeland valley in my lifetime. Viewed from, say, the top of Great Gable it is the ruler-straight boundaries of the forest that shriek out. Nature does not plan in squares and verticals and, since before the war, these sharp edges of the dark carpet have been the only artificial intrusion in a superlatively lovely scene.

[This Pillar Rock ascent was in 1984, when I was 73, but I have been up once or twice since.]

A Very Warm Day

The oppressive heat seemed to reverberate off the rocks on Thornythwaite Fell like sound from a gong. It was not so much like being in an oven – that would have been bearable; more like clawing your way upwards through steaming hot blankets. People lay about, handkerchiefs tied over their heads, recovering, for the next bit, in shady hollows. The bogs were crusted hard, the becks stilled and the sheep sprawled, exhausted, among the rocks, not even bothering to rise when approached. At one time, well remembered, there was no track across Glaramara; now the stony way is six to ten feet wide in places but was avoided by a bee-line, across the bogs, from the top of Raven Crag since the thinnest of single socks, worn because of the heat – were poor protection on the sliding stones. Gable and Pillar reared high, in purple haze, against the blazing western sky; later, on top, the bulk of Great End, a smear of old snow still held in a cleft of Central Gully, and Bowfell, with the sun flooding across the sweep of Flat Crags, looked little more than a stone's throw away. Still not even the slightest zephyr of breeze but all the deep blue tarns were, miraculously, full and the best pool of all, Lincomb Tarn, dramatically cradled in steep, little crags, tempting for a dip. But, even the effort to undress seemed too much this time and, with new friends encountered on top, a slithering descent through the crags, down screes and woodlands, was made to Seathwaite for the consumption, between us, of a dozen cups of tea. The 'wettest place in England' drowsed in the baking heat with the usually flooded Derwent just a trickle among sun-bleached boulders.

[The new friends encountered on top in 1989 were the Astronomer Royal (Sir Francis Graham-Smith) and his wife.]

West of Shap Fells

A buzzard soared in slow spirals above a little crag just west of the Shap Fells road at the start of our round but that was the only moving thing on this hot sultry day – save for the occasional deafening zoom of jet aircraft. We did a slow circumnavigation of the lonely, untracked heights that circle the western reach of Westmorland's Borrowdale and, as expected, saw nobody all day although tourist Lakeland was swarming with people and traffic. Even the sheep were lying down – exhausted by the heat and, no doubt, very thirsty indeed for Borrow Beck was completely dry save for the occasional slimy pool of stagnant water. These modest hills with curious names like Robin Hood, Lord's Seat and Lawyer's Brow are not dramatic places but scrambles on all the steep, little crags of Bannisdale grit were some consolation for all the tussock-trudging and, fortunately, all the bogs were tinder-dry. The pleasure lay in having the whole countryside, as far as we could see, to ourselves, the complete absence of tracks, even footprints, cairns, or litter and the identification of familiar fells – blue, shadowed hills shimmering in the heat – from unusual angles. There are five of these

A lonely valley – the head of Longsleddale.

dead-end roadless dales – although Bannisdale has a farm track – reaching westwards from the Shap Fells road to Grey Crag above Longsleddale and all are worth exploring or circling by horseshoe rounds on days when guidebook places are alive with people – if you like solitude and can use a map. You are a long way from anywhere on these deserted tops where the nearest sign of man may be no more than a ruined farmstead, miles away. Good places to seek out when Lakeland is bursting at the seams.

Lakeland from the Air

One recent summer evening I had the privilege of seeing my homeland hills from a completely new angle – the passenger seat of a light aeroplane. From Kirkbride airfield we flew, in turn, over Skiddaw, the Scafells and Helvellyn, circling a few hundred feet above the summits so that every detail could be studied. About 12 years earlier I had done the same round, the Lakeland 'three-thousands', on foot, taking nearly 20 hours and expending a fair amount of energy; the effortless flight lasted a little over an hour. For the first time I could appraise the Lake District as a whole, rather than piecemeal, and observe, at close hand, the pattern of radiating valleys and linked ridges. All at once, the big, coloured map of the district on my study wall leapt into life, all the familiar fells, crags, lakes and tarns zooming into sharp focus as we swooped and soared above them. More than ever before I sensed the compactness and intimacy of the area – sometimes one view would embrace the whole – and the almost-jewelled perfection of the fell country in its shapes, colours and contrasts. Indeed, the only intrusive, even ugly, note in the scene was the profusion of the paths, unbelievably prominent as dusty streaks across all the fells. These harsh scorings, together with the scars of deserted or working mines or quarries – Force Crag, Honister and Greenside were particularly noticeable examples – thrust themselves into one's view even more forcibly than the great crags that, from this angle, looked not nearly so steep as they seem when you are clinging to their faces. The fells, too, seemed curiously flattened, even tamed, but I looked in vain for people on the summits or the tracks. Perhaps it was too hot for walking.

Droughts and Drenches

AUGUST

Coping with the Heat

It was, perhaps, the hottest day of the year. Frustrated tourists sweltered in their cars crawling in the queues or flopped, perspiring, on grassy banks around roadside 'honeypots'. But, from the heights, blue-remembered hills, flooded in sunlight, crowded the horizon, a gentle breeze cooled the air and there seemed hardly anybody about. Four of us of assorted ages, with 66 years between the youngest and the oldest, scrambled up the rocky east face of Red Screes, climbing every bit of rock in sight, and then did the same on Little Hart Crag before strolling down the deserted length of Scandale, in the broiling sun, to Ambleside. Dips were taken in the idyllic pool of Scandale Tarn – three being brave enough to swim while the oldest contented himself with paddling. We had no swimming trunks but nobody cared for we had the fells to ourselves. Huge blue dragon flies – miniature models of the jet fighters that so persistently harry the fells – swooped and dived just above the tarn but the trout and gudgeon that are said to inhabit the pool were in hiding below the reeds and water lilies. Thereafter, all the way down to the lovely High Sweden packhorse bridge, which a few trippers had reached, we were forever taking off and putting on boots – seated on grassy banks, dotted with tormentil, with our feet in the cooling pools of Scandale Beck, drying out our sweaty socks and idly discussing the welcome absence of the hordes. Later, we looked down through a gap in the woods at the bumper-to-bumper traffic along the A591 and felt a quiet contentment.

[This sweltering August day was in 1988.]

Mountain Springs

The day was stiflingly hot. Salty sweat streamed into my eyes, the rucksack was stuck to my glistening back and the fells, shadowless in the blazing sun, shimmered in the heat haze. A drink was badly needed and I knew where to get one, never-failing in the longest drought – the waterspout at the end of the traverse to Bowfell Buttress. How many thousands of dehydrated climbers and walkers have been revived by this hidden hosepipe in the crags? Recovering on a later summit on a dry Langdale round I thought of other welcoming mountain springs and, most affectionately, of the tiny, brimming rock-saucer near the foot of Intermediate Gully on Dow Crag at which I have regularly quaffed for more than half a century. There is another reliable spring just beyond Kern Knotts on the track to Napes Needle, a cool corner of dripping moss below Gimmer Crag, and Pillar Rock has its Waterfall. Not all Helvellyn walkers know of Brownrigg Well, marked and even named on the one-inch map, the ice-cold source of Whelpside Gill, which may be found perhaps a quarter of a mile west of the summit. Several other mountain springs are indicated on the larger 1:2500 maps and it was knowledge of one of these, between Scoat Fell and Red Pike, that once saved me from melting away on a round of the Mosedale Horseshoe in oppressive heat. I have cached water on the tops in advance of a traverse of the Cuillin ridge in Skye but things are never as serious as this on our far less-demanding fells. All the same, a bit of plastic tubing or a lemonade straw can be useful for sucking up tiny pools of rainwater on the rocks as I found recently on a dusty walk along the baking rocks of Crinkle Crags.

Browney Gill

The tarmac was melting in the stifling heat near Chapel Stile but it was so cool and breezy by the Pike o'Blisco summit cairn that I had to find a sheltered corner for my lunch and even considered replacing my shirt. It was to be an easy day, merely an escape from the oven, but, in the end, I wandered all over the fell, scrambled on most of its ten little crags and finally found the refreshing cool I was seeking in the damp, upper recesses of Browney Gill. Here is the right place on a hot, sultry day – dark pools for revival or for falling into, refreshing spray to clamber through and lovely cold, slimy walls to scale. From Pike o'Blisco the usual white necklace of falls towards the top of the gill seemed to have dried up in the drought but, once inside the ravine, there proved to be enough falling, sliding or gently trickling water to make the ascent interesting. In many years of exploration of this gill and swarms of others – the Oxendale triumvirate are among the best in Lakeland – I had never met other people similarly engaged but, this time, there was an outdoor pursuits party clambering up. Clearly, they were enjoying themselves. One of them had fallen, with delight, from a slightly awkward lower pitch into the pool beneath and, later in the day, I met them again gleefully trying out – premeditated, this time – the swimming potential of Oxendale Beck. The upper pitches of Browney Gill bring you out on the Crinkle Crags track below Great Knott and I thought of making my round more respectable by the descent of Crinkle Gill – until laziness won the day. Instead, I sat in the sun below Kettle Crag.

Idyllic Pools

A glorious dip in Hard Tarn – more of a wallow than a swim – was the one redeeming feature of a recent walk in oppressive heat and wringing humidity. To add to the feeling of clawing through wet blankets there were no views, because of the heat haze, most of the becks were dry, and the windless air was alive with flies. You have to search the one-inch map very closely to find the tiny blue speck of the tarn – unnamed on this scale. It lies in Ruthwaite Cove at nearly 2,400 feet on a rock ledge below the crags of the Helvellyn summit ridge and this day was as welcome as an oasis in the desert – just deep enough for a swim and edged with comfortable rock couches. Neither costume nor towel was needed. Few people seek out the trackless ways to this lovely jewel of the fells. Hard Tarn has long been a favourite bathing place of mine but I could name scores of others where dips have been enjoyed on the hottest days. Ideally, I like to find a pool to restore my well-being at the end of the day, within minutes of the car, and can recall many of these late bathes in such places as Lingmell Beck, Wasdale, the Derwent at Seathwaite, Hayeswater Gill at Hartsop and Mill Gill in Langdale – all of them costumeless, since I do not own one. Occasionally, some ingenuity has been needed to remain concealed from the valley-bound processions. One of the best bathing places in Lakeland is Blackmer Pot in Langstrath – a deep pool beneath vertical rockwalls – but this becomes too popular in heatwaves for my sort of dips, being close to a well-used track. Perhaps the height of enjoyment

Blackmoss (or Blackmer) Pot in Langstrath.

on trying days may be reached by coming unexpectedly upon a pool and, minutes later, rising from cool depths like a giant refreshed.

Evening on Scafell

The fells swam in the heat haze, the towers of Windscale intruded dimly on the edge of the sea, and a transistor set incongruously intoned our Test Match misfortunes from the highest point in England. Down on Mickledore an inexpert party could be seen and heard making heavy weather of Broad Stand, the easiest climb on Scafell, while half-way up the main crag two helmeted climbers were tackling the overhanging Flake Crack on what used to be the hardest climb in the country. The two were the only climbers on the face and, from a sunny patch of turf in Hollow Stones, we watched them, our necks straining upwards, until they reached the traverses, with the finish in sight. They were testing courage and skill in a shadowed, vertical world; we were idling in the evening sunshine debating the contrasting attractions of a dip in Lingmell Gill and a long drink in a low-raftered inn. Finally, we reached a compromise; we would do both – and we did. Earlier, water had been the trouble, with the higher becks dried up but, underneath Pike's Crag, we had found the only spring – a half-inch spout of delicious ice-cold water that made crushed sandwiches almost palatable. The evening sunshine gilded the length of Wastwater, lighted the crags on Great Gable and, as we left, just tipped the topmost cliffs of Scafell.

Collecting Tarns

You can collect ten 2,000 feet summits and visit or bathe in up to 20 tarns or pools in a none too strenuous Glaramara round – on a normal Lakeland day. But recent days, with shrinking reservoirs, scorched fellsides and barely trickling becks, have been far from normal and the usual tally was somewhat reduced on a late July circuit. Worse, one attempt at a dip only stirred up the mud. The rock pools in the gills are better bathing places these dry, dusty days. The half-dozen tarns on the Glaramara ridge – perfect jewels of the fells – are well-known but the pools on Seathwaite Fell, on the return leg from Allen Crags, are rarely visited. Once I counted 12 and there could be more but the other day some had disappeared. To reach your score you go by way of the curiously named Tarn at Leaves on Rosthwaite Fell, and include Sprinkling Tarn, making sure to visit the splendid little tarn set among crags just to the north, with its dramatic 'end-on' view of Great Gable.

Collecting and, ideally, using tarns or the enticing rock pools in the gills is one way of actually enjoying the drought. Stickle Tarn below Pavey Ark was full to the brim on a recent visit. Twenty-five years ago two Grasmere men, one 75 years of age, completed their self-imposed task of bathing in all the Lake District tarns – 463 of them, in their expert opinion. This redoubtable pair who did most of their bathing in winter – and one morning 'did' 14 – only counted the really permanent tarns where you could manage at least a couple of strokes.

[The Glaramara-Seathwaite Fell round was during the drought of 1984.]

A Drenching on the Howgills

Two recent successive days in the fells nicely illustrated the fickle nature of this disappointing summer. The first was spent, stripped to the waist, on a lazy Great Gable round with sun-bathing sessions on every summit or outcrop and a short sleep in a rocky coign on Westmorland Crags. Next day we were battling with the elements – driving rain with hail on the tops, thick cloud and almost continuous thunder and lightning – on an intended traverse of the Howgill Fells, over a dozen summits, from Tebay to Sedbergh. Drenched to the skin, we abandoned the walk at Carlingill and tramped the four miles back to the car along the road, deluged by every car or lorry that passed us in the floods but, by now, not caring. We couldn't get any wetter. The idea had been to show my son these interesting fells, collecting as many as possible in a widely wriggling traverse but we saw none of them – not even the few we reached by compass, except for the few dreary yards around the summit cairns. The other car had been, optimistically, parked at Sedbergh to await our arrival and this one contained my change of clothes; it was some time before I felt reasonably dry. But, like all miserable days, it was thoroughly enjoyed, in retrospect. These are the days you remember when all the perfect days, like our Gable round, have been fused into one hazy memory of sunlit fellsides, warm rocks, shimmering tarns and blue skies stretching to far horizons. A good thing, this very indifferent summer, that this is so. At least this Howgill's thunderstorm jaunt will fit neatly into many other miserable but memorable mountain days.

[The 'disappointing' summer was that of 1985.]

140

The path to Stickle Tarn, Great Langdale.

Climbing for Geriatrics

We abseiled off Lindale Slabs when the crag was suddenly invaded by an outdoor pursuits party and took ourselves off to Humphrey Head. It was probably 50 years since I had last been there and I had forgotten its delights – the great limestone cliff thrusting out into the bay, the varied views from its prow of sea, mountain, woodland and limestone villages and the immensity of the ebb-tide sands. In particular I had forgotten The Cave – a tremendous hole in the cliff like a rotten tooth which, on a climbing crag, would be a famous feature. You scramble under a rock arch like a vaulted cathedral and inch up the back on to the greensward and the fresh air with much the same feeling you get climbing over the snow cornice out of Cust's Gully on Great End. When the tide is in, these cliff scrambles could be even more interesting and, on top of the promontory, with the waves far below, you could, perhaps, imagine yourself on the bridge of a battleship. This is one of the places where the Vikings might have landed a thousand years ago and it is also reputed – although there are later claims – to be the place where the last wolf in England was hunted and slain – by Sir John Harrington in the fifteenth century. There is also a Holy Well, its water once a recommended cure for rheumatism, and, among the brambles and the deadly nightshade, several quite rare plants while, out on the sands, are the feeding birds, notably oystercatchers in their thousands. We walked out to the finger-nail of the promontory and then, for climbing practice and fun, traversed the cliff a few feet above the sands for half a mile, performing feats of dexterity and daring that I, for one, would not have attempted on a proper climb.

The Dove Crag Cave

Drifts of sky-blue harebells, accessible only to rock gymnasts, sprout bravely from the beetling eaves above Dove Crag cave – the most sensational bivouac site in Lakeland. Nearby, some years ago, a peregrine had its nest. Twelve people could sleep here, dry and completely safely – but not somnambulists. For a few paces from the cave the crag drops in fearsome overhangs to the screes 300 feet below. Dove Crag is perhaps the most overhanging large cliff in the country – the only one I know where a stone dropped from the edge will land far out on the screes. You cannot do that on Scafell Crag, Dow Crag or Pillar Rock. Below the cave is the appropriately named Hangover – the first very severe route made on the face and one with desperate memories for me – but today there are far harder routes, among the most fiercely demanding in the country, on the cliff. The other day, on a round of the fells enclosing the lovely Dovedale, I introduced friends to the cave, now equipped with a low wall – to deter sleep walkers? – and an iron box containing the tattered remnants of old visitors' books. From this natural window in the crag the view was quite breath-taking – the wild tangle of steep cliffs and dark hollows immediately below, further away, the hazel woods and splashes of juniper, waterfalls and glorious rock pools, lush green meadows and lazy beds of shingle towards the foot of the dale and, as backcloth, the towers of Angletarn Pikes and the sweep of Place Fell. We scrambled on the splendid, rough rock of Little Hart Crag, bathed in Scandale Tarn and trotted down the steep turf of High Hartsop Dod to traffic-choked Kirkstone Pass.

Unchanged Longsleddale

The dale they saved – it was Richard Crossman who refused the water engineers a second tunnel through the fells – drowsed in the sleepy sunlight of an August afternoon. All the hay was in, lambs cried mournfully for their mothers, sheepdogs sprawled exhausted in the shade, and shirt-sleeved farmers, surveying their neatly cropped meadows, even forgot to grumble about the weather. One mile beyond the fine packhorse bridge at Sadgill, the dale – pastoral, richly wooded and crowded with ancient farms in its lower reaches – changed abruptly into a Scottish glen, or even a wild corner in Afghanistan. The pass wound steeply between towering crags towards red deer country, trees and meadows gave place to screes and soaring fellsides, and through the middle raced the Sprint, a tumult of waterfalls and pools trapped in a hidden ravine. Despite the Haweswater tunnel through its fells, Longsleddale remains much the same as it was 50, or even 100, years ago. Unless you know where to look, the line of the tunnel is completely invisible and, since the dale is a dead-end and what tarmacadam there is remains mercifully narrow, the farmers can get on with their work without the frustration of mass tourism. What a joy to savour a valley without a car-park, bus shelter, public convenience, or caravan site. It hasn't even an inn, a shop, a filling station or an advertisement sign, either – just river, the rocks, and the encircling heights. Here, surely is the best of old Westmorland and, coming down from the crags where the peregrine used to live, one felt nothing but gratitude that so much unspoiled beauty is still there.

The Best Horseshoe

Another disappointing day in our wet and cloudy summer to some extent spoiled a round of the Mosedale Horseshoe with two agile septuagenarians. Steering by compass through the mist, we saw nothing of the dramatic rock scenery on the rooftree of the Pillar fells, and only on little Yewbarrow were we below the cloud. Here, as close to the heart of the sanctuary as the noble ring of the Scafells, Great Gable and

The Wasdale hills and Wastwater, with Great Gable in the centre.

Pillar, is surely the perfect mini-mountain. Steep on all sides, with crags guarding each end of its summit ridge, the soaring wedge of Yewbarrow is the real sentinel of Wasdale Head – almost a little Matterhorn from some angles. Scrambling experience at least is required to traverse the ridge directly over the rocks of Bell Rib, and the northern end is protected by Stirrup Crag which, avoiding the tourist track, can yield an interesting rock route. The summit view is superb – all the Lakeland three-thousanders, notably the bold upthrust of the Scafells and, below your feet, the dark length of our deepest lake, backed by the towering wall of The Screes. Yewbarrow is almost circled by water – the lake lapping its southern skirts and the pools of Mosedale Beck and

144

Over Beck winding round the contours – and when the sea is also seen you might be in the Cuillin looking out across Hebridean waters. Ascent or descent direct from or back to Wasdale Head can be trying, for the boulders cunningly concealed in tall bracken, provide even worse going than the sliding screes. Joss Naylor, the fell runner, has done it in half an hour from Brackenclose but then he lives on the mountain at lonely Bowderdale.

[Another disappointing summer – this one, 1979.]

Searching for Bilberries

Two months ago the bilberry (locally, blaeberry) harvest in the fells looked like being the best for years. Already the berries, hanging like grapes, were beginning to ripen on the steep sides of Doddick Gill on Blencathra, but a picking expedition in July found the whole area closely cropped by clearly adventurous sheep, with hardly a berry to be seen. Success, however, came rather unexpectedly the other day, at the end of a traverse of the north-west fells, with a weighty haul from the slopes of Whiteside above Gasgale Gill – enough, stored in the freezer, to keep us going in bilberry pies for much of the winter. Sheep had, again, been there before us, but we found that where the plants were surrounded by areas of heather the islands of bilberry were uncropped, and whole bags could be won even from a seated or prone position. This Skiddaw slate country is, of course, ideal for the growth of bilberry, heather and other mountain plants and I have long considered that Hobcarton Crag on Hopegill Head is possibly the richest bilberry area in the district. The whole of this vast, crumbling crag is draped with the plant so that the ridges and towers look not unlike a sunken galleon, hanging in slimy seaweed, and rising, prow first, from ocean depths. Some agility and climbing experience, with a taste for rotten rock, are, however, needed to go bilberrying on this crag – or, indeed, to search for the site of the red alpine catchfly. Nowhere else in England does this rare flower grow – one reason why the crag is protected by the National Trust – although it may also be found at the head of Glen Cova in the Highlands.

The Whiteside Ridge from Hopegill Head.

A Changed Newlands

The dead-end valley of Newlands is one of the least-spoiled corners of the fell country – a quite dale, untouched by the scars of tourism, of lonely, tree-sheltered farms, a little, white church and a long, winding beck below encircling heights carpeted with heather and bilberry. Nearly 60 years ago, with youthful optimism, I decided that some day I would retire to this idyllic backwater but, although the dale has remained unchanged throughout my lifetime, events did not turn out that way. Newlands, though, is still a favoured retreat for quietude and seclusion – strange, when it is remembered that for 200 or 300 years this was one of the busiest and most industrialised dales in Lakeland. Starting in the sixteenth century, German, Dutch and English miners, in successive enterprises, tore up the fellsides for copper, lead and other minerals, including some silver and even small quantities of gold, so that the sleepy dale of today must then have been a thriving and populous place, ugly with the noise, excavations, erections and litter of industry. Nature and farming have long since healed the scars and only if you know where to look will you find the spoil heaps, the ruined stone huts and the pony tracks zigzagging up the fells. During a recent round of the heights from Little Town on a wet and misty day I pottered around three of the old mines and tried to picture the Newlands of long ago – before the first tourists came – when the valley meant hard labour for many and great wealth for the few. Goldscope mine – the name comes from Gottesgab or God's gift and not from the gold that might have been found there – was, in fact, last worked during the First World War.

An 'Unknown' Summit

Possibly the least-visited mountain summit in the Lake District lies, incongruously, within half a mile of the highest and most popular summit in England – Scafell Pike. Unnamed on the one-inch map but labelled Pen on the two-and-a-half inch it is a fine, rocky summit perched high above Little Narrowcove – 'La'al Arra' to Eskdale folk – and separated from the Pike by some of the steepest and roughest ground in the district. People go up the Pike every day – many hundreds of them some days in summer – but I would be surprised if more than a handful go on to Pen in a year, and probably only the most determined peak-baggers even know of its existence. Appropriately, no tracks point the way and although the 2,500 feet high summit is graced by a neat cairn there are no beer-can rings, orange peel or sandwich wrappings to indicate the previous presence of civilized man. My first acquaintance with Pen, many years ago, was following a day's climbing on Esk Buttress, the splendid crag below the summit, when the top merely provided a convenient resting place after coping with problems of verticality. Recently, however, ticking off the 'two-thousanders' of the Lake District, I had to seek out the summit again – this time from the Broad Crag col on a day of mist and rain. From the summit I could just see through the cloud the tumbled wilderness of upper Eskdale and, looking round, the dark crags below the highest place in England.

The Best of the Mosedales

The Mosedale that curls enticingly round the skirts of Yewbarrow and Red Pike is the most dramatic and rewarding of all the Mosedales. Here are gorges hung with rowans, sparkling pools, foaming waterfalls and, in the upper reaches of Blackem Head, a wild confusion of crags – in places overhanging the screes. To follow Mosedale Beck from Wasdale to its source below the summit slopes of Scoat Fell is an exhilarating

147

start to a day in the western hills. As you scramble up the steep rake towards the gap in the skyline the rock scenery grows more impressive every few yards and you emerge on the smoothly sweeping switchback of the Pillar ridge almost as an anti-climax. But there is ample reward from the crow's nest summit of Steeple, a little farther on – the Ennerdale forests and the winding Liza more than 2,000 feet below your boots, soaring rock all around, steep coves dipping down to the dale, and the music of falling waters. Through far-flung, but less dramatic, scenery we tramped easily across Haycock and the shoulder of Seatallan to enjoy the gasping splendour of the view from Middle Fell – the dark wall of The Screes above the deepest lake in England and the evening sun gilding the crags of Scafell and Pikes Crag. Home over Hardknott and Wrynose in the dark there was the usual summer hazard – not the incompetent motorists encountered on the outward journey but the sheep, bedded down for the night on the tarmac. They find the hairpins cooler, on warm evenings, than the grass. And then, along the Little Langdale lanes, caught in the headlights, a fox trotting ahead of us and trying to escape, his long brush sweeping the ground.

Grey Crag Memories

Two or three feet from the holds on one of the climbs on Grey Crag above Buttermere is a fine example of the least (or dwarf) willow – the smallest tree in Britain, no more than a couple of inches high. The plant could hardly have survived on a popular crag, suggesting that Birkness Combe is perhaps becoming an old-fashioned climbing ground nowadays. Revisiting the corrie after a long absence the lack of erosion on the faint track through the boulders and up the screes and scant sign of regular use of the climbs seemed to confirm this. Perhaps the climbs – apart from the few very severe ones – are too easy for today's highly technical experts and, sited so high above steep fellsides, not nearly as convenient as roadside crags. So we had the combe to ourselves although wet rocks, drizzle and thick cloud confined our activities to simple pottering. I was reminded of a far worse day many years ago when two of us came upon three elderly gentlemen in rough tweeds and nailed boots repeating the climbs they themselves had pioneered 50 years earlier. We had decided that conditions were far too bad for climbing but, meeting them, felt shamed into following them up one of their routes. All were famous old climbers and one, a nationally known figure, told me that even on a miserable day Birkness Combe could be 'the most wonderful place in the world'. His devotion to the haunts of his youth has long been an inspiration to me. There are few more dramatic and beautiful corners in Lakeland than this high, crag-encircled hollow and, with the mists swirling round unseen depths, I had to agree there is far more to Birkness Combe than tip-toeing up the sunlit rocks of Grey Crag on a windless, summer morning.

An Airy Perch

Huge slabs of rock, piled like a child's blocks, form a certain pinnacled ridge that soars for 600 feet through the mile-long cliffs of St Sunday Crag. For the rock climber and competent scrambler it is the most interesting way to the summit and on a recent return visit seemed nicely within the scope of even a lone, very old mountaineer. Proper climbers, judging by the crampon scratches on the steep rock, use it in winter as an ice-climb but warm, sunlit rock, well furnished with ample holds, is more my scene today. From sound ledges I could look down, between my boots, at Grisedale nearly 2,000 feet below or peer backwards, across the valley, at the splendid coves of Ruthwaite and Nethermost with a corner of Hard Tarn nestling, like a blob of ink on one well-remembered shelf. And, further to the right, I could just make out the processions of tiny matchstick people inching along the towers of Striding Edge. From the summit of the steep, bulky fell there was the stimulating view into the upper corries and crags of the best side of Fairfield while the descent to Patterdale, across the shoulder of Birks, must surely be one of the most panoramic end-of-the-day journeys in Lakeland. Ullswater curved like a silver scimitar around the sweep of Place Fell, the little islands rode like yachts at anchor on the still, blue waters and you could almost sense the holiday bustle along the twisting roads. The sound of barking dogs came up from Grassthwaite How, the Scots pines were clearly reflected in the mirrored surface of Lanty Tarn and a solitary plume of smoke from one of the Patterdale cottages rose slowly in the late afternoon air.

An Ancient Hill Fort

The first mountain in Lakeland if you come in from the north-east is Carrock Fell – a wrinkled hill of volcanic rock surprisingly stuck on the end of the great upthrust of Skiddaw slate. You turn a corner somewhere near Hesket Newmarket and there it is straight ahead – a dome of grass, bracken and heather with the little gabbro crags tucked away above the wooded screes. On a recent visit I used it as the first in a round of the nine, lonely two-thousanders in the 'Back o' Skiddaw' country, easily covered within six hours. There is something for everybody on Carrock Fell – climbers (although the routes are disappointing), geologists, for there are probably more varieties of rock here than on almost any height in England, archaeologists, bird watchers and photographers. The ruins of the ancient fort on the summit are remarkable. They look like a tumble of large scree, draped in necklace fashion around the top, until you realise they can't be scree with no crags above and the boulders so evenly sized. Many, many centuries ago men either carried these thousands of stones to the summit or dug them out of the ground – perhaps as a lookout over northern Lakeland. Fragments of the original masonry still remain and the ring is broken in places where perhaps there were gateways. The fort, they say, could date from the Iron Age – the only hill fort of its kind in this part of Britain – and scattered about the fell are more than 200 tumuli and artificial mounds. While, elsewhere, piles of stones, short stretches of wall and sheep bields have been built from the collapsed ruins of an early civilisation that is still unexplained.

The Other Langdale

The circumnavigation of Langdale – the long, lonely valley in the northern Howgills, not the well-known Lakeland dale – is usually a quiet, upland round of about 13 miles with nothing moving save sheep and Fell ponies, and the song of larks and peewits the only sound. But the other day, for two of us, all this peace and tranquillity was shattered by the hideous roar of swooping jet aircraft – not for a few minutes, but almost continuously during a six-hour round. We have become conditioned to this infuriating disturbance in the Lake District and, knowing all the arguments, have given up complaining but had not, to date, encountered the problem in the secluded Howgill Fells. Perhaps the sorely tried Lakes was being given a respite on this sunny, midweek day but we felt sorry for visitors from afar seeking quietude in these usually peaceful dales and having their days shattered by all this din. But, curiously, I was in these fells three days later doing a Bowderdale round and there was not a sound in the sky. An announcement in the local papers that jet aircraft would be practising in particular areas on certain days might be helpful for some but perhaps impractical since fine, clear weather opportunities may have to be seized at short notice. We wondered, on the bad Langdale day, what effect, if any, the unaccustomed racket would be having on the sheep and Fell ponies. Certainly for us the air circus was disturbing, with planes suddenly swooping around us – and, at least once, below our boots through the trough of Borrowdale – and we had to protect our ears from the piercing blast. After a lifetime in the hills this was the worst day for noise I have experienced – in the quietest fells I know.

Exploring the Howk

There was one tiny corner of the national park, just inside the northern boundary, that, although known by name for years, I had never explored. So, one rather cloudy August day, two of us sought it out and 'discovered' a place that is quite unlike anywhere else in the district. It is called The Howk and you reach it by going through a gate not far from the middle of John Peel's Caldbeck and walking a few yards along a dark track overhung with trees. Suddenly you are in limestone country that could be a corner of Malham Cove or Gordale Scar – loud with the clamour of falling water, buttressed by vertical cliffs and pitted with natural holes and caves. Almost at the entrance to this remarkable ravine stand the ruins of the village bobbin mill – appearing, at first sight, part of the craggy grotto – and then, within the shady woods, you are above the pools and waterfalls, assessing the height of the cliffs and quickly deciding this is far more interesting than John Peel's grave. The river churning through the gorge is Parkend Beck, soon to join the Caldew, but it rises high on the slopes of Knott in the 'Back o' Skiddaw' fells as Roughton Gill – excavated by the first Elizabethan miners – and then, for some distance, becomes Dale Beck – three names in seven or eight miles of changing scenery and rock formations. To fill in a short day you can go up and down High Pike, the most northerly two-thousander in Lakeland, which Chris Bonington, who lives at its foot, does at the run most mornings when he is at home. We took it more easily but still had time for a midday pint.

Pageants and Prospects

SEPTEMBER

Skiddaw Panorama

The finest view into the very heart of the fell country may be that from the top of Skiddaw – or, perhaps better still, from Skiddaw Little Man – on a clear, bracing day. You look straight down steepening slopes to Applethwaite and the wide vale of Keswick, with Derwentwater laid out below you like a map, and the highest mountains in England stretched out, in crinkled purple along the horizon. Borrowdale, with its crowded woodlands, winds through the centre of the picture and, if the lighting is right, Keswick itself – surely the most beautifully sited community in the country – looks like a town in a fairy tale. It was all just like this the other day, and once again one wondered why some people dismiss hoary, old Skiddaw as just a dull, sprawling hump. True, its real values have to be sought out far from the tourist highway but, even for the undiscerning, Skiddaw must exude rare nobility. Perhaps more country can be seen from the top than from anywhere south of the border and it was, of course, up here where they lighted the beacon that 'roused the burghers of Carlisle'. North-west, on this sparkling day sandwiched between the many wet and cloudy ones that have made up our summer, you could clearly see Criffel, the Scottish Lowlands peak across the Solway – curiously unidentified on the new Silver Jubilee summit indicator – but the Isle of Man was hidden in sea mist. Turning round, we admired the tumbled wasteland of the now-treeless Skiddaw Forest, the long line of the Dodds and Helvellyn and, further to the right, the crumpled ram's horn shape of Causey Pike showing black against the sunset.

The Guardian of Wasdale

Perched on the craggy crest of Yewbarrow with the dark depths of Wastwater, 2,000 feet below, reaching out to the sea, it was easy to imagine oneself back in the Cuillin hills looking across Hebridean waters. I had forgotten how steep this little mountain – the real guardian of the shrine of Wasdale Head – really is, and its traverse, including the rocky prow of Bell Rib, seemed quite a challenge. There are few more exciting grandstands than this cock's-comb of a ridge with the finest mountains in England ringed all round you, the huge wall of The Screes above the deepest lake, and Pillar and Gable beckoning ahead. It has been a few years since my last visit, but I had known the hill in the 1930s when we used to run down the Dore Head screes or, if we still had the energy, scramble across the summit on our way back to Wasdale from climbing on Pillar Rock. Dore Head used to be the finest scree run in the district, but is now quite useless as a means of quick descent, all the stones having been kicked, rolled, or washed away – the fate of all over-used scree runs. And something else had changed in the past 50 years – the appearance of the head of the dale. There was no campsite at the head of the lake in the 1930s and very few cars, and the gaily coloured patchwork of tents, seen from the summit of Yewbarrow, seemed to take away, for me, a little of the mystery of the 'secret' valley of our youth. Everybody apparently knows Wasdale nowadays; the sprawl of blue, yellow, and red tents is barely a mile from the very roof of England and cars crowd the lake shore. Things have to change, even in the heart of the sanctuary.

Bikes on Helvellyn

Descending the screes at the side of Browncove Crags down the popular, but boring, trudge from the Swirls car-park to Helvellyn were two mountain bikers wearing white crash helmets. They were trundling or carrying their machines, the scree track being far too rough and steep to ride, and I was surprised to see cyclists in such a place. Indeed, this way up the most-visited mountain summit in England, besides being one of the shortest and possible the least interesting, is also the most uniformly steep. I doubted whether they would be able to ride down any of it – especially since the lower half is now paved with a curving highway of boulders that is even frustrating to trot down. Where had they come from, I asked, for they had obviously crossed or traversed the Helvellyn range, but they had not the slightest idea.

Wasdale Head from the Gable Traverse, with Kern Knotts Crack on the right.

'There was this little path,' they said, 'and we just followed it.' But had they started from the Ullswater side, from Glenridding or Patterdale, or from Dunmail Raise and over Dollywaggon Pike or from Wythburn? – but they had never heard of any of these places. Almost certainly they would not have come by way of Striding Edge or Swirral Edge and the 'little path' might have been the pony track near Keppel Cove but the name meant nothing to them, so I let them pass and carried on to the summit. Clearly it must have been an adventure to cross or traverse the Helvellyn range with mountain bikes – even if the opportunities for riding them must have been limited – but I thought that maps, or even some slight knowledge of the area, might have been more useful than crash helmets.

A Shy Mountain

My favourite way up Esk Pike – the mountain that was not named until 1870 – is the long south ridge from the big bend in Lingcove Beck. You can scramble up the stepped succession of crags – Greenhole, Yeastyrigg and Pike de Bield – making the route as hard or as easy as you chose, and admire the close-up views of the Scafell cliffs and the upper Esk on the easy walking bits. There are only about ten Lakeland mountains higher than Esk Pike but it was not given the dignity of its name on the popular sheets of the Ordnance Survey until about 1964, having to be content, until then, with a dot in the centre of a ring contour and the figure in feet of its quite impressive height – 2,903. A shy mountain, therefore – once regarded as a mere spur of Bowfell – although travellers were using the twin passes on its shoulders, Esk Hause and Ore Gap, long before the days of recorded history. A recent walk to Great End and back from Cockley Beck, taking in the bashful peak and the airy ridge, seemed to underline the tourists' preference for well-trodden ways. Nobody was seen on the outward or return journey until I struck the Esk Hause track to Scafell Pike where, despite the heat, there were processions of them. The Great End gullies, more usually enjoyed under snow and ice, looked strangely innocuous – dusty wastes of scree and easy-angled rock where, in winter, we have sometimes felt quite daring. Returning, the rocky summit of Esk Pike was trodden a second time and Yeastyrigg Gill descended to Green Hole and the Lingcove pools – much easier to cross after this long, dry summer. Mosedale, too, was drier than usual. Because of the heat it had seemed a longish tramp. Many years ago, when the then-nameless summit was often confused with Hanging Knotts, we used to do Esk

155

Pike from Coniston. These days, as the distance seems longer, I think that I must be getting old.

The Oxendale Ravines

Adventurous scramblers who don't mind getting their feet wet – or, in difficult conditions, most of their body – would enjoy exploring the Oxendale gills. There are four of them – Browney, Crinkle, Hell and Isaac – and they come together, two miles from Dungeon Ghyll, at a noble meeting of the waters that is one of the really great corners in Lakeland. From Great Knott to Three Tarns the long switchback of Crinkle Crags sweeps in a semi-circle above a steep, rocky combe with the fan shape of the gills reaching up in dark ravines towards the skyline. The meeting place is usually loud with the clamour of falling waters, but you have to turn corners to peer up the chasms to see what's in store for you. Too much water may make some of the pitches impassable; too little might reduce the adventure. In a recent round I tackled Hell Gill first, traversed across Green Hole from the top of the main ravine, descended Crinkle Gill, crossed Isaac Gill – least interesting of the four – and then climbed Browney Gill to emerge, slightly damp, on the main Crinkle Crags track. The best bits where Whorneyside Force in Hell Gill, climbed to the right of the torrent, the main ravine, shut in by vertical walls and overhanging trees, and the upper water slides of Browney Gill, where neat footwork is needed. Crinkle Gill has spectacular rock scenery but few difficulties, except when in spate. You've got to be in the mood for this sort of ploy and not given to claustrophobia. A jolly, but experienced, party might find it fun, but I've generally enjoyed these unconventional fell days on my own.

[A gill-climbing day in September 1982.]

Exploring Doves' Nest Caves

Recent fine weather – so rare this summer – prompted a visit to Comb Gill, the fine ravine cleaving the upper lip of the rocky dale that points the way out of Borrowdale to Glaramara. But there was still too much water pouring down the main pitches for a solitary scrambler, and an escape was made up the side, followed by an easy perambulation of the surrounding heights. The heavily glaciated side-valley of Comb Gill, girt by crags and outcrops, is one of the best corners in the district for scrambles and fairly undemanding climbs, and I used to consider Doves'

Nest caves an excellent place for adventurous children, properly led. With torches or candles you could climb down into the main cave, ascend to daylight by the Attic Cave, and then scramble, preferably roped, up and down the outer slabs. But on this recent visit I found a notice at the fell gate warning of a new rock-fall on Doves' Nest Crag which has made the place 'extremely dangerous'. From a distance the crag looks unchanged, but the warning is genuine enough and should be strictly observed. The biggest rock-fall ever to take place on the crag was, of course, the fall that made the caves. Apparently, the whole face of the crag became detached, sliding forwards and downwards until it came to rest against the main cliff, leaving the caves inside. The caves and the climbing routes on the outer walls were first explored at the beginning of the century and used to provide a useful practice ground when the higher crags were out of condition. You could always be bone-dry in the caves when it was pouring down outside, but the place, it seems, is a storm refuge no longer.

[The warning notice went up in 1979.]

New Summit Cairns

Somebody has been out in the fells during the last year or so rebuilding summit cairns with something of a craftsman's skill and even, in some cases, the eye of an artist. The latest I have noticed is on the summit of Mardale Ill Bell – a solid, triangular piece of careful, dry-stone masonry topped by a rough wooden cross, not unlike the decoration on many Alpine peaks. High Street, Dale Head, High Spy and several other tops all have rebuilt cairns – some of them slender structures that may not withstand the winter ice and gales but must have involved a great deal of patience and skill. None of these new edifices is offensive, several are aesthetically pleasing, providing graceful foregrounds to a mountain picture, and this recent wave of neat building, using material readily to hand, is vastly to be preferred to the wholesale wrecking of handsome summit cairns carried out a few years ago. The fine cairns on Pike o'Blisco, Lingmell and Dale Head all suffered in this way while the historic Robinson memorial cairn near the foot of Pillar Rock was regularly torn down. Our fells are disfigured by a ridiculous profusion of so-called route cairns – one-tenth the number would be more than ample – and most of them are far too big, unhealthy repositories for discarded sandwiches and apparently sited for tripping the feet in darkness or mist. Further, this surfeit of cairning often swamps the

The Scafells seen across Eskdale.

significance of the few really important ones. But tidy summit cairns harm nobody and can be important navigational aids.

The Biggest Rock-Garden

You could describe Haystacks, sandwiched between the upper reaches of Buttermere and Ennerdale, as the biggest rock-garden in the country. There is more heather on the fell than on many much bigger Scottish mountains, bilberries grow in considerable profusion, mountain flowers and grasses in great variety and even the main crags are unusually vegetatious. And, to complete the picture, the rocky outcrops that sprinkle the summit are linked by some of the most delightful pools in Lakeland. A few hundred feet higher and Haystacks would be one of the great mountains of the district; as it is, many people would hardly call it a mountain, since it fails to achieve 2,000 feet. But it is certainly one of the best of the mini-mountains – buttressed with great crags, crinkled with rocky lookouts, bespattered with tarns – including a perfect gem on the very summit – and surprises round every corner. Haystacks, in spite of its height – and partly because of it – is also one of the superb grandstands of the fell country. From its knobbly summit ridge are remarkable close-up views of the dramatic sides of the big mountains – Scafell, Great Gable, Pillar, and the Buttermere fells. And from where else can the climber see, in one glance, the cliffs of Scafell Crag, Gable Crag, Pillar Rock, and Boat Howe? From a distance Haystacks, with its dark colourings and sunless crags, sometimes appears rather sombre but once on the fell, even in the worst weather, you discover warmth and intimacy.

Our Most Awesome Ravine

The zigzags of the old Sty Head pony track, rarely used today, the Pier's Gill ravines, and the stony way to the Broad Crag col completely avoided Scafell Pike processions. A blazing day in August holiday week but nobody was encountered from Burnthwaite until the last few yards to the summit, which was plastered with recumbent and perspiring humanity. The return, too, was enjoyed in quite, evening solitude by the simple expedient of a trackless line over Lingmell instead of the crowded, dusty slither down the Brown Tongue highway. The tremendous dog-leg gash of Pier's Gill is the most awesome ravine in Lakeland, virtually cleaving in two the north face of Lingmell. Its waterfall pitches would have been climbable this day for I have never seen so little water coming down but, without companion or rope, I scrambled out from the lower rock pools and instead, traversed the edge of the ravine. As height was gained I kept peering down at the yawning walls, pinnacles and water slides and, near the left-hand bend in the gill, the huge Bridge Rock. In particular, I tried to guess the place – between two small pitches in the upper reaches – where, in the remarkably dry summer of 1921, a London visitor, Mr T.C. Crump, injured in two ankles by falls, kept alive for 18 days and nights on one sandwich, a piece of gingerbread, and a trickle of water. And, undoubtedly, by his courage and prayers. At that time Pier's Gill has been climbed only twice, and Mr Crump's rescue and eventual recovery was one of the real miracles of the fells. He was discovered, quite by accident and after all searches had long been abandoned, by three climbers attempting, in a drought similar to this year's, the very first *descent* of the ravine.

A Summer Scramble

The most direct way, for the climber or scrambler, from the neatly repaved track in Grains Gill to the top of Scafell Pike, is by way of the tremendous 600-foot gash of Central Gully on Great End. One hot July, about 30 years ago, I went that way and, half-way up, kicked steps for perhaps 20 feet up a slope of still-hard, old snow. The other day, for a change, the ascent was repeated – not in any expectation of finding snow this time but merely to see what the ice pitches looked

Dale Head from Eel Crags.

like in summer and to escape Esk Hause processions to the Pike. At first, on entering the gully, the sudden transition from bright sunlight to dank gloom seemed a waste of a good morning but, to a lone scrambler, the pitches proved interesting enough without being too frightening. There was little or no evidence that the gully is used in summer – plenty of loose rock and the scrapes of crampon points the only scratches – and not the slightest sign of litter anywhere. Despite the gloriously dry September there was a fair amount of water trickling down and the well-known ice-pitches had been converted into walls of dripping moss in which one hopefully prodded for holds. At the point

160

where the gully divides the left fork was taken but, higher up, a move was made towards the right exit from which, at the top of a short scree slope, one finally emerged into the sunshine again with the Pike straight ahead. It was just 104 years since the ubiquitous W.P. Haskett Smith had first gone this way – at the same time of year. Few since then have bothered with the place in summer – as a rock climb it has no merits except its length – but Central Gully is certainly the best-known and most popular snow and ice climb in Lakeland.

[Haskett Smith's first ascent of Central Gully, Great End, was in August or September, 1882.]

Great Rock Falls

An undemanding but interesting climbing route from Birkness Combe to the summit of High Stile is by way of Chockstone Ridge on Grey Crag and the upper crags – steepish, airy, sunlit on the right day, and landing you a few yards from the summit cairn. For a solo climber on deserted crags the other day it seemed sporting enough and there was the added interest of studying, at close quarters, the great rock-fall that shattered these crags a few years ago. Hundreds, possible thousands, of tons of rock peeled off the side of Slabs Ordinary Route and crashed down the screes, destroying the first pitch of Chockstone Ridge on the way. You now have to scramble over the debris to get on to the climb. Many of these rock-falls are unseen, happening at night or on winter days when the fells are comparatively deserted, but this one, I'm told, was witnessed by people who had a narrow escape. The disintegration of our crags, rived or loosened by the winter ice, has been going on for thousands of years but the disappearance of prominent features is always an awe-inspiring warning of nature's inexorable power. One of the biggest rock-falls occurred about 20 years ago when one of the towers above the Wastwater Screes crashed down towards the lake with a roar that was heard, I was told, at Strands. And, two or three years ago, a considerable portion of Plaque Route on Bowfell Buttress toppled down on to the screes, completely altering the climb. Increasing thousands of boots are slowly kicking our fells to death, but the swelling ice in the crevices wreaks far more destruction on the crags every winter, and springtime visitors should carefully test every hold.

161

[The rock-fall on Grey Crag occurred in the 1970s and that on Wastwater Screes probably in the 1950s.]

Remembering Scawdel Fell

The craggy mountain wall that shuts out the setting sun from the middle of Borrowdale was known to us in the 1930s as Scawdel Fell and I notice that the Bartholomew map, as recently as 1968, was still using this name. But, for many years now, the mountain, or at least the summit, has had the Ordnance Survey-authenticated name of High Spy although whether everybody in Borrowdale is aware of this is doubtful. Certainly, in my younger days, it was always 'Scawd'l' to the dales-folk and perhaps still is. One wonders who invented the name High Spy and why. Was it to avoid confusion with High Scawdel, the shoulder of fell to the south, and Low Scawdel, the long line of crags to the east? Certainly, High Spy is a good, descriptive name for an airy perch that looks down the precipices of Eel Crags but Scawdel Fell always seemed to have a genuine, local ring about it. Eel Crags appears as the summit name on some maps – including a 1913 Ordnance Survey half-inch 'road map' – and at one time Lobstone Band, the name of the shoulder slanting down to Borrowdale, was wrongly given to the summit. Wainwright gets the name right, adding 'also variously known as Eel Crags, Lobstone Band and Scawdel Fell' but Baddeley, Ward Lock, Poucher, Palmer and Symonds, although occasionally mentioning Scawdel Fell, had clearly never heard of High Spy. One interesting feature of the fell, to a cragsman, is that a route on its east-facing crags – a desperate wall known, for some reason, as Footless Crow – was regarded, in the 1970s, as the hardest climb in Lakeland, which means England.

Surviving the Drought

The deepest lake in England –Wastwater, which plunges to more than 250 feet – was full to the brim the other day, as if the drought had never happened. So, too, were Buttermere and Crummock Water, as well as most of the larger lakes while mountain tarns like Easdale, Goatswater and Blea Water – the deepest of them – were lapping their shores as if after months of rain. Easy, however, to see evidence of the long, dry summer in the reservoirs. Haweswater, the biggest in the country, was so low that the ruins of the drowned hamlet of Mardale were revealed, while part of the old road that ran along the shore of

Haweswater drawn down during the drought of August 1984. Harter Fell is in the background.

Thirlmere before it was nearly trebled in size towards the end of last century was again visible. Sheep grazed on dried turf normally several feet below the surface and the ugly, exposed shores glared white in the sunshine – sucked down by the thirst of Manchester industry and a million consumers. Seathwaite Tarn in the Coniston fells which supplies Barrow-in-Furness seemed, from the surrounding tops, drawn down about ten feet but Levers Water, tapped to meet the needs of the High Furness villages, looked only two feet down. Stickle Tarn in the Langdales was two-thirds its normal size, its eastern corner a waste of mud, but Hayeswater under High Street which supplies Penrith was full, although its outflow had partly dried up. Fox Tarn, high up in the Scafells, the smallest tarn in Lakeland to have a name, has completely disappeared while the river Derwent at Seathwaite, notorious as the wettest place in England, was the other day, a bed of dry stones.

[The drought described here was that of 1976.]

'Professor of Adventure'

With an hour to spare after a round of the Derwent Fells, a visit to the Castle Crag caves seemed a good idea. I hadn't been there since before the war when Millican Dalton, 'Professor of Adventure', lived there. Sometimes I would bump into him at Rosthwaite post office as he collected his shopping, piling it on to an old bicycle, already overladen with tents, ropes, and other paraphernalia. He was a devil-may-care figure in homemade clothes, the trousers torn off at the knees, with Tyrolean hat and jaunty pheasant's feathers, deeply tanned face, and a little pirate's beard. When not taking novices on the crags or exploring Doves' Nest caves, he would be shooting Derwent rapids on a home-made raft, sailing on Derwentwater, or scrambling up the Lodore waterfalls in spate. He lived for much of the year in the Castle Crag caves in the old quarries on the north side of the fell. You could always tell when he was in residence by the plume of blue smoke rising among the trees high above the Borrowdale road. He was a first-class cook and camper and a most hospitable host. Castle Crag, barely 1,000 feet in height, is one of the boldest and most aggressive little hills in Lakeland. It squats, like a gigantic woolly-gloved thumb, exactly above the great bend in the Derwent and in the very throat of the dale. Splendidly girt with cliffs and scree, the fell is cloaked elsewhere in thick woodlands that hide the old quarry scars. The summit – a superb, even dramatic viewpoint – is a war memorial for the men of Borrowdale, and the caves are a reminder for some of us of kindly old Millican, Gentleman of the Hills, who had opted out of the rat race before it began.

[Millican Dalton died in 1947 at the age of 80.]

Grass Tracks Once Again

After years of rough-shod stumbling along eroded, stony ways how delightful to be treading grass tracks once again. Half a century ago most of our fell paths were like this. I was traversing the switchback wedge of High Rigg from the A591 to Tewet Tarn and back – little hills that are passed and ignored by thousands of motorists, and most walkers, each year – enjoying an easy afternoon of quiet delights. Up through the old Scots pines went the winding track, past tiny tarns and along lush turf, speckled with the dainty tormentil and an occasional splash of heather, while the peewits wheeled overhead. Straight ahead soared the sharp ridges of Blencathra and you could peep, to the right, into the well-remembered recesses of the ravine of Sandbed Gill or, leftwards, to the sweep of Bleaberry Fell and the Armboth tops. It is the sort of easy, scenic walking that elderly pedestrians, no longer quite fit enough for Scafell Pike or Great Gable, might enjoy. To avoid retracing your steps you can come back along another pleasant grass track to the west of St John's Beck or, with the luxury of a non-walking driver, carry on just past the tarn to the car waiting at the appropriate milestone on the A66, a couple of hours or so later. Apart from two climbers on one of the very hard routes to the left of the Gangway on Castle Rock of Triermain I saw nobody all afternoon — a weekend — and the grassy ways suggested that these modest fells, enclosed by speeding highways, are, fortunately, largely ignored. The old, local name, Naddle Fell, seems no longer used by the map-makers but I think that High Rigg is, properly, merely the name of the summit.

Long Distance Views

The remarkable clarity of distant views on several recent days – following the heat haze of the long drought – has been aesthetically welcome but is not normally a good sign. When I can clearly see, from my study window, the stone beacon on Thornthwaite Crag, ten miles distant as the ravens fly, bad weather, with heavy rain, is usually not far away. Today the beacon stands sharp against an almost cloudless sky, the cairns on Ill Bell are plain to see and I can easily pick out the features of Bowfell Buttress, 17 miles away. It will probably rain soon. These distant views are by no means exceptional. Often I have been able to identify cultivated land, as distinct from bare upland, in the Isle of Man from the Coniston fells and, more than 50 years ago, from the summit of Scafell, I saw the hills of Scotland, Ireland and Wales. It was just after dawn – we had spent a shivering night on top, perched above a sea of white cloud – and it was the first time I had seen the Irish hills. We moved 100 yards along the ridge to another viewpoint and, there, beyond the rim of the sea, were the mountains of Snowdonia. Many years later a man who had read of our sighting told me, in confirmation, that he had once seen, from the summit of Carnedd Llewelyn, not only Ireland, the Isle of Man, the whole of Wales, with the Bristol Channel beyond, and the Pennines but 'away to the north, two or three peaks sticking out of the sea – very small but absolutely clear – and one of them must have been Scafell'. Of course, the Scottish hills are frequently visible from Lakeland fells and the shape of Criffel, across the Solway, is well known to many of us. This autumn and winter clarity

– exceptional views are less usual in summer – is wonderfully satisfying but, regrettably, rarely long lasting.

[The correspondent who had seen Scafell from Carnedd Llewelyn was Christopher Goodall of York who first wrote to me in 1967, having read of our four countries' sighting in one of my early books. He wrote to me again about it in January 1990.]

From Sea to Sea

During a sorry summer, when the fells have been hidden in cloud and rain more often than not, it is heartening to hear of a correspondent's recent 'unbelievable view from sea to sea' from the seemingly unlikely viewpoint of Nine Standards Rigg above Kirkby Stephen. Perched on this two-thousander near its line of Dalek-like stone cairns, he thought he could pick out both the Solway Firth and Hartlepool power station and, with long valleys to peer down on either side, this is perfectly feasible. The theoretical maximum distance for intervisibility between this height and sea level is something like 65 miles while, under perfect conditions, with nothing in between, it should be possible to see the top of some other two-thousander up to 120 miles away from this one. In theory, too, maximum sightings of up to 145 miles are conceivable between three-thousanders – say Scafell Pike and Ben Lomond or the Carnedds in North Wales – and once, more than 50 years ago, I saw the mountains of Scotland, Ireland and Wales at dawn from the top of Scafell – but from two points about 100 yards apart. It has been claimed it is possible to see both the Irish Sea and the North Sea from Cross Fell, but in fact, because of its flattened dome shape, you can see nothing from the cairn except a quarter of a mile of dull foreground and then the limitless sky. Although, from rather lower elevations, long views might well be visible on either side. Ben Lomond has been fairly positively identified, on a remarkably clear day, from Red Pike in the Buttermere fells, and the Mourne mountains and the peaks of Snowdonia are said to be regularly seen from Black Combe (only 1,969 feet) but it has always been raining whenever I've been up there.

Boyhood in Furness

It was a nostalgic, return visit to my roots – the breezy Furness peninsula I had left in the early 1930s after a long boyhood of mischief, desultory wanderings and a little mild adventuring. There, near the foot of the Hoad at Ulverston was the ironstone crag where two of us did our first rock climbing – dangerously, looking now at its steep nose, without a rope – and, across the dancing, sunlit waves from the Roa Island lifeboat station, the crumbling pile of Piel Castle on its tiny island where we had often scrambled up the ancient walls. Regrettably, there was a notice restricting visits to the castle because of 'renovation' work so we couldn't make the crossing this time but the castle ruins looked unchanged since my boyhood visits and the old inn, smacking of smuggling days, was still there. It was said you could get a drink here at any hour of the day or night since raiding policemen, being rowed across the channel, could always be observed in good time to hide the glasses. In 1487 – an anniversary missed by the press last year – Lambert Simnel made his abortive bid for the English throne, landing by sea with his troops on Piel Island and temporarily establishing his 'government' in the castle. Simnel had decided to impersonate the young prince murdered in the Tower of London by Richard III but the rebellion was quickly overthrown and for 500 years the island and its castle have been forgotten – except by the people of Walney Island, Roa Island and Rampside who see them every day. The channel between the island and the mainland was crowded with a great many windsurfers the other day while Black Combe – my first hill – filled the northern horizon.

[Written in September 1988.]

Black Combe Memories

Black Combe had been my first mountain – 57 years earlier. We had walked, two youngsters with our father, from The Green, along the Whicham valley road and then straight up the steepest side. There were no tracks, we had no map and it seemed a tiring slog with many false summits. From the top we looked down on the Furness peninsula spread out below us like a map, across the Irish Sea to the Isle of Man and, turning round, to the Lakeland fells. We did not know that Black Combe was hardly a real mountain, being less than 2,000 feet high, or that Wordsworth had claimed that from its summit could be seen the best and longest view in England. But it had always been a familiar sight from our home – a great, sprawling hump standing guard over the Duddon estuary – and had always been a mountain to us. Since that first day I have often revisited Black Combe – sometimes followed by a sea bathe at Silecroft – by the easy track from Whicham or, more interestingly, round the combe which, as youngsters, we believed to be an extinct volcano and, the other day, from the old smugglers' road and over Swinside Fell. This last route must be a dreary plod in good weather but, in drizzle and thick cloud, provided interesting compass work and an excuse to revisit the extraordinary Swinside Circle. The summit view was restricted to five feet but it used to be claimed that, on the clearest days, 14 counties could be seen and that the recorded sight, from the top, of Jack Hill near Hanley, Staffordshire, was the longest continuous overland view in England. Mountains in Scotland, Ireland and Wales have been seen from this ancient outpost which is sometimes even visible from as far away as the North Pier at Blackpool.

[This was written in September 1982 so it is now 65 years since I first went up Black Combe, and I can still remember the day quite clearly.]

Crossing the Sands

Far out on the sands at low tide, with distant shores a vague blue on the horizon and the hills hidden in mist, it seemed a long way from anywhere and even lonely – although there were two hundred in the party. Certainly, without the Queen's Guide to the Sands, we would have been lost and compasses unavailing. For not only was there no distant aiming point but we took a curious curving course – half-way to Morecambe, it seemed – and then swung back, perhaps eight miles in all. We did this to cross the river channels at no more than knee depth and avoid the shifting quicksands that, over the centuries, have claimed many lives. This was the way to the Lakes long before the coming of the railways – and from at least the time of Henry VIII. Coaches ran daily over the sands at one time, as well as private carriages – the Duke of Edinburgh has driven a team across – and herds or flocks of sheep and cattle were guided or swum through the channels. The day before our crossing the guide had surveyed the route – the channels are constantly changing – and marked out the safe places with laurel branches, seen in the distance as black specks. He halted us before each crossing for instructions – 'spread out between the markers and keep behind me' – and then we waded into the current – grannies and children among us with the dogs happily paddling across. Vast flocks of birds – unidentifiable at this distance – were feeding in the far shallows and scurrying shapes towards the horizon were picked out, through binoculars, as the tractors of the fluke fishermen. Most crossed

in bare feet or in trainers. I wore old mountain boots that took a week
to dry out, and collected toe blisters from the chafing salt and sand.

*[Cedric Robinson of Guides Farm, Cart Lane, Kent's Bank, is the affable and
very competent Queen's Guide to the Sands.]*

Autumn Sunshine

OCTOBER

Contouring the Crinkles

From a perch on Little Stand, high above Cockley Beck, it is possible to pick out a sort of terrace that contours the knobbly fells south and west of Crinkle Crags at about the 2,000 feet level and provides a slightly adventurous, untracked route from Three Tarns to the Three Shires Stone. Up to a dozen crags and outcrops *en route* might be climbed, scrambled up or down or avoided altogether and the best of them, in my view, is Gaitkins – 'the crag of the little goats' – high on the shoulder of Cold Pike. Years ago, when I was more agile, two of us paid many visits to this and other crags around Gaitscale Gill, climbing up and down the beautifully firm, steep rock and exploring every corner of this splendid outdoor gymnasium. The other day we merely pottered on the easiest scrambles, admired the lovely, little tarns not even shown on the 1:2500 maps, dozed in sun-drenched corners and, from many an airy ledge, watched the processions on the eroded track to the Crinkles up to a mile away. Otherwise, on these untracked heights, we saw nobody all day and nothing moved except the quietly cropping Herdwicks and, occasionally, the soaring contrails of unseen aircraft. The crags bordering the upper Esk and the Dunnerdale and Coniston fells turned blue towards evening, there were strings of sparkling pools in the gill and the great corrie of Adam-a-Cove was a deserted sun-trap. Dozens must have traversed the Crinkles that day but we seemed to have the whole of its southern continuation to ourselves. Completely avoiding stony ways we kept to good rock or turf all day and only returned to 'civilization' at the traffic-congested Three Shires Stone where the real perils of the day – not the crags – began.

Waterfall in Cowcove Beck, upper Eskdale.

Bilberry and Heather

The easy, grassy tracks around the Grasmoor heights are always a pleasant change from the grossly eroded highways that so disfigure the

Striding Edge with Helvellyn behind.

Scafells, Great Gable, Helvellyn, and the Langdale tops. These shapely hills to the north of Buttermere, although steep-sided, provide remarkably simple walking enabling several summits to be linked together with little exertion, thus allowing full concentration on changing views of lakes and winding dales. I had set my sights on what looked like an amusing scramble through the Mellbreak crags only to find that the road had collapsed at Hause Point on Crummock Water, preventing access to Kirkstile. The road, I learned, is likely to remain closed, to allow extensive rebuilding, until the end of the month – you cannot now drive from Cockermouth to Buttermere – so, not to waste the day, I wandered up Whiteless Pike and along the higher tops. These have always been, for me, especially colourful fells – the varying greens and purple, in season, of bilberry and heather, the grey, blue, and brown of the rocks and scree, and the grey sheep grazing the steep grass among the crags. They say that Grasmoor – the mountain of the wild boar, the derivation having nothing to do with grass – probably grows more differing flora than any other fell and I dare say, if you tried hard enough, you could find 40 or 50 different plants or flowers in just one corner. The Ordnance Survey have been making some nomenclature changes around here, preferring the old name of Wanlope for the more usual Wandope and changing the fell most of us have known all our lives as Eel Crag to Crag Hill. This latter is correct – Eel Crag is merely the cliff at the northern end of the fell – but ask a local shepherd the way to Crag Hill and he won't know where you mean.

[The Buttermere road collapsed in 1981 but I have still not done my fancied scramble through the Mellbreak crags.]

Quarrying Worries

Many years ago there was a pleasant, little-used track from tiny, reed-choked Boo Tarn up the south-east slopes of Coniston Old Man. The route zigzagged ingeniously along grassy terraces, past a small disused quarry, and on to the summit, completely avoiding the processions up the popular, stony route through the big quarries, spoil-heaps, and dereliction on the east face. During the last 20 years, however, the quiet, secluded track has gradually lost its appeal by the development of the little, old Bursting Stone quarry – 'Brussen Staen', locally – into a huge industrial scar of vast excavations, spoil-heaps, quarry buildings, machinery, vehicles, and a steep road winding up the fellside. The other day they were bulldozing huge blocks of discarded rock down the slopes close to the track and, every time I pass the site, the scale of the operations seems to have increased. It is the same sad story with the Kirkstone quarries, where small disused excavations have been developed since the war into a massive disembowelling that has completely changed the appearance of Snarker Pike. Other examples of the widespread scenic damage caused by the reopening of innocuous old quarries could be quoted, and now the Lake District Special Planning Board has given the go-ahead for the development of another long-abandoned excavation in the Coppermines Valley, despite urgent objections from conservationists. Slate quarrying is an important traditional industry in these parts but, once planning permission is given for these enterprises, control over the extent of the subsequent workings seems to be extremely limited. Even the planning board must be appalled at the lasting damage done to the environment at Kirkstone and Bursting Stone.

[I am just as concerned about these matters as when I wrote this piece in October 1982.]

A Longsleddale Round

Among the finest 'surprise' views in our fells must be that from the cairn on the south-east ridge of Harter Fell in the ascent from Adam Seat and Gatescarth Pass. One moment you are trudging up a featureless slope with nothing to be seen ahead; the next, you are looking down the long length of Haweswater, the lake appearing almost vertically below your boots, with the Northern Pennines in the distance. On a recent, still day of hazy autumn sun, the fells asleep in the curious quiet before winter, unrippled waters of ultramarine contrasted with the blue wash of distant hills. Not a blade of grass stirred; not even a slither of scree from a careless sheep. Except for russet smudges of bracken, miles away, it could have been high summer. The round of Longsleddale from the packhorse bridge at Sadgill to take in this splendid view makes an easy day. First, up Great Howe and on to Tarn Crag above the Buckbarrow cliffs, the descent to the pass, the walk over Harter Fell, and then the rest of the horseshoe over Kentmere Pike and Shipman Knotts. On a leisurely mid-week round two people were met on Kentmere Pike; otherwise, only the Swaledales and the ravens. Peregrines used to nest on Buckbarrow but not any longer. Forty years ago I remember two of us roping down to a nest on this crag to mark the eggs with dye to make them unsaleable but, since then, unscrupulous thieves and collectors have driven the peregrine out of many of its haunts. In compensation, we now have the golden eagle and from one point on my round I looked across miles of fells to their crag.

Hunting Above Mardale

Hounds were out on Whelter Crags above Mardale, the red deer had gone to ground, but the Fell ponies grazed, undisturbed, high up in Riggindale. Mardale Waters, the cluster of teeming becks east of the High Street ridge, foamed and leapt down the contours towards the largest reservoir in England, but the sheep grazed among the ruins of the farms flooded so long ago, and you could see the old lanes again and recall memories of the drowned dale. Haweswater, a mile shorter now – in October, 1976 – than its length on the map and only one-third full, will take a long time to recover. I chose a sporting route up the craggy, north face of Harter Fell – a rocky water course, a damp gully, an airy ridge with a bonus of clean, rough rock – and, from the summit, looked down on the now ugly lake, with its acres of bare, grey

Blea Water on High Street, the deepest tarn in the Lake District at 207 feet.

shores. On to Mardale Ill Bell and High Street and easily down Long Stile and Rough Crag to the valley. The dalesmen, scanning the fells through field-glasses for a sight of the hunt, had gone, but the car trippers were there – searching the skies, unavailingly, for eagles. High up at the head of Riggindale, with no hunters about, I had come across two of the hounds, frenziedly quartering the steep screes and baying as they went, but the fox eluded them. They would have a long, lonely walk back to kennels – hours after the rest of the hunt. Mardale with its ring of lonely fells maintains a largely unspoiled beauty with quiet serenity.

A Rocky Picture-Frame

From half-way up Skew Gill, above the Corridor Route to Scafell Pike, you get a remarkably revealing view of Great Gable. You are looking down on Styhead and across the dale, about a mile away, to Napes Needle – from this angle, an airy pinnacle on the skyline of the ridge.

With good eyesight you might be able to spot climbers on the top block, matchsticks on a steeple, clear against the sky, but there was nobody up there the other day, and nobody on the grey wall of Kern Knotts. Several people, though, were on the Styhead track or scurrying down the eroded screes from the summit like ants on a rubbish heap. The southern front of Gable was flooded in sunlight with blue cloud shadows chasing across the crags and screes, and the view was exactly framed by the vertical rock walls of the gill – the full colour, intimate statistics of a single mountain viewed from the shadowed depths of the ravine. Skew Gill provides an exhilarating scramblers' route to the top of Great End – one of the easiest of our mountain gills with no problem pitches and not enough water to sweep you off. In winter under snow it is even better. But not one in a thousand pilgrims to the roof of England, crossing the foot of the ravine, turns aside to explore the place and there are no tracks, scratches, or litter. Several people passed its foot while I sat lunching above the tourist track but didn't even bother to look up the gill. Much of the best of Lakeland can only be enjoyed by diversions from the popular ways – and by using one's eyes. There was thick cloud on the stony summit of Great End but sunshine again on Esk Hause and by the waterfalls in Grains Gill – and double parking, even in October, in the Seathwaite lane.

Avoiding the Grass

There was far too much water crashing down Borrowdale's Sour Milk Gill the other day to make its ascent a reasonable expedition. But in drier weather this can be a feasible and enjoyable route for the competent climber-scrambler seeking an unorthodox way to the heights. Moreover, if this semi-aquatic introduction can be combined with the ascent of Rabbit's Trod, a moderate climb up the northern flank of Gillercombe Buttress, the summit of Grey Knotts may be attained after 1,800 feet entirely on rock – an almost unique opportunity in the Lake District. By avoiding most of the gill, where a bathing costume would have been appropriate, and the upper pitches of the climb which were wet, it was nevertheless rewarding, on a warm, sunny day after heavy rain, to make at least half this height in scansorial fashion. Easy rock with its changing, little problems delightfully eases the ennui of endless grass or eroded tracks. Two climbers met on top of the Buttress had travelled from Stirling for the weekend. 'We got tired of Glencoe in the wet,' the explained, 'so we come to the Lakes where the crags are lower and drier.' From Brandreth the dome of Great Gable blocked

176

the view to the south but elsewhere the giants of the fell country, Pillar, Great End, Skiddaw, and Helvellyn, straddled the horizon, bathed in the afternoon sunlight. School parties, anxiously shepherded by their teachers, crept down the Green Gable ridge but Base Brown was deserted save for a worried couple, off route and trying to find Honister Pass. Down at the bustling Seathwaite road-end the narrow lane was packed tight with cars. The first really fine day for a fortnight had brought out the worshippers in force.

The Longest Scramble

The precipitous face of Ill Crag overlooking the wilderness of upper Eskdale is an obvious challenge to the exploring scrambler or climber. From the foot of Little Narrowcove – 'La'al Arra' to the locals – the crags and screes rise 1,600 feet to the rocky summit but there are no tracks or recorded climbs. Some people make the easy diversion to the cairn from the tourist route to Scafell Pike but the steep Eskdale face is almost unknown. On a sunny autumn day with clearing morning mists two of us climbed the cliff up easy slabs, pleasant walls of sound, rough rock and shattered outcrops, finding little difficulty, and many other routes seem equally feasible. Prominent in the view as we ascended was the bold, little peak of Pen, just across the dark hollow of the cove – possibly the least-visited summit in the district but only a rough half-mile from the crowded top of Scafell Pike. We watched the shy summit sink slowly beneath us as we swarmed up our south-facing wall until we could look over the top to the winding shoals of the Esk reaching down the long dale to the sea. All this area immediately to the east of the roof of England is among the steepest, roughest and most desolate country in the district but that day it had all the magic of high, lonely places – silence, solitude, exciting depths, sunlit views to far horizons and slowly moving cloud shadows purpling the heights. Climbing to the summit, we saw the first people we had seen all day – the processions going up and down the well-trodden highway to the Pike. And the pools of the upper Esk, the waterfalls of Lingcove Beck and the Mosedale bogs were our only company on the homeward journey.

On the Crags Again

The neat ascent, finger and toe, of sunlit rock is always a strangely satisfying delight and especially so, I found, after a long absence from technical climbing. A warm, windless day, with sunshine from dawn to dusk, was selected and Grey Crag in Birkness Combe above Buttermere chosen as a place where undemanding routes, within the ambit of a rickety septuagenarian, might be found. The young expert, laden with ironmongery, was even prepared to allow the old-timer to lead alternate pitches and three linked climbs, totalling about 700 feet, eventually put us on top of the mountain. It was carefree, cheerful climbing here in the early 1930s with our old hemp ropes, and black plimsolls; this day, it was all chocks, runners and hand-jams with complicated rope engineering replacing old-fashioned techniques. But the magic of well-remembered joys was still there – the feel of warm, rough rock, the thrill of the drop between one's feet, the route-finding, the bilberry eating between climbs, the airy perches and the beck winding through the combe far below. From one high stance we could look right over the summit of High Crag, just across the corrie, to the Langdale Pikes and then, by turning the head slightly, could enjoy the splendid panorama of all the north-west fells, with Skiddaw and Blencathra in the background, and, down in the dale, the toy cars scurrying over Honister Pass. Now and again we spotted the little black matchsticks of walkers moving along the splendid ridge and, once, could hear their voices. In 50 years nothing had changed – except that once-familiar holds seemed to have shrunk in size and, strangely, to have moved further apart.

[These climbs were done when I was 75 – the last time I can remember using 'ironmongery' on rock.]

Rock Nostalgia

Two helmeted climbers were poised just below me on the steep, final pitch of Trident on Dow Crag – a favourite route of mine in the old days. Further down the crag two others were engaged on some desperate modern route that I could not even name. I was merely walking round the Coniston fells and felt sadly out of touch. Many, many years ago, a handful of us considered this 'our' crag, spending almost every weekend on it and knowing every route. I recalled the day, more than 60 years ago, of my first close-up view of this great crag. I had cycled to Torver from Barrow, walked up the Old Man by the Cove quarries, and, looking across the corrie at the steep buttresses of Dow, saw little dots scurrying down the screes and – almost unbelievably to me then – the coloured blobs of climbers slowly working their way up the steep walls. It looked a fascinating, exciting game, with its neat precision and the balancing on tiny holds. Suddenly, I knew this was what I wanted to do. Soon, I started learning how to climb, and, for much of a lifetime, rock became almost my whole world but, nowadays, although fingers sometimes itch for the feel of rock, memories have to suffice. Climbing today, with all its equipment and techniques, is a different game from the one we knew and the routes they are now doing, scores of new ones every year, frighten an old climber. Thrilling, though, to look, from a safe perch, at some of these vertical places above yawning depths and ponder how on earth they do it – even with all their safeguards. I continued my plodding round, remembering happy, carefree days, and eventually came down to old, familiar Coniston where, in the pub, they were lighting the first fire of the winter.

Crashing Cataracts

Those twin tributaries of the Derwent – Langstrath Beck and Greenup Gill – are among our finest mountain streams and they unite at one of the most exciting places in the district, just below the rocky bulk of Stonethwaite's Eagle Crag. Complementary in character – Langstrath, with its winding, pastoral reaches and superb pools, and the steeper Greenup, a necklace of waterfalls and water slides pouring through a miniature tree-lined gorge – the two, in confluence and in spate, suddenly become a wild cataract crashing through a rock corridor in angry confusion. You see them at their best immediately after heavy rain – we have had plenty of this recently – and the other day, at Galleny Force, the surging power of the newly united torrents, swollen by dozens of short-lived becks tumbling down the fellsides, seemed irresistible and overpowering. And yet, a few miles further on, the racing flood, now the Derwent, had become a broad stream slowly winding, past shingly shores, through the Borrowdale birches. I had come down to the twin becks from a round of the tops just in time to see a fat ewe, up to her neck in the swirling waters, struggle across the shallower rapids above the force. And it reminded me of a wet winter's day, nearly 50 years ago, when three members of a university mountaineering club met tragedy at just this point. Missing the bridge across Langstrath Beck in the mist and rain and finding the bridge across Greenup Gill washed away they had tried to cross the confluence in flood. After a

Langstrath Beck.

five-hour struggle one died from exposure and exhaustion, and the other two almost lost their lives trying to get him across.

October Heat-Wave

The first really fine day in the fells for what seemed weeks and, although mid-week in mid-October, processions were winding over the eroded Langdale tracks. It was hot enough without a shirt and Stickle Tarn was a perfect mirror for the crags but, after the long rains, Mill Gill's boiling, white torrent crashed noisily down the fellside. Perspiring visitors rested by the falls, skimmed stones across the tarn or lazed in the sunshine on the shore. A low orange tent below the screes suggested enterprise. Away from the almost-crowded tracks by the beck the grassy zigzags of the old pony trod were deserted and a scramble up the rocks of Tarn Crag had provided a more interesting route to the heights. The final stages were an ascent of the easiest gully on Pavey Ark, where a hooded anorak was needed to survive the miniature waterfall behind the first chockstone, and a delightful scramble up the unscratched, east rock ridge of Harrison Stickle – the right sky-line edge as seen from the dale. Perhaps the fells were 'wick wi' foak' but my unconventional route was quiet and lonely. In a rocky combe below the summit a pair of ravens perched on a boulder 30 feet below and only took off in a leisurely glide when I kicked a stone. Two people in shirt-sleeves sat sunbathing by the cairn. Stilled waves of blue-grey fells reached out to hazy horizons. Not enough wind to snuff a match. A careful descent of the south-facing crags – the moss and lichen still damp despite the hot sun – led down to over-trodden slopes. Even in the crowded Langdale Pikes it is possible to find lonely ways, remote from orange peel and beer-can rings.

Circling Kentmere

The day, at the end of an appalling summer in these parts, could hardly have been better – warm sunshine, remarkably clear views, and not enough wind on the tops to blow out a match. Even more impressive on this hill day-in-a-thousand, was still silence – a magical stillness almost as complete as on those windless days in winter when the fells are gripped in snow and ice. In a six-hour round of the Kentmere Horseshoe, I heard only one sound on the heights: the distant murmuring of the little waterfalls near the source of the River Kent, just audible from the summit of Ill Bell, one mile away; otherwise, not even

181

a whisper of wind in the crags or the rustle of grass. Later, from the useful sheep-trod that contours the lip of the fine corrie of Hall Cove below High Street, I studied once again the source of the Kent that flows 25 miles to the sea from these lonely fells as perhaps the swiftest river in the country. On large-scale maps the actual source is shown just below Bleathwaite Crag at about 1,850 feet above sea-level; but if the gathering grounds are closely examined on the ground – especially after the sort of precipitation we have had to endure in recent months – it will be seen that one main tributary begins at a point well above the 2,000 foot contour near the western end of Gavel Crag. In both cases the river that flows majestically through the middle of Kendal – and regularly flooded the streets before costly remedial measures were adopted – begins as tiny springs seeping through bright green mosses that never dry up even in the longest drought. Kentmere Reservoir, with a capacity of 250 million gallons, could never run dry.

[But, sometimes, the reservoir is deliberately drained to permit inspections or remedial work on the dam.]

Sifting out History

The broad, hurrying waters of Kendal's River Kent – in spate, one of the fastest-flowing rivers in England – begins as an inch-wide trickle on the shoulders of High Street. To reach the source, you scramble around the lovely pools and waterfalls of the head-waters of the river beyond Kentmere Reservoir until you reach the fine corrie of Hall Cove. The river is born in springs that ooze out of bright green mosses, loosely carpeted with scree, at more than 2,000 feet above sea-level. When I was there recently, I traced the highest source but, a few yards higher up and just underneath the upper lip of the corrie, I could still hear the water trickling and gurgling out of some unseen, never-failing cavity deep in the rocks. To round off the day I came down the side of Rainsborrow Crag to Hartside and stumbled on the archaeologists who, for some time, have been painstakingly excavating what appears to have been an ancient settlement at Bryant's Gill. Rough stone floorings and ruins of old walls have been found hidden in the bracken and careful sifting of every ounce of soil has revealed fragments of house-hold articles. Apparently, people were living and working in this remote corner in the 'Dark Ages' between the Romans and Vikings – probably 1,200 years ago, when the dale had its lake south of the present hamlet and was thickly wooded. I understand the archaeologists began their work in Kentmere by mapping and recording everything that was not natural including heaps of boulders. Some of the larger heaps – clearly not walkers' cairns – are believed to have special significance and, when dismantled, could well yield secrets of a long-lost way of Lakeland life.

South of the Crinkles

From the unnamed summit of the bold knuckle of grass and rock overlooking Cockley Beck – Little Stand and Red How are the names of encircling crags, not the top – I looked across at walkers nearly a mile away, making for the popular Crinkle Crags – Bowfell ridge. They would, I knew, be following broad eroded tracks all the way and meeting many other walkers, whereas my rocky summit was trackless and, in spite of many visits, I have never seen anybody else up there. And yet my lonely summit, with Stonesty Pike just to the north, is really part and parcel, and the real start, of the Crinkle Crags ridge. It is only the height-saving lure of Wrynose Pass that fortunately channels the processions past Red Tarn, leaving the delights of this unspoiled area for connoisseurs happy to seek out solitude at the expense of a little extra toil. Perhaps I had cheated on this windy autumn day by parking at the Three Shires Stone instead of at Cockley Beck but, on my way to the true ridge, I had avoided the main highway by a scrambling detour over Cold Pike, Gaitkins and Red How and an exploration of the charms of Gaitscale Gill. About 30 years ago I described Gaitkins – 'the crag of the little goats' – as an especially favourite corner of mine, and I still hold to this opinion. Splendid sweeps of rough grey rock, tiny tarns in the hollows, and sheep grazing the grassy ledges high above the beck combine to make this the perfect eyrie for an afternoon's scrambling, sketching, dozing or just quiet contemplation away from the crowds. Too windy, though, on this recent day for lazing about so I picked a mildly adventurous route up the Red How cliffs and then steered due north along the long, long ridge.

The Other Borrowdale

Half the length of the Borrowdale of Shap Fells – not the popular Borrowdale reached from Keswick – is outside the Lake District national park but must be the most beautiful valley in old Westmorland beyond the inner shrine. The other day, with not a soul about but Hugh Walpole's Borrowdale probably chock-a-block with tourists and traffic, the Westmorland one seemed almost preferable to the 'real' Lake District. Borrow Beck chattered over the stones and here and there widened into deep, inviting pools, the autumn colours in the woods almost shrieked to be admired and black Fell ponies could be seen, outlined against the sky, on most of the surrounding tops. The Whinfell ridge, enclosing the dale to the south, is known to some who prefer less-crowded heights but the fells to the north of the valley remain untracked and largely unknown. Two of us collected the half-dozen modest heights of this sprawling ridge, returning down the long length of the dale to the car, seeing nobody but concerned about the appearance of a second monstrosity on the Whinfell ridge. The first one, the British Telecom radio repeater station, is a huge, ugly contraption looking like something out of space fiction: the new Mercury one, a quarter of a mile away, is even higher and looks like Blackpool Tower. More incongruous erections, on a lovely skyline, would be difficult to imagine. A further irritation was that upper Borrowdale, the lower slopes of Mabbin Crag and Castle Fell are, clearly, being afforested. We knew that, despite protests, Ashstead Fell was to be clothed with conifers but this was something new. Together, these intrusions slightly marred an enjoyable outing.

Long Distance Views

My recent Diary note about exceptional mountain views prompted a minor spate of letters and telephone calls, all providing further evidence of the occasional intervisibility of Lakeland, Scotland, Ireland and Wales – if you happen to be in the right place at the right time. The ascent of Scafell – my own viewpoint in about 1930 – is apparently not necessary for these distant sightings. One reader identified the mountains of Snowdonia from Fell Head in the Howgill Fells and another, who duplicated my four countries tally from High Stile above Buttermere, believes he could even pick out Ben Lomond, far beyond the Lowland hills. A mountaineering friend writes of seeing Ben Hope, 98 miles away, from Ben Macdhui when every mountain on the summit indicator was visible – I have enjoyed the same view – and tells me he has clearly seen the Orkney Islands from Cairngorm. Much more surprising, he has a friend with a photograph of Kilimanjaro taken from the top of Mount Kenya, about 250 miles away. A elderly lady mountaineer of my acquaintance recalled seeing the Irish Sea and the North Sea from Little Scoat Fell in the Pillar range, and the same claim has been made for the summit of Cross Fell where the horizons must be 120 miles apart. But, in fact, from the cairn on Cross Fell – because of the domed shape of the plateau – you can only see a quarter of a mile of dull foreground and then the limitless sky. Perhaps if you walked about a bit, on the right sort of day, you might be able to see both seas – but not from the same viewpoint. I could just pick out the Scottish hills beyond the Solway from Blencathra the other day but the sunlit Scafells, beyond Borrowdale, looked more interesting.

A Meeting of the Waters

From Lincolm Tarn, the finest pool on the Glaramara–Allen Crags ridge, I dropped down to the lonely head of Langstrath where adventurous sheep-trods are the only paths. Here, in a green hollow below soaring fells, is an impressive meeting of the waters – Allencrags Gill tumbling steeply from Esk Hause, Angletarn Gill with its narrow, curving ravine and the unnamed beck that drops down the crowded contours of Glaramara with ruler-straight determination. The three meet at a quiet pool, shadowed by rowan and holly and here, primed by never-failing springs, begins Langstrath Beck, one of the noblest of our mountain rivers. In this upland corner, loud with the music of falling waters, the long drought seemed a distant memory. Every yard of the way down the long, winding dale were waterfalls, pools, swirling depths or smoothly sliding shallows, crashing torrents and flooded gorges – all hurrying on, in furious spate, to get round the corner, miles ahead, and swing into Borrowdale and the Derwent. From the foot of the Stake there were people, well-trodden paths, and the famous pools of Blackmoss (or Blackmer) Pot, Swan Dub and Tray Dub, where, in less crowded days, we bathed costumeless without a thought. But this sunny afternoon I felt that the real charm of the dale lay among the quieter head-waters in which you could laze all day and see nobody. A few hours earlier I had passed the shrunken bath-tub of Thirlmere with its acres of mud and rock but here, underneath the crags of Esk Pike and Hanging Knotts, unending supplies of water, stored by nature in underground crevices, were gushing out of the fellside in ceaseless streams.

A Child's Mountain

Forty-odd years ago I took our daughter up her first 'mountain'. She was two and a half years old, the hill was little Catbells and she walked all the way up, refusing to be carried. Since then she has climbed, or at least seen, many real mountains in different countries but still, I think, feels affection for her very first hill. She is over on holiday with us now – straight out of the earthquake-shattered heat of Los Angeles to the downpours and fresh gales of Lakeland – and if we ever get a dry day she hopes we will be able to go up little Catbells together again. Since the fell is regularly ascended by toddlers and old men with walking sticks it can hardly be a mountain but it is shaped like one and, for all its modest height, commands one of the most airy views in the district. It can also be the start of splendidly rewarding rounds of the higher fells. Catbells is a family hill – a place for children and grand-fathers, for early morning exercise or fresh air on a still, summer's evening, for shy lovers, picnic parties and yelping dogs. From its rocky top Keswick looks a fairy town in a magic landscape and the lake, ringed with wooded fells and dotted with islands and boats, an enchanting place for youthful adventure. Catbells is a pretty name for a child's mountain – the fell where Beatrix Potter's Mrs Tiggy-Winkle had many adventures and some of Sir Hugh Walpole's heroes ran up through the bracken to watch the sun setting behind Grasmoor. Walpole himself had his home on its slopes for many years: 'a little paradise on Catbells', and, in his books, often described scenes he could see from the windows of his study above the garage where he did his writing.

His First 'Walk'

It was the first time my son-in-law from Vancouver had climbed a hill, anywhere. Hundreds of days skiing down them, in two continents, after ascents by chair-lift or cable car, but no pedestrianism. On a bright but breezy day all the Langdale Pikes were collected and a few scrambles thrown in for fun. My daughter, who used to climb, accompanied us and entered into the conspiracy so that Tony is still under the impression that our ascent of Jack's Rake and descent of part of the Dungeon Ghyll ravine are the easiest tourist ways. Once or twice, hauling himself up on greasy hand holds or lowering a boot through the spray he would mildly enquire whether this really was walking but we maliciously assured him that it was and he seemed satisfied. Perhaps he secretly sighed for the mechanical uplift of Mount Whistler but, surprisingly, his balance and footwork were impeccable – despite his huge, heavy Canadian boots being worn for the very first time. (I was wearing my magic 'carpet slippers' which I now realize have their limitations.) The day, including the ritual real-ale session that rounded it off, was hugely enjoyed by the three of us although the young people

Little How Crags and Great How Crags above Levers Water.

seemed unused to the chill breeze on the summits. But two days later, on a round of the Gables, driving rain, battering winds that almost blew us off our feet and the usual mist put things in a different perspective. I had promised easy summit wandering and matchless views but the going, on a vile day, proved hard and we saw nothing. On the drive home, though, under the skirts of Skiddaw and Blencathra and along the Ullswater shore, the clouds were blown away and sunlit fells below a sky of deepest blue at least gave the visitors a sight of Lakeland at her best.

Winter on the Way

NOVEMBER

First Snow of Winter

On the very clearest days a tiny triangle of fell, in the dip between Sallows and Red Screes, may be seen from our windows, and long ago I worked out that it must be St Sunday Crag. It was bright and clear the other morning after a wild night of driving rain and gale-force winds, and I could easily pick out the little sliver of fell for it was white – the first snow of the winter. There was also a slight dusting of snow on the eastern shoulder of Mardale Ill Bell. This first sign of snow on the fells each back-end is a thrilling sight for those of us who especially enjoy the winter scene and the delights of skiing, ice climbing, or roaming the white-plastered hills. Unlike the rest of the country we love snow – any sort of snow but especially crisp, crystalline stuff – except when its presence on the roads prevents our getting among it. The day after this rather late first sighting – I have kicked steps up a snow gully in Nethermost Cove and found six inches of new snow on Helvellyn in September – I wandered up the Trout Beck to Threshthwaite Mouth and studied the horizon of hills from the ridge above. It was a strange sight because Helvellyn and its satellites were plastered with snow – probably enough for a few skiing turns in places – but most of the rest of the Lakeland fells were completely clear. Nothing on the Scafells, the highest land in England, or on Great Gable, the Coniston fells, Bowfell, or even on Great End where in a hard winter it can pack 20 feet deep in the gullies. Clearly the snow had fallen in a north-east gale before reaching the west.

[This occasional view of part of St Sunday Crag was from the windows of my previous home.]

Great Gable and Kirkfell from the High Stile ridge before the snows.

New Snow on Bowfell

The first mountain snows of the winter came, with blizzard ferocity, on a wild day of gales and floods. There had been no hint of it in the weather forecasts and thick cloud blotted out the tops the next morning so that the new white blanket, first glimpsed from Ambleside during a temporary clearance, came as a complete surprise. Two hours later I was trudging through it, knee-deep in places, on the roof of Bowfell – delighted to be in the snow again, in spite of the nil visibility and a gusting wind that made balance on the hidden boulders slightly awkward. Unaware of the snow, with the fells in cloud, I had left home without winter equipment and found myself floundering about in my lightweight, summer 'carpet slippers' and feeling rather vulnerable, without the security of an ice-axe, when I went exploring above and around Bowfell Buttress. Deep, soft, untrodden snow is tiring stuff and the carpet was only crusted on the top few feet of the summit rocks making the freezing level that day at about 2,900 feet. The depth of the wind-blown drifts, in one day's snowfall, was astonishing and the cornice at the top of the south gully – ready to avalanche at any

189

moment – actually reached to the vertical for the top ten feet or so. New snow provides the perfect opportunity for determining earlier wanderings. It was clear from the few tracks, that only one or two people had ascended that day from Three Tarns and that one other party had come up the Great Slab – indeed, I met the latter party later on the summit. Elsewhere across the top, the only tracks were my own and the Ore Gap ascent or descent, for example, had not been used since the snow came down. Two ravens, briefly perched on top of the south gully cornice, were the only other living things about.

A Deepdale Snow Round

Overnight snow had transformed the fells, throwing the crags into black relief against newly whitened slopes looking steeper than they had the previous day. The high corrie of Sleet Cove at the head of Deepdale was shadowed and cold, a stark, black-and-white picture of soaring crags and steepening gullies but the summit snows around the rim of the cirque glistened in the morning sunlight. Within the corrie, there was shelter from the wind but clouds of spindrift blowing off Fairfield and Cofa Pike told of the gales higher up. With its twin hanging valleys, splendid climbing crags, ravines, pools and waterfalls and a refreshing absence of tracks, Deepdale is an exhilarating corner on a summer's day. But in winter, its gullies packed with snow and ice, rocks glazed, gills frozen and even the fellsides requiring care, these high corries become a challenging wonderland. There are, though, easy places and this can be a good area for teaching beginners the use of ice-axe and crampons. This day, in fact, I had gone into the cove to assess likely snow conditions for a later visit with a novice winter climber. The snow proved rather disappointing but plods up Black Tippet and down Flinty Graves at least kept me warm; the neighbouring snow gullies were insufficiently consolidated. Between ascent and descent there was a brief visit to the windswept summit of Fairfield with the gale trying to pitch me over the crags. Several years ago two girls stumbled over here in a snowstorm and it was weeks before their bodies were found by bloodhounds. This day, however, visibility seemed limitless and only the biting wind sent me scurrying down Flinty Graves and away from the glorious distant views of alpine Lakeland.

November Perfection

From the snow-crusted summit of Wetherlam the sunlit table-top of Ingleborough, 40 miles away, seemed to hang in the sky above a sea of fog. All round the horizon the Lakeland fells, patterned in snow, basked in the afternoon sunshine as they had done for much of a bright November but, far to the south, fog and mist were creeping up the valleys. Motorists would already be coping with fog in Lancashire and Yorkshire, but up in the fells, even on distant Ingleborough, the almost unbroken sunshine continued. Wetherlam was glazed in ice, necessitating cutting the occasional step with the axe, and the descent of the snow-packed crags of Steel Edge was pleasantly alpine. From a sunny, sheltered luncheon place by the frozen tarn above Steel Edge, I had seen, beyond the black, shadowed wall of the Old Man range, the sunshine sparkling on the silvered sea, the long blue lengths of Windermere and Coniston Water reaching south towards the fog and, by turning my head, the glistening top of Ingleborough high in the heavens. Many Lakeland days were like this last month – sunlit and cold, windless except on exposed tops and incredibly clear; a November of up to a score of near perfect days. There is a magic in early winter – the low-angled sun and long shadows giving a new sculpturing to the scenery, the westering sun sinking behind the long line of purple hills sharp cut as stage scenery, and the northern and eastern corries lightly carpeted in snow. But, after such an enchanting November – and by the law of averages – there could be a hard winter ahead.

[This perfect November was that of 1988.]

The Bowfell Hut

The old stone hut on Bowfell, rediscovered the other day nearly 50 years after I had first found it, fitted my vague memory of that early sighting. Somehow, despite dozens of visits to the mountain, I had not stumbled on it again during the intervening years. I had referred briefly to the hut in one of my early books, giving its rough location, and then forgot all about it – until a friend casually mentioned recently that it was still there. Perhaps I should seek it out again, I thought – a good excuse to revisit a familiar fell. But when, after three trips, I had failed to locate it I began to wonder whether, in fact, I had imagined the place. But the last attempt had been in deep snow and thick mist, hiding everything so a final, determined bid was launched after a trudge up the steep fellside from the Mickleden sheepfold. The hut, I thought,

191

must be somewhere to the north of the North Gully of Bowfell Buttress but several detailed searches of the broken crags, and two descents into the gully failed to yield anything man-made, not a cairn, a scratch on the rocks nor even a beer can-ring. There was much abortive scrambling on loose, lichen-covered slabs until, on the final descent, I looked for the third time, but more closely, into a likely rock corner – and found it. It is a very crude shelter, walled and roofed with great chunks of stone, making it barely distinguishable from the surrounding crag, with a narrow entrance into which I could just squeeze, after removing my rucksack. Perhaps some shepherd had built it a hundred, two hundred years ago as a shelter if overtaken by blizzard or darkness, although the area, among crags at 2,800 feet, seems an unlikely pasturage even for Herdwicks.

The Smuggler's Hut

The last remains of the so-called smuggler's stone hut near the summit of Great Gable seem to have disappeared. On a recent tramp across the top I scrambled down to the site above Central Gully on Gable Crag, but could find no trace of the building. Fifty years ago you could pick out its shape for some of the walling remained and, much more recently, some of the stones still lay on the ledge above the gully – but now there's nothing to be seen. Probably we will never know the real story of the hut. Was it used by Moses Rigg, the legendary Honister quarryman turned whisky distiller and smuggler – he of the well-known Moses' Trod – and, if so, was it a store for whisky or wadd (plumbago from the Borrowdale mine) or even a lookout post or shelter? Many authorities have discounted all these theories; the place, they thought, was far too precariously perched to be accessible to nineteenth-century dalesmen, but the late George D. Abraham of Keswick, the pioneer climber and photographer, did not agree. Mr Abraham, whose daughter is a Country Diary colleague, once told me he was quite sure that Moses had actually had a still on that wild ledge on Gable Crag. Towards the end of the last century the hut, he said, had had a roof, was stone-flagged, and showed signs of having contained a still. Moreover, it was common talk in the dales at that time that this was where Moses made his brew – from the bog water on Fleetwith Pike, and indeed Mr Abraham knew one Dan Tyson who claimed to have worked with Moses. But other evidence suggests that Moses was already a legend last century in the day of Auld Will Ritson of the Wastwater Inn – in spite of the claim of Ritson, a noted storyteller, that as a lad he had known him.

[George Abraham's daughter, Mrs Enid Wilson of Keswick, was a Guardian 'Country Diary' contributor for many years until her death in 1988. Mr Abraham died in 1965 at the age of 93.]

Manchester's 'Lake'

Our most recent 'lake' – Wet Sleddale Reservoir – came into service just 21 years ago and, walking round it the other day, I was again satisfied that its creation was one of the more enlightened concepts of the old Manchester Waterworks authority, so often the villains of the piece. You can't see the triangular stretch of water, perhaps two-thirds of a mile long, from the main road but only the thin line of the dam, stretched across the mouth of the dale, and this has been quite effectively camouflaged with greensward and woodlands. The lake, shaped like a flowing pennant, nicely fills the lower floor of a dale that lacked spectacular beauty, with little bays and rocky beaches, the blue-green water lapping gently sloping meadows grazed by sheep and cattle. Nobody, not even the engineers, would claim that the 2,000-feet-long dam has added to the scenery but at least it was built with sympathetic hands and, from the surrounding heights, the pool looks a pleasant feature and never seems drawn down with the ugly rim that so often disfigures the far larger Haweswater. An ancient packhorse bridge would have been drowned by the rising waters but Manchester dismantled it and rebuilt it, with considerable care, further up the dale. More unsightly than this sparkling wedge of water dancing in the morning sunlight, it seemed to me, was the eroded circuit of a motor-cycle track that circles the boggy land surrounding Seat Robert, the highest summit in these parts. This lonely fell is topped by an Ordnance Survey 'ring' at ground level, instead of a triangulation pillar, and a rampart of thousands of stones – either a tumulus or some sort of fort.

[Wet Sleddale reservoir came into service in 1967.]

Lodore in Spate

Just 170 years ago the Poet Laureate, Robert Southey, brilliantly described, in 147 different ways, exactly 'how the water comes down at Lodore'. Those who have recently seen Lodore Force in surging spate will agree with the accuracy of all his adjectives. For this is the time, after continuous heavy rain, for looking at waterfalls – one of the compensations of wet weather. Lodore is not the biggest nor the best of our falls but, with Aira Force, among the most popular. The longest single fall is probably Scale Force near Crummock Water – sufficiently remote to have been more a favourite with Victorian tourists than the motor-car trippers of today. Seeing the disappointing trickles of Lodore, or many of our 'guide-book' falls, during a dry summer must make the casual tourist wonder what on earth the poet was getting so excited about. But, after one of the wettest summers and 'back-ends' that I can remember – that of 1980 – the sight of thousands of tons of water crashing angrily down the rocks every few seconds at least emphasizes the awesome might and majesty of Nature. Perhaps the best falls are not mentioned in the guidebooks. The upper falls of Dungeon Ghyll, for example, are more impressive than the 'tourist' fall at its foot, the hidden falls in the Oxendale ravines are often both beautiful and dramatic, and some of the necklaces of falls and waterslides in the high fells that only appear under exceptional conditions can be quite sensational. On some recent days the fell country has been alive with the sight and sound of hundreds of new runners, becks and gills – millions of tons of water out of control but dazzling in their abandon.

Breaking-In Boots

Good weather recently for breaking in new boots – streaming fells, deep, squelchy bogs and flooded becks. If boots are still painful after a day or two in these conditions they'll never be right. My initial breaking-in was on Wetherlam with pouring rain and thick cloud to complete the cure. Nothing and nobody to be seen, but at least it was comfortable to have dry feet. My old, discarded boots had been letting in water on even moderately damp ground. Before the baptism of the new pair I had soaked them, inside and out, with vegetable oil. In the old days, we always used goose grease – carefully saved after Christmas by wives or mothers. Dubbin or mineral oil, we were told, rotted the stitches. Once I broke in a new pair of very stiff, steel-shanked climbing boots by an extremely painful round of the Fairfield Horseshoe. About a mile from the end of the walk I stood knee-deep in Rydal Beck for several minutes until the boots were filled with water, and then fastened the laces as tightly as possible. It was a completely crippling last mile but the boots never gave me the slightest trouble afterwards – once my feet had recovered. The recent floods in the fell country finally put the seal on a disappointing summer and autumn; even the cows, still scratching at the last of the grass, look miserable, although the Herdwicks, long accustomed to hard lying, seem more stoically resigned to their fate. Lawns have never been so matted with moss and, everywhere, hedges remain uncut. Workers say it has always rained on their precious weekends and several recent glorious Mondays, sandwiched between bad days, can only have added to their desolation.

[The disappointing summer and autumn of 1979.]

The Tigers' Cliff

The overhanging and thickly vegetated north face of Goat Crag in Borrowdale, half a mile west of the tourist-defiled Bowder Stone, is not a place for ordinary mortals. Here, a quarter of an hour's walk from car or tent, is the resort of the 'hard men' of the climbing world – incredible routes through the dark overhangs, many of them pioneered within the last 12 years, with the aid of pitons or even expansion bolts. To view the climbs in detail and try to catch their flavour – in imagination only – two of us recently found the scrambling ascent of the neighbouring ridge of Nitting Haws a suitably unusual way to the rewarding perch of High Spy. Goat Crag climbers, deeply involved in maintaining precarious contact, have little opportunity for viewing the scenery; we, on the other hand, far less preoccupied with survival, could survey in comfort the wonderful autumn pictures largely denied them – the wooded sweep of the dale with glimpses of the winding Derwent through the yellowing birches, sunlit crags above Derwentwater and, due south, the soaring backcloth of the highest fells. Ravens and rooks zoomed or squabbled above our heads, toy cars edged up the valley far below, and tiny insects whirred among the juniper. Scansorial problems were modest for we avoided the final upthrust of the crag by a greasy groove to the right, crossed the old drovers' track to the Blea Crag ridge, and then strolled to the bold, new cairn on High Spy. A lone dipper, delicately threading the windings of Tongue Gill, cheered our descent through the old quarries and over the bastion of Castle Crag. Borrowdale was bustling with traffic but we had seen nobody all afternoon. Even the 'hard men' had shunned the damp walls of Goat Crag.

A Familiar Round

Wonderfully rewarding to sit on the summit cairn of Brown Pike only a week ago, stripped to the waist and basking in the warm sunshine. Not a breath of wind, Blind Tarn, far below, a black mirror burnished by a segment of sunlight, and the crags of Scafell, blue-grey against the autumn gold, looking almost within throwing distance. Then, a couple of hours later, during a leisurely round of the Coniston fells, standing in the crisp snow on the north side of Swirl How and looking across the whole of our mountain heritage from Skiddaw to Morecambe Bay. There have been several recent November days like this in the fell country – days of fog and morning mists in the valleys but cloudless blue skies, unbroken sunshine and lonely quietude on the tops as the hills settle down to their winter sleep. Strangely, the Isle of Man which, on a clear day, peeps over the summit of Grey Friar from this viewpoint, was invisible, hidden behind horizon haze, and the line of the temperature inversion hung across the sky suggested a weather change soon. Too perfect on the sunlight tops to hurry down at dust so we did the last hour in the dark, stumbling over a black shoulder of the fells.

Lost on Bowfell

A round of the Langdale fells, starting with Jack's Rake on Pavey Ark and finishing with the descent of Hell Gill, was enlivened by a curious encounter on Hanging Knotts. The day, for a change, had been clear with gusty winds on the tops but, after an interesting scramble through the crags above Rossett Gill, I emerged into thick cloud on the summit plateau, quite close to Ore Gap. Almost at once I met another lone walker, picking his way in the direction of Esk Pike but, as he admitted, hopelessly lost. Could I help, he asked. He had left his girlfriend below in the mist, after walking along something called The Belt, and had been trying to find her for the last hour without success. No, he had no compass. 'Could it have been The Band?' I asked and he thought that might have been the name, so I had to tell him he was about a mile out of his way and going in the opposite direction. With obvious relief, he agreed to accompany me over Bowfell and, eventually, some distance above Three Tarns, we found his companion who seemed to have weathered the wait with fortitude, despite the cold. There was a touching reunion. This young man was not the first to have gone astray in mist on the extensive Bowfell summit plateau – or in many places in

196

Harrison Stickle and Pavey Ark behind Stickle Tarn. The prominent groove in Pavey Ark is Jack's Rake.

the Lakeland fells in poor conditions. One wonders, indeed, how many casual walkers in the hills carry compasses and know how to use them. Accurate compass work is the most satisfying reward of a day in the clouds and a very necessary insurance. If regularly taught in schools compass navigation could save lives, avoid distress – and provide fun. And, despite reports to the contrary, compasses *do* work accurately on Bowfell – provided they are held in the hand and not placed, in certain places only, on the rock.

Looking at Waterfalls

November, so often a quiet time of fading autumn colours and clear, dry days in the fells, has this year been a depressing month with far more than its share of incessant rain, cloud and high winds. Holiday-makers from the south met during an afternoon round of Striding Edge on one of the few dry days claimed they had quite enjoyed their frequent wettings – but they were the hardier sort. For such enthusiasts even bad weather can have its rewards for there is always the chance that lifting mists and suddenly clearing skies will produce views, if only for moments, of quite striking beauty. And another bonus for the more determined visitor, after continuous heavy rain, is to seek out waterfalls. The cataracts and cascades of Lakeland cannot compare in size and splendour with the great waterfalls of Europe or even the Scottish Highlands – the Falls of Glomach in Ross and Cromarty are more than three times as high as our longest falls – and some of them, in a dry summer, can be little better than rather ordinary splashes or depressing trickles. But see Lodore, Aira Force, Scale Force, Stock Gill, Stanley Force or many others in the sort of weather we have been having and the tremendous power and thunder of the falls can make the most miserable day amply rewarding. Better still, make an expedition of it by visiting, not the popular tourist falls, close to roads or tracks, but the often far more beautiful and impressive cataracts in the ravines or among the crags. As an example, the glorious Oxendale trinity of Browney Gill, Crinkle Gill and Hell Gill have recently been in most spectacular spate with enough excitement and interest to make the pouring rain seem unimportant.

A Pillar Rock Day

So still and quiet on top of Pillar Rock the other day you could use unshielded matches and hear the murmur of becks nearly 2,000 feet below. And yet, an hour later, on the higher summit of Pillar, the mountain, we could hardly stand against the south-westerly gale and barely converse without shouting. The gale presumably had been blowing all afternoon but the Rock, sheltered by the mountain wall, was a haven of quietude on a wild day of scurrying cloud on the highest tops and spraying becks in the dales. Not a good day for climbing because of greasy rocks but, once on top of the Rock, we could sprawl at our ease, look down the dark, conifer carpet to the lake and the sea, see the upper crags in Birkness Combe across the dale lighted by a shaft of sunlight and count the tarns on Haystacks. Reaching the whaleback summit of Pillar was a double exhilaration – first, after the stillness, the buffeting gale, and, second, the fantastic skyscape. The sea and the Wasdale hills were blotted out by a gigantic curtain of ink-black cloud, topped by a level blanket of white cotton wool. And this blanket, lighted from above by the westering sun, glowed with fire – a rim of gold below the blue vault of the sky. In a few moments we were enveloped in cloud and trotted down to the valley in clammy greyness and gathering dark, but we had had our brief reward. And later, splashing down flooded tracks to Wasdale Head, we had our second reward – a full moon, huge and shining, peeping over the shoulder of Great End and lighting our way, through familiar evening smells and sounds of woodsmoke and falling waters, to the lights of the inn.

Perfection on the Pike

The day before the first snows of the winter came to the fell country achieved almost magical perfection. Still lakes shone like burnished mirrors reflecting the gold and russet pageant of autumn sunlit hills, carved sharp as monoliths, crowding the horizon, and a thousand becks, full and fresh after recent rains, splashed merrily down the contours. Down in the dale the Borrowdale birches hung motionless over shingle-shored pools and it was warm work, in shirt sleeves, clambering to the heights, but on the highest point in England a fresh wind from the sea brought out sweaters and anoraks. The views were as sharp as through a telephoto lens – the Napes Needle on Great Gable, two miles away, the Isle of Man beyond Wastwater and the sea, and, to the north, across the Solway Firth, the blue shape of the Scottish hills. All the way north-eastwards up and down the ridges, the sunshine lighted our footsteps. Down to Esk Hause, with a pair of ravens for company, over Allen Crags, past some of the finest mountain tarns in Lakeland and across the hummocks of Glaramara we ambled until the shadows lengthened and the fells turned purple at the darkening. Then, helter-skelter, down the steep front of Thorneythwaite Fell to the Seathwaite intake fields and the end of a day when our familiar homeland hills had never looked more beautiful. Thirty hours later came the snow, wiping out the rich warmth of autumn but bringing a new magic to a countryside that changes every day.

First Trip over Wetherlam

Where to take a friend of mature years for an introductory walk in the Lakeland fells? Walna Scar, Brown Pike, along the top of Dow Crag with all its climbing memories and back over the Old Man to Coniston was rejected when the morning turned out cloudy and rather wet. Instead we went over dear old Wetherlam – from Tilberthwaite on to Birk Fell, up Wetherlam Edge and down Steel Edge and a stroll down the far side of the gill, splashed with autumn colour and loud with the tumult of the beck. We arrived on the summit with the sun – the

Cove Bridge on the Walna Scar track, with Brown Pike in the background.

forecasters had got it right this time, the clouds lifting from the waves of hills, the Scafells clear, a splash of sunlight on Helvellyn, the trough of Greenburn in burnt sienna, the Holme Fell woodlands rich and warm and tiny cars creeping over Wrynose far below. The little tarns on Swallow Scar, neatly rimmed with tiny crags, were perfect mirrors of the clearing sky and, an hour or two later, the long length of Windermere not even rippled and, miraculously, quiet and still. Nothing moved on the lake within a magic few minutes – the scene, with its shadowy shores, might have been a Japanese painting – and it had been the same on the hill – not a whisper of wind and the sheep quietly seeking out their cosy bields for the night. On the way home the westering sun, the sky ablaze, dazzled through the rear mirrors of the car and lit the Glen Mary woods with brush strokes of golden light. Yew Tree Tarn, empty for weeks, was full again and a heron took off from the far shore and skimmed low across the water. Autumn perfection in mid-November, warm enough for shirt-sleeves on the tops, and the rocks, after days of downpours, gently steaming in places and drying nicely ready for a good, hard winter.

Homage on Great Gable

Perhaps 300 of us stood bareheaded in the first snow of the winter for the two minutes' silence on the mist-wreathed summit of Great Gable. How many, one wondered, were aware that the real memorial is not the handsome bronze plaque, but the thousand acres of mountain land above 1,500 feet on both sides of Styhead presented to the nation nearly 70 years ago in honour of climbers who had given their lives in war. The protection for all time – as a unique national heritage – of the brave heights of Great Gable, Kirk Fell, Lingmell, Broad Crag, and Great End, and freedom for all to roam them at will is the true shrine for which those who go to the hills should always be grateful. It was a still, late autumn day of much quiet beauty. Below the summit clouds, little patches of wintry sun briefly illuminated in turn a corner of the Ennerdale forest, the shoreline of one of the Buttermere lakes or, in a sudden flash of silver, a high tarn on Haystacks. Once, from the old sled-gate of Moses' Trod, we saw the bold prow of Honister Wall, a fine rock-climb near the pass, sharply outlined in gold against the dark background of fellside. Little groups of returning pilgrims sat in the lee of rocks for their sandwiches and coffee and looked down the long western dales towards the sea, admiring the profile of Pillar Rock, or the contrasted beauty of shadowed Warnscale and smiling Buttermere. A few of us remembered Ennerdale before the forests transformed the dale and quietly wondered about changing priorities. Most had been delighted to be out in the first snow. At least it concealed the grossly-eroded tracks – the modern price we have to pay for our freedom of the hills.

[The memorial land – 1,184 acres of 12 summits on both sides of Styhead Pass – was purchased by the Fell and Rock Climbing Club as a memorial to members who had fallen in the First World War and handed over to the National Trust. The summit tablet was unveiled on Whit Sunday, 8 June 1924, by the then club president, Dr A.W. Wakefield of Keswick, not long after he had taken part in one of the early Everest expeditions. Unsuccessful attempts had been made earlier to purchase, as a memorial, for the nation, either Pillar Rock or Napes Needle.]

An Easy, Grassy Height

In the foreground of the view from my study window, framed between two old ash trees and squatting like a footstool below the soaring bulk of Red Screes, is the rocky ledge of Reston Scar. As the raven flies it is barely three miles from my home – five minutes in the car – but, until the other day, I'm ashamed to say I'd never been up there. Hundreds of times I must have driven below it on the way to crags and mountains but, except for wondering whether there might be a bit of a scramble on the low cliff, I had always ignored this little hill. In fact, it took some temporary foot trouble, which has made me seek out grassy ways, for a time, instead of crags and rocky tracks, to send me there. It was late on a glorious, autumn afternoon with the sun still shining on the new snows and flooding the dale with golden light. I was planting roses, annoyed about the waste of a good mountain day and worrying about my feet when, looking up from my labours, I saw Reston Scar. 'Of course,' I thought, 'nice, grassy tracks. The very place for my feet,' and, dropping the spade, I drove off to catch the last of the light. You can easily get to the summit cairn from Staveley within 20 minutes and even after a leisurely round of all the little tops of Hugill Fell, with its tarns and springs, I was back home well within two hours – almost relieved that it was now too dark to finish off the roses. These quiet, grassy fells, like so many of the modest foothills that we tend to ignore in our search for more challenging heights, were exactly as delightful as I had expected – soft, gentle turf, superb views of the high, snow-capped fells, the road and the railway winding far below, nobody about and very, very peaceful.

[Reston Scar was in the view from the windows of my previous home and this quick afternoon trip was in November 1986.]

Blind Mountain Man

We photographed him sitting astride the narrowest part of Striding Edge, a huge smile on his face and his legs dangling over the drop on either side. He will proudly show the picture to his friends but Peter Richardson, a young Bradford schoolteacher, will never see it himself, and saw nothing of the splendid view from his perch with Red Tarn far below, for Peter is completely blind. The pleasant task of escorting him, with the help of three friends, up Helvellyn by way of Striding Edge and down by Swirral Edge proved a most rewarding experience. On the easy places he strode along, a hand on one of our arms, with great confidence – he'd have gone quicker if we'd let him – and on the rock scrambles he followed our directions exactly: a foothold at knee-level, perhaps, a right handhold high up. There was hoar frost and some verglas on the rock but his only slight slips, immediately corrected

Red Tarn and Striding Edge from the summit of Helvellyn.

by one of us, were on the descent of Swirral Edge where falling snow, turning to rain, did not help. For Peter the ascent was a joyous romp with the changing scene, described to him as we went along, clearly pictured in his mind. The descent must have been a little trying at times, but he never complained about the occasional knock and apologized for every slight mistake. We had a short length of line for emergencies but never used it, and I don't think many of the people we encountered realised that one of us was blind. He noticed things we missed – birdsong, the sound of running water, the wind in the crags, the movements of other parties, the direction of the sun – and was profuse in his gratitude to us for helping him to realise an old ambition. We all thought him a most cheerful and courageous companion.

The Other Borrowdale

The other Borrowdale – the one that cuts across the Shap Fells road – is always deserted, even at weekends. No doubt it looked exactly the same a hundred years ago except that High Borrowdale, now a sad cluster of derelict buildings sheltered by trees, was then being farmed.

Today there's only one farm in the dale, the lonely farm track, fine woodlands at one end, the meandering Borrow Beck with its splendid pools, two bridges, and the steep fellsides soaring up on either side. Even five hundred years ago it must have looked much the same – except for the bridges. Nearly two thousand years ago the Romans had a fort near Low Borrow Bridge, but neither this occupation nor the passage of the railway and then the motorway across the skirts of the dale seem to have had any impact on this loneliest of valleys. And only once, in my memory, was Borrowdale in the news – when they threatened, unavailingly, several years ago, to turn it into a reservoir. Recently, on a day of sunlit snows, two of us intended a circumnavigation of Borrowdale, traversing the fells on either side. But, because of a late start, we shortened the round after walking the five summits of the Whinfell ridge by strolling back up the dale. The views from the ridge, from Pillar to Whernside, showed that the eastern hills – Harter Fell, High Street and the Northern Pennines – had collected most of the snow, much of it blown by northerly winds on to south and west slopes which, gleaming in the sunshine, seemed thickly plastered. Borrowdale was quiet, still, and lonely with just the soft murmuring of the beck and the slow movement of distant sheep on the steep fellsides, and it's always like this.

'Snow on High Ground'

DECEMBER

A Familiar Round

After the worst and wettest autumn for years the first sizeable snowfalls heralded a complete change in the weather – hard frost, unbroken sunshine and picture postcard views. Overnight winter had arrived and magically the beckoning fells loomed closer and, with the snow, seemed twice as high. Not enough snow yet for skiing or climbing but perfect for the familiar round of the Coniston fells. Near the Banishead stone circle I chatted with a farmer getting down the last of his sheep, the dogs scampering down the snow ledges on the little crags with holiday abandon. Yes, he agreed, a 'turble clarty back-end' but today, what a morning! A steepish snow slope, topped by the beginnings of a cornice, led interestingly to Brown Pike with its superb view of the long, wooded length of Dunnerdale and the battlemented Scafells, etched boldly in white and grey against the bright blue sky. Smoke curled lazily from unseen cottage windows in distant woodlands, purple tarns glistened on the lower fells, sunlit sands reached out far away to the glittering sea, and the vapour trail of an aircraft crept in a slow arc high over Helvellyn. Sandwiches were eaten in a sunny belvedere, sheltered from the wind by a rock outcrop, just below Goats' Hause. The tarn, edged with snow, looked by contrast even blacker than usual and the soaring, white face of the Old Man appeared almost alpine. And from the Brim Fell ridge Coniston might have been a Swiss lakeside town, sparkling in the sunlight. Far to the south the sun touched a window or a car windscreen somewhere near Morecambe Bay and the signal was semaphored to me high up in the snows.

New Snow on the Crinkles

Over the Crinkles to Bowfell on a bright December morning was a switchback of delight – the ravines opening out below one's feet, the sunlit Langdale Pikes flanking the shadowed dale and, away to the left, the long line of the Scafells, spattered with snow. Here is the best ridge-walk in south Lakeland – the five rocky bumps of Crinkle Crags, two of Shelter Crags, the triangular peak of Bowfell and, for extra measure, the rocky tors of Cold Pike and Gaitkins or the scattered crags of Pike o'Blisco. Seen from my windows on clear summer evenings it is a blue, knobbly ridge stretched across the sunset – not unlike a section of the Cuillin ridge in Skye. In winter it becomes a fairyland of icing sugar towers sparkling in the sunshine or a progression of dark crags starkly outlined by plunging snow gullies. From a car parked by the Three Shires Stone the traverse is an exhilarating stroll; more rewarding is an ascent by one of the Oxendale ravines or the remote corries on the Eskdale side. The other day the views, after weeks of miserable weather, were of magical clarity – moving specks visible a mile away, the Scafells seemingly within hailing distance, the glittering sea right to the horizon. And you could watch the crags drying out, gently steaming in the sunshine, while the becks, in roaring spate, could be heard foaming down the contours a thousand feet below. I came down the snow in Mickle Door, the gully between the second and third Crinkles – not enough depth for good climbing – scrambled up the crags of Gladstone Knott and wandered homewards across the delightful outcrops of Gaitkins and Cold Pike before the clouds rolled in.

Pavements to the Heights

From the frost-bound top of Harrison Stickle on this still December morning, the nearer summits looked close enough to touch and the fells crowding the horizon as sharp against the sky as if cut out of cardboard. Only south-east was the prospect blurred, a thin haze of fog and mist hanging over the winding miles of Windermere reaching out towards the sea. The top few hundred feet of the ascent had been a fingers-and-toes climb of the summit crag after a sedate approach up the new 'staircase' high above the true-left side of Dungeon Ghyll. These rebuilt Langdale paths, most skilfully paved, culverted and graded, remind one of the thousands of steps up various holy mountains out east and you feel rather like a pilgrim, keeping to the straight and narrow way, as you use them. Their provision, in the more popular corners of the Lake District, seems the only alternative to allowing the fells to be kicked to death by the hordes but there is little or no feel of fell-walking in their use. Indeed, most of the journey to Stickle Tarn nowadays is hardly different from walking upstairs a few hundred times, although the scenery may be better. One must admire the skill and strength used in the building of these staircases – the steps, for instance, have been carefully tilted so that water and small stones can run off – while hoping that this major surgery can be restricted to the worst-eroded, most popular areas. But, although Jack's Rake on Pavey Ark, which I used for descent, has become dangerously loose through increased popularity, a staircase or ladders up here would be unthinkable.

The Best Winter?

Overnight the snow blanket on the fells had changed, as if by a magician's wand, from knee-deep powder to hard packed crust – perfect for winter mountaineering. From the icing-sugar cairn on Dow Crag we looked north across miles of untracked snow and distant black cliffs to the roof of England and south, beyond soft brown valleys and dark misty woodlands, to the sea. Beneath our feet familiar gullies, packed with snow, plunged between icy walls to the black pool of Goats Water and we assessed the pitches for a later ascent in this best outdoor winter for years. Looking down on Low Water later – frozen, this time, right across with white ice – we pondered on the difference in water temperature caused by an extra 200 feet in height. A pair of ravens – they mate for life – followed us along the ridge, occasionally giving an aerobatics exhibition above the corries and, many thousands of feet higher silent aircraft crept across the blue zenith like silver darts in slow motion. As the sun sank behind the Dunnerdale fells we strapped on crampons for the descent of a steep gully of frozen snow on a shadowed east face. No sound except the satisfying crunch of pointed steel on the smooth white carpet and the hiss and slither of chips of ice sliding down towards the darkening valley. The descent taking longer than expected it was dark when we reached the intake fields. Coniston, not far below, looked a cluster of fairy lights and, over our left shoulders, the North Star high above Wetherlam gave us another bearing.

[This 'best outdoor winter for years' was that of 1976.]

Above the Kent

We call them the Troutbeck fells, although their best sides overlook Kentmere, perhaps because they are so familiar from the Kirkstone road – a switchback skyline of smooth, shapely hills looking, under snow, rather like a blown sail leaning backwards against the sky. I see them, end on, from my house every day – except when the clouds are down – and the morning after the snows came I went along the ridge for some necessary exercise. In places the snow lay deep and powdery, elsewhere, crisp and frozen, making the traverse a pleasant progression of satisfying crunches – the first few thousand footprints in a new white world. The clustered battlement-like cairns on the summit of Ill Bell which always identify the mountain from afar might have been made out of icing sugar and High Street, straight ahead, surfaced like a great white whale. Ill Bell – wrongly named Hill Bell on the two-and-a-half inch map not so many years ago – probably derives its name from 'eel' or 'e'il' meaning evil but there was nothing dark or foreboding about the mountain this glorious winter's day. Sunshine sparkled on successive waves of white peaks reaching to the horizon, the shadows were blue-grey against the snow and, on the return trip, the long length of Windermere's silvery snake meandered, far below, through neat woodlands and bright meadows, into the distant sea haze. Back down in the dale the Kent – one of England's fastest rivers when in spate – raced, in full flood, past winding lanes still golden, here and there, with the last leaves of autumn, but winter had come to the fells, already turning purple at the darkening.

Gable for Geriatrics

The easiest way to the top of Great Gable – I know octogenarians who manage it without discomfort – is from Honister Pass, the motoring saving a thousand feet of ascent. And to make a more interesting round trip the rock-spattered summits of Grey Knotts and Brandreth can be included, the mountain traversed to Beck Head, and the pleasant meanderings of Moses' Trod followed back to the pass. Two of us did the round in mist which makes it even more interesting. Picking the right line for Beck Head from the summit of Great Gable with only a few feet of visibility needs a little care – many people have come below the mist to find themselves headed for Wasdale Head – and the twists and turns of Moses' Trod are not always obvious to the stranger – largely due to the recent proliferations of tracks and cairns. If in doubt it is better to hold a firm compass course and ignore the confusing tracks. Low cloud on the tops provides the interest and satisfaction of accurate compass work and the occasional delight of unusual views if the mists are torn aside. One hole in the cloud curtain, lasting for seconds only, on this recent walk exactly framed the whole length of Wastwater, but excluded everything else, even The Screes. Just a glistening, white expanse entirely surrounded by dark, grey cloud. Later brief pictures were of the summit rocks of Haystacks with a corner of Innominate Tarn and, towards the end, a tiny intimate view of the top pitch of Honister Wall, low down on the slopes of Dale

Dale Head from High Spy.

Head. Identification of miniature features like these, spotted through windows in the clouds, brings added interest and reward. Trudges over familiar fells, in mist and rain, can have their own highlights – more subtle than those on sunny days.

Mountain Chandeliers

The summit of St Sunday Crag – the rocks, every blade of grass and every clump of heather or bilberry – was decorated, the other day, with millions of frost fingers, each one about three inches long. It looked as if many tons of goose feathers had been heaped on the top few acres – and then meticulously arranged so that each feather was pointing exactly to the east. But only Nature can do things like this. There had been a light snow covering on the highest slopes facing north and east and this had been converted by frost and an icy wind, perhaps following a thick thaw, into this extraordinary summit scene that glistened like a lighted chandelier in the thin winter sunlight. I had gone up the mountain, following the east ridge out of Deepdale, to check whether it was the actual summit of the fell or the top of the subsidiary summit of Gavel Pike that I can just see, on the very clearest days, from our windows. A reader had kindly shown interest. Unfortunately, a cloud over the snow-wreathed Fairfield crags and the Kirkstone fells prevented my getting a sight of the area of our bungalow, 14 map miles away, but a view through binoculars from our windows of the tiny triangle of fell the previous day and a close study of the ground on this latest visit persuaded me that it is the actual summit we can sometimes see. The lower summit of Gavel Pike is too pointed and rocky to fit. This is by no means the most distant mountain sighting from our home. Esk Pike and the shoulder of Great End, 18 miles away as the raven flies, are clearly visible on the good days. The top hundred feet or so of St Sunday Crag are just an added bonus.

[As seen from my previous home.]

Christmas Card Patterdale

It was a magical, glittering morning in Patterdale with the valley looking exactly like the Christmas cards that had been thudding daily through the letter-box. Trees stood bedecked in snow, sunlight sparkled on white roofs, and the smoke rose straight from cottage chimneys. And high above the dale the familiar fells had been transformed into alpine peaks, with even the steeper crags hung in snow and ice. The ascent to Striding Edge was the usual, long trudge but the Edge itself was far too interesting for boredom – all the towers cloaked in frozen snow and ice, Red Tarn far below, frozen right across, and Helvellyn straight ahead, soaring up like a great white whale. This popular summer horseshoe round, including Swirral Edge, becomes a worthwhile expedition under snow and ice – no technical difficulties for the winter climber, but demanding competence with ice-axe and crampons in severe conditions. Fortunately, there was not a breath of wind this December day, and I was able to climb with confidence and enjoyment over all the crusted towers and down the icy chimney at the end of the Edge. The steep rise to the Helvellyn ridge on frozen snow, the stroll along the top of the cornices, and the descent of Swirral Edge all went easily in crampons. There were few marks of earlier traffic, and I met nobody on the road. From the summit the Lake District seemed a sea of great white waves reaching to the horizon. The descent to the dale in the growing dusk – with a flaming red sky to the west behind the now darkened east wall of the ridge, patches of white cloud hung across the tops, and the moon rising over Place Fell – was a magical journey in a winter wonderland.

Above the Fog

From the multi-cairned summit of Ill Bell the fell country was a grey-white feather bed of mist etched across with dark ridges reaching, in succeeding waves, towards an unseen horizon. The scene might have been a Japanese painting – all the valleys filled with fog, the horseshoe ridges just peeping above, the distance a blur of sky and cloud, little or no colour, and everything quiet and still. We were traversing the Troutbeck fells on a dull, dank December day, the only movement all afternoon the vague shape of a car crawling up the Kirkstone corners two miles away, not a breath of wind, no sheep, no people, not a sound. The bogs were still frozen across making walking easy – a hands-in-pockets stroll along familiar ground. A double temperature inversion, one above the other, hid the high ground, including the Scafells, only the nearer heights of 2,000 to 2,500 feet being visible, but the table-top of Ingleborough peeped up behind a shoulder of Gragareth and the Howgills tops appeared as a far scattering of islands in a grey-white sea. From deserted Kentmere – only one other car parked by the church – we avoided tracks, reaching Yoke through the cluster of crags that give so much character to its eastern slopes and, at the end of the ridge, working down steep hanging valleys to the fell road. Seeing nobody all day, even in the distance, was a mid-week bonus – these fells would be swarming with folk at the weekend – but we were a little disappointed by the continued absence of the snow that so magically transforms the fells in winter. But the weather forecast that night sounded hopeful.

[The snows came late in the winter of 1989.]

Enjoying the Mist

The last time I had done a circuit of the Kentmere fells had been ten months before on skis – a perfect alpine day with views across dazzling snows to far horizons. Today was rather different – sodden turf, streaming rocks, and thick cloud almost down to the intake fields. The scramble up the ridge of Rainsborrow Crag on greasy rock needed care and the summit had to be found by compass. Ill Bell and Froswick were easy to find but Mardale Ill Bell proved curiously elusive, although it is a summit I see from my house every day – except during such a clarty back-end as this one. But once the source of the River Kent, a bright green moss just below the ridge, had been identified, a north-east bearing led easily to the recently rebuilt cairn. Mountain walking in thick cloud is strangely satisfying. Small features, until you reach them, are grotesquely magnified, outcrops become crags, and yawning depths may be no more than faint depressions. Bits of rock, hardly noticed in good weather, take on special significance and the mere ticking off of familiar summits seems oddly rewarding. Sandwiches eaten in the shelter at the top of the Nan Bield, with the view restricted to a few yards, were as enjoyable as usual, and the pull up to Harter Fell at least good exercise. You remember or picture the views you should be having and content yourself with the thought that it is purely a navigational exercise – a stolen day just to keep the muscles in trim. The reward came later with the dale suddenly leaping up through clearing mists and a glint of watery sunshine lighting the lane down to Hartrigg. At least, in this wettest of late autumns, there had been no rain.

A New Mountain 'Sport'

Climbers and hill walkers are concerned about a new mountain sport that is reported to be particularly popular in the Lake District. They call it 'boggling' and I understand it involves the use of specially adapted four-wheel-drive vehicles that are driven up, down, or across the fells. Green roads or rough tracks are traversed and sometimes, I'm told, the vehicles are taken up the fellsides, over grass and heather, to the summits. Walkers have spotted them on High Street, Walna Scar, and other places, and perhaps it is the ultimate frustration to struggle to a mountain top on foot only to find a motor vehicle parked there.

Of course, Bren gun-carriers and tanks lurched about the slopes of Skiddaw during the war for training purposes and, regrettably, motor-cars have been driven to the summit – as stunts, rather like John Leeming's landing of an aeroplane on Helvellyn just over 50 years ago. I've even met a one-legged motorcyclist on top of Coniston Old Man – and admired his courage and skill. But it would be a sad commentary on modern values if the lonely fells ever become a playground for motor sportsmen. Where would it all end? The mind, indeed, boggles.

[John Leeming landed his aeroplane on Helvellyn – with Bert Hinkler as passenger – on 22 December 1926.]

Changing Fell Fashions

Fashions in our use of the fells are always changing. Two favourite walks of the Victorians were to Scale Force, 'Lakeland's highest water-fall', from Buttermere and to Bowscale Tarn from the Mungrisdale road – but the original paths are now disused. Gone, too, are the refreshment huts half-way up Skiddaw and near the edge of Easdale Tarn. I remember both and, especially, the man in the hut by the tarn who sold lemonade and entertained his visitors by bending six-inch nails into almost any required shape. At the same time new paths through the fells are continually appearing. Before the war there was no track over Glaramara and the crossing, in thick mist or bad weather, used to provide useful compass practice. Today, the path is unmis-takable. The other day I went up Sergeant Man from Far Easdale and returned to Grasmere over Tarn Crag. Not long ago, certainly since the war, the route from the head of the dale to the former prominent cairn on the Man – it used to be the boundary between Cumberland and Westmorland – was quite untracked, and so was the descent through heather and bilberry, past rocky tors, to Tarn Crag. Today, well-cairned paths make the ways clear, although I notice the well-built cairn on Sergeant Man, formerly visible for miles, had been pulled down into a small heap, suffering the fate regularly dealt to the fine summit cairns on Lingmell, Pike o'Blisco and Dale Head. There is a fine example of the way our fell tracks are degenerating into highways on the Causey Pike ridge between Sail and Scar Crags. At one time, well within my memory, this was a pleasant, narrow track, perhaps two feet in width; today it is a jumble of parallel paths up to 30 feet wide in places.

213

Golf Course Panorama

From the highest green on Kendal Golf Course, ten minutes' steep walking from my roof-tops eyrie, the view on a recent crisp, sunny afternoon, despite nearly a life-time's familiarity, was almost breathtaking. Surely this hilly course, high above the old grey town, must have the most magnificent and extensive views of any club in England. This afternoon, with the roofs of Kendal and the lovely dale of the Kent far below flooded in sunlight, the fells crowding the horizon, washed with gold on western slopes, were sharp against the sky as if cut out of cardboard. Almost due west was the shapely pointed peak of Caw and then, working round the compass, the stately procession of the Coniston fells, Crinkle Crags, the triangle of Bowfell, picture postcard Langdale Pikes, the steep upthrust of Red Screes, the Troutbeck fells, High Street, the nearer heights of Brunt Knott and Potter Fell, the knobbly Whinfell ridge, a huddle of Howgills and the sprawling shape of Middleton Fell. Behind and to the right of Bowfell soared the dome of Great Gable looking rather like a nuclear explosion and the summit of Scafell Pike, the highest land in England, peeped above the rim just to its left. Then, by strolling to the seventh green, you could see all the rest – flat-topped Ingleborough, the Kent estuary with Heysham power station in the distance, far across the sands, and, on the edge of the sea, the dark bulk of Black Combe. In the immediate foreground were the immaculately laundered greens and fairways, the immense backcloth, the loveliest mountain land in the country, not a road or a motor-car to be seen, and not a sound except the occasional drone of unseen aircraft.

Lunch in the Cave

The rain filled the valley and trickled depressingly down the side of the cliff, but it was snuff-dry and cosy inside the remarkable cave above the overhangs of Dove Crag. Lunch in the cave on a wet day is well worth the effort because it is always dry – even after the continual heavy rain we have had to endure recently. People often spend the night there nowadays – it could sleep a dozen at a pinch – but somnambulists should be warned. A few sleep-walking steps would project them over the overhangs and on to the screes 300 feet below. Two of us 'discovered' the cave about 40 years ago when we were working on a climbing guide to the area although generations of shepherds and foxhunters must have known the place. But I believe my friend, George

Spenceley, was the first to cache food there and use it regularly overnight. Nowadays there is emergency food and fuel in a metal box, with a visitors' book which shows the popularity of the cave among Outward Bound and school parties. I hope the earliest visitors' books are still preserved; they record details of the first climbs on this tremendously imposing crag – probably the steepest in the Lake District. Lying flat on your stomach on the cliff top, above the overhangs, you can drop a stone straight on to the screes, which you cannot do on Scafell Crag, Dow Crag, or Pillar Rock. A recent refinement is a low stone wall, intended either as a barrier against the icy north winds or as a slight deterrent to persistent sleep-walkers. Inexperienced fell-walkers who do not know the route to the cave, should not go scrambling about the cliffs. To the initiated, however, it is the perfect eyrie, unique in Lakeland, with a spectacular view down rugged Dovedale to Ullswater and the distant Northern Pennines.

Breaking Records

It was interesting to discover the other afternoon that the summit of Red Screes, just over one thousand feet above Kirkstone Pass, is within one hour from my home. A short break in the wet weather was the temptation, and the knowledge that Jorge Bolet was playing Rachmaninov on BBC 2 at four o'clock the reason for some haste. The motoring, without speeding, took 22 minutes and the ascent, by a scramble to the left of Kilnshaw Chimney, exactly 37 minutes. A younger man or a fell-runner would have been far quicker. There was only one other person about – a Windermere man, Don Austin, met on the summit who told me it was his 199th ascent of the fell. My own visits have been far fewer but, over many years, I have found Red Screes a particularly convenient place for easily accessible snow or ice climbing and even for skiing in the south-east corrie. Quick visits have often been paid on either Christmas Day or Boxing Day to enjoy the winter conditions, and perhaps the availability of alcoholic refreshment at nearly 1,500 feet has occasionally been an added attraction. Not so many years ago the craggy east face was quite trackless and you usually had the mountain to yourself. I've sometimes been up there in winter with sunlit views across snowbound Lakeland and the air so still you could hear voices down at the Kirkstone Inn. Red Screes – you can see screes from the inn and the colour is particularly striking after rain – is a slowly crumbling mountain, every year more tons of rock tumble down from the shattered crags, but the snow and ice hold it together in winter, and this season is always the best time for enjoying this handy hill.

[My own 'record' for the ascent of Red Screes from Kirkstone Pass is now 30 minutes. The motoring, however, takes a few minutes longer from my new home but the summit can still be reached in an hour – when I am in form. Don Austin must, by now, have been on top far more than 200 times for I've twice met him up there since writing this piece in 1985.]

Loughrigg on Boxing Day

Years ago I would be up betimes on Boxing Day to enjoy the challenge of rock, ice or snow but nowadays there's the increasing temptation of a later start and the gentler delights of something like Loughrigg Fell. You could describe Loughrigg, with its little crags, tarns, woodland and sprinkling of summits, as Lakeland in miniature and on most Boxing Days you are also likely to get, in addition to the scenery, the sight or sound of a foxhunt. It there's sunshine and snow as well you are especially rewarded and the views from the main top, although little more than a thousand feet up, embrace most of the Cumbrian hills as well as the unmistakable flat top of Ingleborough. Another feature of Loughrigg, just above Rydal Water, is the tremendous cave which, in the event of lightning, cloudburst or other natural phenomenon, could easily shelter all the people on the fell, as well, if need be, as the entire population of Ambleside. Since Loughrigg is mostly the resort of unambitious walkers or first-time visitors it is odd that most of the multitude of paths seem to lead everywhere except to the summit which must have eluded many. I remember once, in thick cloud and heavy rain, failing to find it – defeat on a familiar, thousand-footer. But this Boxing Day, if it's sunny with snow, there'll be plenty of people about and, with an early start, one might fit in Silver How as well – the perfect winter round on gentle, switchback heights high above the shining lakes and the pools of the Rothay and the Brathay.

Searchlight on Grasmere

A thousand feet above Grasmere, brimming a grassy shelf of Heron Pike and enclosed by tourist tracks and sheep trods, is the unremarkable pool of Alcock Tarn. Usually it does little more than mirror the sky and provide a foreground for the distant winding length of Windermere but the other afternoon, from a nearby outcrop, it yielded a magical bird's-eye view of the dale where so many painters, poets and writers, over the centuries, have made their home. It was a dull, windless day, with Bowfell and the Crinkles black against the sky and the Coniston fells hidden in thick cloud but, to the south-west, a thin shaft of sunlight suddenly burst through a rent in the dark veil and briefly floodlit the floor of the dale. It was as if the lights had been turned on to a stage. Everywhere else – Easdale, Greenburn, the Langdales and Loughrigg – was shadowed and gloomy but, astride the Rothay, the square fields of Grasmere, the houses, farms and hotels, were flooded for moments in golden sunlight. A photographer, with camera at the ready, might have caught the picture of a lifetime – the tiny, central heart of Lakeland alone under a searchlight – but the magic was quickly switched off and December gloom descended. Alcock Tarn (curiously spelled Allcock on the Ordnance Survey's 1:25,000 map but nowhere else) was called Butter Crags Tarn a hundred years ago but renamed after a Mr Alcock who lived nearby, had it dammed, enlarged and stocked with trout. Fell runners in the annual Grasmere Guides Race have to round a flag on Butter Crags before their helter-skelter descent to the sports field.

Exploring Browncove Crags

A damp clinging blanket of cloud reduced the view to two yards of wet stones but the sudden appearance of new snow gleaming faintly through the grey murk was just enough to indicate the drop on the left. I was wandering along the bare top of Helvellyn and the very thin covering of snow – restricted to the east side of the summit ridge high above Red Tarn – was the start of the huge cornices that will hang over the face later this winter. Sometimes these cornices build up to a width of 20 feet with a vertical, or even overhanging, lip that collapses in thaw conditions. But for this sudden white warning in the grey gloom this winter morning a feckless walker could easily have stepped over the edge. Descending Lower Man later, with no ideas on how to fill in the day, a tiny triangle of blue sky unexpectedly windowed the cloud just long enough to frame Brown Cove Tarn far below to the right – and give me the suggestion for an hour's scrambling. Brown Cove is one of the eastern coves of Helvellyn but Browncove Crags are on the opposite side of the ridge and not associated with the cove in any obvious way. The crags are a favourite winter climbing ground of mine – the three modest snow gullies can often be soloed – but I had never explored the cliff out of season. In a few minutes I was trotting down below the cloud into wintery sunshine with a fresh breeze already

Below Striding Edge.

drying out the rocks. And so, for the next hour or so, I busied myself with some fairly simple pottering up and down a strangely neglected crag – probably far beneath the attention of modern climbers but, it seemed to me, a pleasantly rough, out of the way place, ideal on a warm, sunny day, for a cautious, old-fashioned mountaineer.

Exercise above Deepdale

The knuckled fist of Fairfield's northern crags thrusting deep into the wilderness of upper Deepdale seems to attract more than its fair share of mist and cloud. Indeed, I have rarely been there in clear weather in winter, although the neighbouring heights have mostly been sunlit. And it was the same the other day – sunshine gilding the snows of St Sunday Crag, soaring into blue skies, and sharply silhouetting the ridge of Hartsop-above-How, but Greenhow End, The Step and Hutaple Crag, whither I was bound, were cloaked in dark, grey cloud. I often go this way for my first snow outing of the year – up Black Tippet and down Flinty Graves, or the other way round – and find the trip a useful refresher in coping with steepish snow, in ascent and descent, and in strengthening the calf muscles in crampon work. Beginners in winter

218

mountaineering, with the necessary equipment, and, ideally under instruction, could benefit from this round but I have never found any steps in either gully. This is rather surprising for they must be about 800 feet high, and are often full of hard-packed snow presenting no technical difficulties of any kind but giving excellent crampon practice in confident movement up and down snow slopes with some feeling of exposure. For a lone climber with the necessary equipment and experience the round can be a delight even though – as happened with me the other day – you can only see a yard or two ahead. From the top of Black Tippet it was an easy tramp along frozen snow to the summit of Fairfield and then to the steepening gulf of Flinty Graves but a compass proved necessary for the cloud was very thick and the snow still untracked. Once down below the cloud in Sleet Cove, however, the dale could be seen for miles, reaching east towards the sunset glow on the Patterdale fells.

Homeland Hills

Around the turn of the year I took my last walk along my homeland hills. Within a few days I leave my fellside eyrie with its views into four counties and move into a flat looking on to town roofs. Overnight, you might say, I will change from a countryman, of long standing, into a townsman. It is only a move of two or three miles but, soon, the long limestone scars that start above the house and edge for miles south to the estuary will no longer be my homeland heights. Soon, too, the friendly pheasants that daily invade the garden, the curlews that quarter the field behind the hedge with their sad cries, and the breath-taking view of a horizon crowded with hills from the top of the scar, just minutes away, will be no more than nostalgic memories. Barely half a mile away from our hedge, at the foot of the scar, is a bright green tarn on which, in almost forgotten winters, I have often skated and just beyond the tarn an old, stately hall, with ancient yews among which, it is locally rumoured, Henry VIII wooed the young Katherine Parr. As I passed there on my walk the other day I could pick out some of the spy holes and arrow-slits in that part of the defences that still remains in the old hall – the nearest habitation to ours in one direction. From the top of the scar the view was the same as it must have been before the first tourists 'discovered' the Lake District – ancient windswept yews cringed against the crumbling limestone crags, screes sloping steeply to miles of patterned farmland and, here and there, the sunlight glinting on tiny tarns and lazy streams. Six miles away was the

219

The Lakeland hills from the scar behind my former home.

The roofs of Kendal from my present home.

hidden trough of Windermere and beyond it, stretched across the horizon against the sunset, the familiar blue outline of the hills from Black Combe to Shap Fells with the rooftree of England reared up behind them. Far behind me was the unmistakable table-top of Ingleborough, at my feet the green and white turf and limestone, and straight ahead, brown woodlands, grey stone walls, blue fellsides and the silvered pools of distant waters.

[This last walk along Cunswick Scar and Scout Scar from my home, for 30 years, at the foot of these limestone crags was just before my move in New Year 1989, to a flat in Kendal, following the passing of my dear wife of more than 50 years. I thus exchanged views from our windows of hills in the four former counties of Cumberland, Westmorland, Lancashire and Yorkshire for a scene of town roofs and the Town Hall clock. Many times since, from my new abode, I have repeated the walk, with variations, but the feeling of being among my own homeland fells — the top of Cunswick Scar was within ten minutes' walk from my garden fence — is, sadly, no longer there.]

Index